Praise for *THR3E* and
Ted Dekker's Previous Novels

"Dekker delivers another page-turner . . . masterfully takes readers on a ride full of plot twists and turns . . . a compelling tale of cat and mouse . . . an almost perfect blend of suspense, mystery and horror."

—*Publishers Weekly*

"*Three* is a rare suspense story that is truly suspenseful, and absolutely impossible to put down! Dekker outdoes the masters of the thriller genre with a plot so compelling, so effective, so full of twists and turns that readers are kept on the edge of their seats right to the last few pages."

—BOB LIPARULO
New Man Magazine

"Well, well, well, guess what I've found? A fiction writer with a rare knack for a compelling story, an expansive reservoir of clever ideas, and a unique wit that makes me laugh."

—FRANK PERETTI
Best-selling author of *This Present Darkness* and *The Oath*

"Ted Dekker is clearly one of the most gripping storytellers alive today. He creates plots that keep your heart pounding and palms sweating even after you've finished his books."

—JEREMY REYNALDS
Syndicated columnist.

"Someone recently asked if I would be interested in reading the hottest new fiction writer on the market. I asked who that might that be, expecting a writer along the lines of John Grisham or Stephen King. Instead, I was introduced to *Blink*, the new novel by Ted Dekker. They were right. . . . Ted Dekker has caused me to miss some serious sleep the past three nights! Dekker is awesome. I will own everything he writes."

—TOM NEWMAN
Film Producer and Founder of Impact Productions

"Ted Dekker is the most exciting writer I've read in a very long time. *Blink* will expand his fan base tremendously. Wonderful reading . . . powerful insights. Bravo!"

—TED BAEHR
President, *MOVIEGUIDE®* Magazine

"Cloaked in the mystery of Saudi Arabia, this tale woven by Dekker is compulsively readable. Written with an arresting hybrid of suspense and love, *Blink* casts a sweeping light on a surreal world where the future is buried by the past. Saudi Arabia was my home for twelve years. Dekker has an uncanny ability to capture the true essence of the world's most mysterious land in this hauntingly beautiful story. You will be astonished."

—JEAN SASSON
New York Times Best-selling Author of
Princess: A True Story of Life Behind the Veil in Saudi Arabia

"Ted is a great weaver of stories that are believable yet tinged with the mystery of the unseen."

—TIM WAY
Senior Book Buyer, Family Christian Stores

"Dekker is an emerging powerhouse among fiction writers. *Blink* is a thrilling tale that grabs your attention immediately and is near impossible to put down."

—LARRY J. LEECH II
Christian Retailing

"[*Blessed Child* is] superbly written and deeply captivating."

—*CBA Marketplace*

" . . . page-turning, action-packed suspense and adventure."

—*Lifewise Magazine*

"[*Thunder of Heaven* is] a real page-turner . . . scenes read like the best of David Morrell . . . his description is upsettingly precise."

—*Booklist*

THR3E

TED DEKKER

THOMAS NELSON
Since 1798

THREE

Published by WestBow Press, a division of Thomas Nelson, Inc., P.O. Box 141000, Nashville, Tennessee 37214.

WestBow Press books may be purchased in bulk for educational, business, fundraising, or sales promotional use. For information, please email SpecialMarkets@ThomasNelson.com.

Library of Congress Cataloging-in-Publication Data

Dekker, Ted, 1962–
    Three / by Ted Dekker.
      p. cm.
    ISBN 0-8499-4372-8 (HC)
    ISBN 0-8499-4449-X (IE)
    ISBN 1-5955-4137-3 (mass edition)
    ISBN 0-8499-4512-7 (SC)
    I. Title.
    PS3554.E43T48 2003
    813'.6—dc21

              2003003818

Printed in the United States of America

06 07 08 09 RRD 13 12 11 10

1

THE OFFICE HAD NO WINDOWS, only electric lanterns to light the hundreds of spines standing in their cherry wood bookcases. A single lawyer's lamp spread its yellow hue over the leather-topped desk. The room smelled of linseed oil and musty pages, but to Dr. John Francis it was the scent of knowledge.

"Evil is beyond the reach of no man."

"But can a man remove himself beyond the reach of evil?" Kevin asked.

The dean of academic affairs, Dr. John Francis, gazed over bifocals at the man who sat opposite him and allowed a small smile to nudge his lips. Those blue eyes hid a deep mystery, one that had eluded him since their first meeting three months earlier when Kevin Parson approached him after a philosophy lecture. They'd struck up a unique friendship that included numerous discussions such as this one.

Kevin sat with his feet flat, hands on knees, eyes piercing and un-moving, hair ruffled despite a compulsive habit of running his fingers through his loose brown curls. Or because of it. The hair was an anomaly; in every other way the man groomed himself perfectly. Clean shaven, fashionably current, pleasantly scented—Old Spice, if the professor guessed right. Kevin's ragged hair begged to differ in a bohemian sort of way. Others fiddled with pencils or twirled their fingers or shifted in their seats; Kevin ran his fingers through his hair and tapped his right foot. Not now and then or at appropriate breaks in the conversation, but regularly, to the beat of a hidden drum behind his blue eyes. Some might consider the idiosyncrasies annoying, but Dr. Francis saw them as nothing more than enigmatic clues to Kevin's nature. The truth—rarely obvious and almost always found in subtle-ies. In the tapping of feet and the fiddling of fingers and the movement of eyes.

Dr. Francis pushed his black leather chair back from the desk, stood slowly to his feet, and walked to a bookcase filled with the works of the ancient scholars. In many ways he identified with these men as much as he did with the modern man. Put a robe on him and he would look rather like a bearded Socrates, Kevin had once told him. He ran a finger over a bound copy of the Dead Sea Scrolls.

"Indeed," Dr. Francis said. "Can man step beyond evil's reach? I think not. Not in this lifetime."

"Then all men are condemned to a life of evil," Kevin said.

Dr. Francis faced him. Kevin watched, unmoving except for his right foot, tapping away. His round blue eyes held steady, stared with the innocence of a child's, probing, magnetic, unabashed. These eyes attracted long stares from the secure and forced the less secure to avert their gaze. Kevin was twenty-eight, but he possessed a strange blend of brilliance and naiveté that Dr. Francis could not understand. The full-grown man thirsted for knowledge like a five-year-old. Something to do with a unique rearing in a bizarre home, but Kevin had never been forthcoming.

"A lifetime *struggle* with evil, not a life of evil," Dr. Francis clarified.

"And does man simply choose evil, or does he create it?" Kevin asked, already many thoughts beyond his initial question. "Is evil a force that swims in human blood, struggling to find its way into the heart, or is it an external possibility wanting to be formed?"

"I would say man chooses evil rather than creates it. Human nature's saturated with evil as a result of the Fall. We are all evil."

"And we are all good," Kevin said, tapping his foot. "The good, the bad, and the beautiful."

Dr. Francis nodded at the use of the phrase he'd coined, which referred to the man created in God's nature, the beautiful man, struggling between the good and the bad. "The good, the bad, and the beautiful. Indeed." He stepped for the door. "Walk with me, Kevin."

Kevin ran both hands past his temples and stood. Dr. Francis led him from the office and up a flight of steps to the world above, as Kevin liked to call it.

"How is your paper on the natures progressing?" Dr. Francis asked.

"Guaranteed to raise your eyebrows." They stepped into the empty main hall. "I'm using a story to illustrate my conclusion. Not conventional, I know, but since Christ preferred to use fiction to communicate truth, I figured you wouldn't mind if I borrowed from him."

"As long as it makes the point. I look forward to reading it."

||||

Kevin walked with Dr. John Francis down the hall, thinking that he liked this man beside him. The sound of their shoes striking the hardwood floor echoed through the chamber steeped in tradition. The older man strolled casually, his ready smile hinting at wisdom far beyond his words. Kevin glanced up at the paintings of the divinity school's founders along the wall to his right. Bold, gentle giants, Dr. Francis called them.

"Speaking of evil, all men are capable of gossip, don't you think?" Kevin asked.

"Undoubtedly."

"Even the bishop is capable of gossip."

"Of course."

"Do you think the bishop does gossip? Sometimes?"

The dean's answer waited three steps. "We are all human."

They came to the large door that opened to the central campus and Dr. Francis pushed it open. Despite the ocean breezes, Long Beach could not escape periodic stretches of oppressive heat. Kevin stepped out into the bright midday sunlight, and for a moment their philosophical bantering felt trivial in light of the world before him. A dozen seminary students walked across the manicured park, heads bent in thought or tilted back with smiles. Two dozen poplars formed an avenue through the expansive lawn. The chapel's steeple towered over the trees beyond the park. To his right, the Augustine Memorial Library glistened in the sun. The Divinity School of the Pacific, South, was at a glance statelier and more modern than its parent, the Episcopal seminary in Berkeley.

Here was the real world, made up of normal people with sensible histories and ordinary families pursuing an admirable profession. He, on the other hand, was a twenty-eight-year-old convert who really had no business attending seminary at all, much less leading a flock one day. Not because he didn't have honorable intent, but because of who he *was*. Because he was Kevin Parson, who had really only discovered his spiritual side for the first time three years ago. In spite of his whole-hearted embrace of the church, he still felt no holier—and maybe less—than any drunk on the street might. Not even the dean knew his whole story, and Kevin wasn't sure the man would be so supportive if he did.

"You have a brilliant mind, Kevin," the dean said, gazing out at the grounds. "I've seen a lot of people come and go, and few of them have your same tenacity for the truth. But believe me, the deepest questions can drive a man mad. The problem of evil is one of those questions. You'd be wise to court it slowly."

Kevin looked into the graying man's eyes, and for a moment neither spoke. The dean winked and Kevin offered a slight smile. Kevin liked this man as much as he might like a father.

"You're a wise man, Dr. Francis. Thanks. I'll see you in class next week."

"Don't forget your paper."

"Never."

The dean dipped his head.

Kevin took one step down to the concrete landing and turned back. "Just one last thought. In absolute terms, gossip isn't so different from murder, right?"

"Ultimately, no."

"Then the bishop is ultimately capable of murder, isn't he?"

The dean lifted his right eyebrow. "That's a bit of a stretch."

Kevin smiled. "Not really. Neither is more evil."

"You've made your point, Kevin. I'll be sure to warn the bishop against any sudden urges to kill his fellowman."

Kevin chuckled. He turned and walked down the steps. Behind him the door closed with a soft thump. He turned back. The steps were empty.

He was alone. A stranger in a strange world. How many grown men would stare at a flight of steps just vacated by a professor of philosophy and feel utterly alone? He scratched his head and ruffled his hair.

Kevin headed for the parking lot. The sense of solitude left him before he reached his car, which was good. He was changing, wasn't he? The hope of change was why he'd chosen to become a priest in the first place. He'd escaped the demons of his past and begun a new life as a new creature. He had put his old self in the grave and, despite the lingering memories, he was coming to life, like an aspen in the spring.

So much change in so little time. God willing, the past would remain buried.

He swung his beige Sable out of the lot and merged with the steady flow of traffic on Long Beach Boulevard. Evil. The problem of evil. Like traffic—never ending.

On the other hand, grace and love weren't exactly running scared, were they? He had more to be thankful for than he ever imagined possible. Grace, for starters. A fine school with fine teachers. His own home. He might not have a rack of friends to call on at his every whim, but he did have a few. One at least. Dr. John Francis liked him.

He humphed. Okay, so he had a ways to go on the social front. Samantha had called him, though. They'd talked twice in the last two weeks. And Sam was no slouch. Now there was a friend. Maybe more than a—

His cell phone chirped loudly from the cup holder. He'd gotten the thing a week ago and had used it once, placed a call to his home phone to see if it worked. It had, but only after he'd activated the voice mail, which had required a call to the salesman.

The cell rang again and he picked it up. The thing was small enough to swallow if you got hungry enough. He pushed the red button and immediately knew it was the wrong one. Ignore "Send" above the green button. Green is go and red is stop, the salesman had said.

Kevin lifted the phone to his ear, heard silence, and tossed it on the passenger seat, feeling foolish. It was probably the salesman, calling to see if he was enjoying his new phone. Then again, why would a salesman bother to check on a nineteen-dollar purchase?

The phone chirped again. Behind him, a horn honked. A blue Mercedes crowded his bumper. Kevin punched the accelerator and picked up the phone. Red brake lights cut across all three lanes ahead. He slowed down—the Mercedes would have to chill. He pressed the green button.

"Hello?"

"Hello, Kevin."

Male voice. Low and breathy. Drawn out to accentuate each syllable.

"Hello?"

"How are you doing, my old friend? Quite well from what I can gather. How nice."

The world around Kevin faded. He brought the car to a halt behind the sea of red taillights, felt the pressure of the brakes as a distant abstraction. His mind focused on this voice on the phone.

"I . . . I'm sorry. I don't think—"

"It doesn't matter if you know me." Pause. "I know you. In fact, if you really think you're cut out for this seminary foolishness, I must say I know you better than you know yourself."

"I don't know who you think you are, but I don't have a clue what you're talking—"

"Don't be stupid!" the voice yelled into his ear. The man took a deep, scratchy breath. He spoke calmly again. "Forgive me, I really don't mean to yell, but you're not listening to me. It's time to quit pretending, Kevin. You think you have the whole world fooled, but you don't have me fooled. It's time to let the cat out of the bag. And I'm going to help you do it."

Kevin could hardly comprehend what he was hearing. Was this for real? It had to be a practical joke. Peter? Did Peter from Intro to Psych know him well enough to pull a stunt like this?

"Who . . . who is this?"

"You like games, don't you, Kevin?"

There was no way Peter could sound so condescending.

"Okay," Kevin said. "Enough. I don't know what—"

"Enough? Enough? No, I don't think so. The game is just starting. Only this one is not like the games you play with everyone else, Kevin. This one's for real. Will the real Kevin Parson please stand up? I thought about killing you, but I've decided this will be much better." The man paused, made a soft sound that sounded like a moan. "This . . . this will destroy you."

Kevin stared ahead, dumbfounded.

"You may call me Richard Slater. Ring any bells? Actually, I prefer Slater. And here's the game Slater would like to play. I will give you exactly three minutes to call the newspaper and confess your sin, or I will blow that silly Sable you call a car sky-high."

"Sin? What are you talking about?"

"That's the question, isn't it? I knew you'd forget, you stupid brick." Another pause. "Do you like riddles? Here's a riddle to jog your mind: *What falls but never breaks? What breaks but never falls?*"

"What? What's—"

"Three minutes, Kevin. Starting . . . now. Let the games begin."

The phone went dead.

For a moment, Kevin stared ahead, phone still plastered to his ear. . A horn blared.

The cars ahead were moving. The Mercedes was impatient again. Kevin pressed the accelerator, and the Sable surged forward. He set the phone down on the passenger seat and swallowed, throat dry. He glanced at the clock. 12:03.

Okay, process. Stay calm and process. Did this really just happen? Of course it just happened! Some madman who called himself Slater just called my cell phone and threatened to blow up my car. Kevin grabbed the cell phone and stared at its face: "Unavailable, 00:39."

But was the threat real? Who would really blow up a car in the middle of a busy street over a riddle? Someone was trying to scare the snot out of him for some maniacal reason. Or some sicko had randomly chosen him as his next victim, someone who hated seminary students instead of prostitutes and really intended to kill him.

His thoughts spun crazily. What sin? He had committed his

sins, of course, but none that stood out immediately. *What falls but never breaks? What breaks but never falls?*

His pulse pounded in his ears. Maybe he should get off the road. Of course he should get off the road! If there was even a remote chance that Slater meant to carry out his threat . . .

For the first time, Kevin imagined the car actually filling with a blast of fire. A shaft of panic ripped down his spine. He had to get out! He had to call the police!

Not now. Now he had to get out. Out!

Kevin jerked his foot off the accelerator and slammed it down on the brake. The Sable's tires squealed. A horn shrieked. The Mercedes.

Kevin twisted his head and glanced through the rear window. Too many cars. He had to find a vacant spot, where flying shrapnel would do the least damage. He gunned the motor and shot forward. 12:05. But how many seconds? He had to assume three minutes would end at 12:06.

A dozen thoughts crowded his mind: thoughts of a sudden explosion, thoughts of the voice on the phone, thoughts of how the cars around him were reacting to the Sable jerking along the road. *What falls but never breaks? What breaks but never falls?*

Kevin looked around, frantic. He had to dump the car without blowing up the neighborhood. *It's not even going to blow, Kevin. Slow down and think.* He ran his fingers through his hair several times in quick succession.

He swung into the right lane, ignoring another horn. A Texaco station loomed on his right—not a good choice. Beyond the gas station, Dr. Won's Chinese Cuisine—hardly better. There were no parks along this section of road; residences packed the side streets. Ahead, lunch crowds bustled at McDonald's and Taco Bell. The clock still read 12:05. It had been 12:05 for too long.

Now true panic muddled his thinking. *What if it really does go*

off? It's going to, isn't it? God, help me! I've got to get out of this thing!
He grabbed at his seat belt buckle with a trembling hand. Released
the shoulder strap. Both hands back on the wheel.

A Wal-Mart sat back from the street a hundred yards to his left.
The huge parking lot was only half-filled. A wide greenway that
dipped at its center, like a natural ditch, surrounded the entire lot.
He made a critical decision: Wal-Mart or nothing.

Kevin leaned on his horn and cut back into the center lane with
a cursory glance in his mirror. A metallic screech made him duck—
he'd clipped a car. Now he was committed.

"Get out of my way! Get out!"

He motioned frantically with his left hand, succeeding only in
smashing his knuckles into the window. He grunted and swerved
into the far left lane. With a tremendous *thump* he crashed over a
six-inch-high median and then into oncoming traffic. It occurred to
him that being rammed head-on might be no better than blowing
up, but he was already in the path of a dozen oncoming cars.

Tires squealed and horns blared. The Sable took only one hit in
its right rear fender before shooting out the other side of the gauntlet.
Something from his car was dragging on the asphalt. He cut off a
pickup that was trying to exit the lot.

"Watch out! Get out of my way!"

Kevin roared into the Wal-Mart lot and glanced down at the
clock. Somewhere back there it had turned. 12:06.

To his right, traffic on Long Beach Boulevard had come to a
screeching halt. It wasn't every day that a car blasted through oncoming traffic like a bowling ball.

Kevin sped past several gaping customers and zeroed in on the
greenway. Not until he was on top of it did he see the curb. The Sable
blew a tire when it connected; this time Kevin's head struck the ceiling. A dull pain spread down his neck.

Out, out, out!

The car flew into the ditch and Kevin crammed the brake pedal to the floor. For a fleeting moment he thought he might roll. But the car slid to a jolting halt, its nose planted firmly in the opposite slope.

He grabbed at the door latch, shoved the door open, and dove to the turf, rolling on impact. He scrambled to his feet and raced up the slope toward the lot. At least a dozen onlookers headed his way from the sea of parked cars.

"Back! Get back!" Kevin waved his arms at them. "There's a bomb in the car. Get back!"

They stared at him for one moment of fixed horror. Then all but three turned and fled, screaming his warning.

Kevin swung his arms furiously at the others. "Get back, you idiots! There's a bomb!"

They ran. A siren wailed through the air. Someone had already called the cops.

Kevin had run a good fifty paces from the greenway before it occurred to him that the bomb hadn't gone off. What if there wasn't a bomb after all? He pulled up and whipped around, panting and trembling. Surely three minutes had come and gone.

Nothing.

Was it a practical joke after all? Whoever this caller was, he'd done almost as much damage through the threat alone as he would have by detonating an actual bomb.

Kevin glanced around. A gawking crowd had gathered on the street at a safe distance. The traffic had stalled and was backing up as far as he could see. Steam hissed from a blue Honda—presumably the one that had hit his right rear fender. There had to be a few hundred people staring at the nut who'd driven his car into the ditch. Except for the growing wail of sirens, the scene had grown eerily silent. He took a step back toward the car.

At least there was no bomb. A few angry motorists and some bent fenders, so what? He'd done the only thing he could do. And really, there still could be a bomb. He'd leave that for the police once he explained his story. Surely they would believe him. Kevin stopped. The car tipped into the dirt with its left rear tire off the ground. From here it all looked kind of stupid.

"You said bomb?" someone yelled.

Kevin looked back at a middle-aged man with white hair and a Cardinals baseball cap. The man stared at him. "Did you say there was a bomb?"

Kevin looked back at the car, feeling suddenly foolish. "I thought there—"

A deafening explosion shook the ground. Kevin instinctively crouched and threw his hands up to protect his face.

The bright fireball hung over the car; boiling black smoke rose into the sky. The red flame collapsed on itself with a soft *whomp*. Smoke billowed from the charred skeleton of what was only a moment ago his Sable.

Kevin dropped to one knee and stared, dumbstruck, wide-eyed.

2

WITHIN THIRTY MINUTES the crime scene was isolated and a full investigation launched, all in the purview of one Detective Paul Milton. The man was well built and walked like a gunslinger—a Schwarzenegger wannabe with a perpetual frown and blond bangs that covered his forehead. Kevin rarely found others intimidating, but Milton did nothing to calm his already shattered nerves.

Someone had just tried to kill him. Someone named Slater, who seemed to know quite a lot about him. A madman who had the forethought and malice to plant a bomb and then remotely detonate the device when his demands weren't met. The scene stood before Kevin like an abstract painting come to life.

Yellow tape marked a forty-yard perimeter, and within it several uniformed police officers gathered pieces of wreckage, labeled them with evidence tags, and stacked them in neat piles on a flatbed truck to be transported downtown. The crowd had grown to well over a hundred. Bewilderment was fixed on some faces; other spectators wildly gestured their version of the events. The only injury reported was a small cut on a teenage boy's right arm. As it turned out, one of the cars Kevin had clipped in his mad dash across the street was none other than the impatient Mercedes. Once the driver learned he'd been following a car bomb, however, his attitude improved significantly.

Traffic on Long Beach Boulevard still suffered from curiosity, but the debris had been cleared.

Three news vans were in the lot. If Kevin understood the situation correctly, his face and what was left of his car were being televised live throughout the Los Angeles Basin. A news helicopter hovered overhead.

A forensic scientist worked carefully over the twisted remains of the trunk, where the bomb had clearly resided. Another detective dusted for prints on what was left of the doors.

Kevin had spilled his story to Milton and now waited to be taken down to the station. By the way Milton glared at him, Kevin was sure the detective considered him a suspect. A simple examination of the evidence would clear his name, but one minor fact haunted him. His account of events omitted Slater's demand that he confess some sin.

What sin? The last thing he needed was for the police to begin digging into his past for some sin. Sin wasn't the point. The point was that Slater had given him a riddle and told him that phoning the newspaper with the riddle's answer would prevent Kevin from being blown sky-high. That's what he'd told them.

On the other hand, willfully withholding information in an investigation was a crime itself, wasn't it?

Dear God, someone just blew up my car! The fact sat like an absurd little lump on the edge of Kevin's mind. The front edge. He smoothed his hair nervously.

Kevin sat on a chair provided by one of the cops, tapping his right foot on the grass. Milton kept glancing at him as he debriefed the other investigators and took statements from witnesses. Kevin looked back at the car where the forensic team worked. What they could possibly learn from that wreckage escaped him. He stood unsteadily, took a deep breath, and walked down the slope toward the car.

The forensic scientist at the trunk was a woman. Black, petite, maybe Jamaican. She looked up and lifted an eyebrow. Pretty smile. But the smile didn't alter the scene behind her.

It was hard to believe that the twisted pile of smoldering metal and plastic had been his car.

"Whoever did this had one heck of a chip on his shoulder," she said. A badge on her shirt said she was Nancy Sterling. She looked back into what was left of the trunk and dusted the inside lip.

Kevin cleared his throat. "Can you tell me what kind of bomb it was?"

"Do you know bombs?" she asked.

"No. I know there's dynamite and C-4. That's about it."

"We'll know for sure back at the lab, but it looks like dynamite. Leaves no chemical signature that ties it to a specific batch once it's been detonated."

"Do you know how he set it off?"

"Not yet. Remote detonation, a timer, or both, but there's not too much left to go on. We'll eventually get it. We always do. Just be glad you got out."

"Boy, no kidding."

He watched her place tape over a dusted fingerprint, lift it, and seal the faint print on a card. She made a few notations on the card and went back to work with her flashlight.

"The only prints we've found so far are in places where we would expect to find yours." She shrugged. "Guy like this isn't stupid enough not to wear gloves, but you never know. Even the smartest make mistakes eventually."

"Well, I hope he made one. This whole thing's crazy."

"They usually are." She gave him a friendly smile. "You okay?"

"I'm alive. Hopefully I don't hear from him again." His voice shook as he spoke.

Nancy straightened and looked him in the eye. "If it's any consolation, if this was me, I'd be in a pool of tears on the sidewalk. We'll get this one, like I said; we always do. If he really wanted to kill you, you'd be dead. This guy's meticulous and calculating. He wants you alive. That's my take, for what it's worth."

She glanced up to where Detective Milton was talking to a reporter. "And don't let Milton get to you. He's a good cop. Full of himself, maybe. Case like this will send him through the roof."

"Why's that?"

"Publicity. Let's just say he has his aspirations." She smiled. "Don't worry. Like I said, he's a good detective."

As if on cue, Milton turned from the camera and walked straight for them.

"Let's go, cowboy. How long you here for, Nancy?"

"I have what I need."

"Preliminary findings?"

"I'll have them for you in half an hour."

"I need them now. I'm taking Mr. Parson in for a few questions."

"I'm not ready now. Half an hour, on your desk."

They held stares.

Milton snapped his fingers at Kevin. "Let's go." He headed for a late-model Buick on the street.

||

The station's air conditioner was under repair. After two hours in a stuffy conference room, Kevin's nerves finally began to lose the tremble brought on by the bomb.

An officer had fingerprinted him for comparisons with the prints lifted from the Sable, then Milton spent half an hour reviewing his story before abruptly leaving him alone. The ensuing twenty minutes of solitude gave Kevin plenty of time to rehash Slater's call

while staring at a large brown smudge on the wall. But in the end
he could make no more sense of the call than when it had initially
come, which only made the whole mess more disturbing.

He shifted in his seat and tapped the floor with his foot. He'd
spent his whole life not knowing, but this vulnerability was somehow
different. A man named Slater had mistaken him for someone else and
very nearly killed him. Hadn't he suffered enough in his life? Now he'd
fallen into this, whatever *this* was. He was under the authorities' micro-
scope. They would try to dig into his past. Try to understand it. But
even Kevin didn't understand his past. He wasn't about to let them try.

The door banged open and Milton walked in.

Kevin cleared his throat. "Anything?"

Milton straddled a backward chair, slapped a folder down on the
table, and drilled Kevin with his dark eyes. "You tell me."

"What do you mean?"

Milton blinked twice and ignored the question. "The FBI's bringing someone in on this. ATF wants a look, CBI, state police—the lot
of them. But as far as I'm concerned, this is still my jurisdiction. Just
because terrorists favor bombs doesn't mean every bomb that goes off
is the work of terrorists."

"They think this is a terrorist?"

"I didn't say that. But Washington sees terrorists behind every tree
these days, so they will definitely go on the hunt. It wouldn't surprise
me to see the CIA picking through the files." Milton eyed him,
unblinking, for a few long seconds, and then blinked three times in
rapid succession. "What we have here is one sick puppy. What con-
fuses me is why he picked you. Doesn't make sense."

"None of this makes sense."

Milton opened the file. "It'll take a couple days for the lab to complete their work on what little we found, but we have some preliminary findings, the most significant of which is nothing."

"What do you mean, nothing? A bomb about blew me to pieces!"

"No evidence of real investigative value. Let me summarize for you—maybe it'll shake something loose in that mind of yours." He eyed Kevin again.

"We have a man with a low, raspy voice who calls himself Richard Slater and who knows you well enough to target you. You, on the other hand, have no idea who he could possibly be." Milton paused for effect. "He constructs a bomb using common electronics available at any Radio Shack and dynamite, rendering the bomb virtually untraceable. Smart. He then plants that bomb in the trunk of your car. He calls you, knowing that you're in the car, and threatens to blow the car in three minutes if you can't solve a riddle. *What falls but never breaks? What breaks but never falls?* Right so far?"

"Sounds right."

"Due to some fast thinking and some fancy driving, you manage to drive the car to a relatively safe location and escape. As promised, the car blows up when you fail to solve the riddle and phone it in to the newspaper."

"That's right."

"Preliminary forensics tell us that whoever planted that bomb left no fingerprints. No surprises there—this guy's obviously not the village idiot. The explosion could have caused significant collateral damage. If you'd been on the street when it blew, we'd have some bodies at the morgue. That's enough to assume this guy's either pretty teed off or a raving lunatic, probably both. So we have smart and we have teed off. Follow?"

"Makes sense."

"What we're missing is the most obvious link in any case like this. Motivation. Without motivation, we've got squat. You have no idea whatsoever why anyone would want to harm you in any way? You have no enemies from the past, no recent threats against your well-being, no reason whatsoever to suspect why anyone on this earth might want to hurt you in any way?"

"He didn't try to hurt me. If he wanted to kill me, he could've just blown up the bomb."

"Exactly. So we're not only clueless as to why someone named Slater might *want* to blow up your car, we don't even know why he *did*. What did he accomplish?"

"He scared me."

"You don't scare someone by nuking their neighborhood. But okay, say he just wanted to scare you—we still don't have motivation. Who might want to scare you? Why? But you don't have a clue, right? Nothing you've ever done would give anyone any reason to hold anything against you."

"I—not that I know of. You want me to just make something up? I told you, I really don't know."

"You're leaving us high and dry, Kevin. High and dry."

"What about the phone call?" Kevin asked. "Isn't there a way to track it?"

"No. We can only track a call while it's being made. What's left of your cell is nothing more than a lump of plastic in an evidence bag anyway. If we're lucky, we'll have a shot next time." He closed the file folder. "You do know there'll be a next time, don't you?"

"Not necessarily." Actually, the thought had plagued him, but he refused to give it any serious consideration. Freak occurrences like this happened to people now and then; he could accept that. But a deliberate, drawn-out plot against him was unfathomable.

"There will be," Milton said. "This guy went to great lengths to pull this trick. He's after something, and we have to assume he didn't get it. Unless this was random or some kind of hellacious mistake, he'll try again."

"Maybe he mistook me for someone else."

"Not a chance. He's too methodical. He staked you out, wired the car, knew your moves, and blew it with careful deliberation."

True enough. Slater knew more than even the police knew. "He scared me. Maybe that's all he wanted."

"Maybe. I'm open to anything at this point." Milton paused. "You're sure there's nothing else you want to tell me? We don't have much on you. Never been married, no record, college grad, currently enrolled in seminary. Not the kind of person you'd expect to be involved in a crime of this nature."

Slater's demand crossed his mind.

"If I think of anything else, trust me, you'll be the first to know," Kevin said.

"Then you're free to go. I've put in an order to tap your phones as soon as we can clear the red tape—the boys should be out first thing tomorrow morning. I may also place a black and white outside your house in Signal Hill, but I doubt we're dealing with anyone who would approach your house."

"Tap my phones?" They were going to dig, weren't they? But what was he afraid of, as long as they didn't start prying about his past?

"With your permission, of course. You have any other cell phones?"

"No."

"If this guy makes contact in any other way, I want to hear about it immediately, you understand?"

"Of course."

"And pardon my insensitivity, but this isn't just about you anymore." His eyes twinkled. "We have reporters all over the place and they want an explanation. You might have some media attention. Don't talk to them. Don't even look at them. Stay focused, *capice?*"

"I'm the victim here, right? Why do I get the feeling I'm the one under investigation?"

Milton placed both of his palms on the table. The air condition-ing kicked in above them. "Because you are. We have a monster out there and that monster has chosen you. We need to know why. That means we need to know more about you. We have to establish moti-vation. That's the way it works."

Kevin nodded. Actually, it made perfect sense.

"You're free to go." The detective handed him a card. "Call me. Use the cell number on the back."

"Thanks."

"Don't thank me yet. Do you always stare people down while you're talking to them, or are you hiding something?"

Kevin hesitated. "Has it ever occurred to you that you have a ten-dency to terrify your witnesses, Detective?"

The man did one of his flash-blink routines—four this time. Paul Milton might have political aspirations, but unless the people decided to turn the country over to vampires, Kevin didn't think the detective had a chance.

Milton stood and walked out.

3

A FRIENDLY COP NAMED STEVE ushered Kevin out the back and took him to the Hertz rental-car agency. Twenty minutes later Kevin held the keys to a Ford Taurus, nearly identical to the Sable that was no more.

"You're sure you're okay to drive?" Steve asked.

"I can drive."

"Okay. I'll follow you home."

"Thanks."

The home was an old two-story that Kevin had purchased five years earlier, when he was twenty-three, using some of the money from a trust fund established by his parents before the car accident. A drunk driver had slammed into Ruth and Mark Little's car when Kevin was only one—their deaths had reportedly been immediate. Their only son, Kevin, had been with a baby-sitter. The insurance settlement went to Ruth's sister, Balinda Parson, who received full custody of Kevin and subsequently adopted him. With a few strokes of a judge's pen, Kevin ceased being a Little and became instead a Parson. He had no memories of his real parents, no brothers or sisters, no possessions that he knew of. Only a trust account beyond anyone's reach until he turned eighteen, much to Aunt Balinda's chagrin.

As it turned out, he had no need to touch the money until he turned twenty-three, and by that time it had grown into a sum in excess of three hundred thousand dollars—a small gift to help him build a new life once he got around to discovering he needed one. He'd called Balinda "Mother" until then. Now he called her his aunt. That's all she was, thank God. Aunt Balinda.

Kevin pulled into the garage and stepped out of the Taurus. He waved as the cop drove by, then closed the garage door. The timed light slowly faded. He stepped into the laundry room, glanced at a full hamper, and made a mental note to finish his laundry before he went to bed. If there was one thing he hated, it was disorder. Disorder was the enemy of understanding, and he'd lived long enough without understanding. How meticulous and organized did a chemist have to be in order to understand DNA? How organized had NASA been in reaching out to understand the moon? One mistake and *boom*.

Mounds of dirty clothes reeked of disorder.

Kevin walked into the kitchen and set the keys on the counter. *Someone just blew up your car and you're thinking about doing laundry.* Well, what was he supposed to do? Crawl into the corner and hide? He'd just escaped death—he should be throwing a party. Let's toast life, comrades. We have faced the enemy and we have survived the bomb blast down by the Wal-Mart.

Please, get a grip. You're babbling like a fool here. Still, in light of the past several hours, it was a blessing to be alive, and gratefulness was warranted. *Great is thy faithfulness. Yes indeed, what a blessing we have received. Long live Kevin.*

He stared past the breakfast nook with its round oak dinette, through the picture window that overlooked the front yard. An oil pump sat dormant on a dirt hill beyond the street. This was his view. It's what two hundred thousand dollars bought you these days.

On the other hand, there was that hill. Kevin blinked. With a pair of binoculars, anyone with a mind to could park himself at the base of that oil pump and watch Kevin Parson organize his laundry in complete anonymity.

The trembles were suddenly back. Kevin rushed over to the window and quickly lowered the miniblinds. He spun around and scanned the main floor. Besides the kitchen and laundry room, there was the living room, the bathroom, and sliding glass doors, which led to a small lawn encircled by a white picket fence. The bedrooms were upstairs. From this angle he could see right through the living room into the backyard. For all he knew, Slater could have been watching him for months!

No. That was stupid. Slater knew of him, maybe something from his past—a demented motorist he'd hacked off on the highway. Maybe even—

No, it couldn't be that. He was just a kid then.

Kevin wiped his forehead with his arm and stepped into the living room. A large leather sofa and a recliner faced a forty-two-inch flat-screen television. What if Slater had actually been *in* here?

He scanned the room. Everything was in its place, the coffee table dusted, the carpet vacuumed, the magazines in their rack beside the recliner. Order. His *Introduction to Philosophy* text sat on the dinette beside him. Large two-by-three-foot travel posters covered the walls in a hopscotch arrangement. Sixteen in all, counting the ones upstairs. Istanbul, Paris, Rio, the Caribbean, a dozen others. An unknowing person might think he ran a travel agency, but to Kevin the images were simply gateways to the real world, places he would one day visit to broaden his horizon.

To expand his understanding.

Even if Slater had been here, there would be no way to tell, short of dusting for prints. Maybe Milton should send out a team.

Easy, boy. This is an isolated incident, not a full-scale invasion. No need to tear the house down yet.

Kevin paced to the couch and then back. He picked up the remote control and turned on the television. He preferred to spin through the channels on the huge Sony picture tube rather than settle on any particular channel for long. The TV was yet another window into life—a wonderful montage of the world in all of its beauty and ugliness. Didn't matter; it was real.

He flipped the channels, one every other second or so. Football, a cooking show, a woman in a brown dress showing how to plant geraniums, a Vidal Sassoon commercial, Bugs Bunny. He paused on Bugs. *I say, what's up, doc?* Bugs Bunny had more truth to speak about life than the humans on the tube. "If you stay in the hole too long, it becomes your tomb." Wasn't that the truth. That was Balinda's problem—she was still in the hole. He flipped the station. The news . . .

The news. He stared at the aerial images, fascinated by the surreal shots of the smoldering car. His car. "Wow," he mumbled. "That's me." He shook his head in disbelief and ruffled his hair. "That's really me. I survived that."

What falls but never breaks? What breaks but never falls? He will call again. You do know that, don't you?

Kevin clicked the tube off. A psychobabblist once told him that his mind was unusual. He'd tested with an IQ in the top one percentile—no problems there. In fact, if there was a problem—and Dr. Swanlist the psychobabblist certainly didn't think there was a problem at all—it was that his mind still processed information at a rate normally found in others during their formative years. Age normally slowed down the synapses, which explained why old folks could be downright scary behind the wheel. Kevin tended to view the world through the eyes of an adult with the innocence of a child. Which was really psychobabble for nothing of any practical value, regardless of how excited Dr. Swanlist got.

He looked at the stairs. What if Slater had gone up there?

He walked to the stairs and took them two at a time. One master bedroom on the left, one guest bedroom that he used as an office to his right, and one bathroom between the two. He headed for the guest bedroom, flipped on the light switch, and poked his head in. A desk with a computer, a chair, and several bookcases, one with a dozen textbooks and the rest heavy with over two hundred novels. He'd discovered the miracles of stories in his early teens, and ultimately they had set him free. There was no better way to understand life than to live it—if not through your own life, then through another's. There was once a man who owned a field. Brilliant, brilliant, brilliant. Not to read was to turn your back on the wisest minds.

Kevin scanned the fiction titles. Koontz, King, Shakespeare, Card, Stevenson, Powers—an eclectic collection. He'd read the books eagerly in his recent renaissance. To say Aunt Balinda didn't approve of novels was like saying the ocean is wet. She would feel no better about his philosophy and theology textbooks.

The travel posters in this room boasted of Ethiopia, Egypt, South Africa, and Morocco. Brown, brown, green, brown. That was it.

He closed the door and walked into the bathroom. Nothing. The man in the mirror had brown hair and blue eyes. Gray in bad light. Somewhat attractive if he was any judge, but generally average looking. *Not the kind of person stalked by a psychopath.* He grunted and hurried to his room.

The bed was made, the dresser drawers closed, the shade open. All in order. *You see, you've been hearing ghosts.*

Kevin sighed and peeled off his dress shirt and slacks. Thirty seconds later he'd changed into a pale blue T-shirt and jeans. He had to get back to a semblance of normalcy here. He tossed the dress shirt into the laundry bin, hung up his trousers, and headed for the door.

A flash of color on the nightstand caught his eye. Pink. A pink ribbon peeked out from behind the lamp.

Kevin's heart responded before his mind did, pounding into overdrive. He walked forward and stared at the thin pink hair ribbon. He'd seen it before. He could swear he'd seen this ribbon. A long time ago. Samantha had given him one exactly like it once, and it had gone missing years ago.

He spun around. Had Sam heard about the incident and driven down from Sacramento? She'd phoned recently but hadn't mentioned coming to visit him. The last time he'd seen his childhood friend was when she'd left for college at age eighteen, ten years earlier. She'd spent the last few years in New York working in law enforcement and had recently moved to Sacramento for employment with the California Bureau of Investigation.

But this ribbon was hers!

"Samantha?" His voice echoed softly in the room.

Silence. Of course—he'd already checked the place. Unless . . .

He snatched up the ribbon, ran for the stairs, and descended them in three long strides. "Samantha!"

It took Kevin exactly twenty seconds to search the house and rule out the possibility that his long-lost friend had paid him a visit and was hiding like they had as children. Unless she had come, left the ribbon, and then departed, intending to call him later. Would she do that? Under any other circumstance it would be a wonderful surprise.

Kevin stood in the kitchen, perplexed. If she'd left the ribbon, she would have left a message, a note, a phone call, something.

But there was no note. His black VTech phone sat on the kitchen counter. Number of messages: a big red "0."

What if Slater had left the ribbon? He should call Milton. Kevin ran a hand through his hair. Milton would want to know about the ribbon, which meant telling him about Samantha, which meant opening up the past. He couldn't open up the past, not after running from it for so long.

The silence felt thick.

Kevin looked at the pink ribbon trembling slightly in his hand and sat slowly at the dinette. The past. So long ago. He closed his eyes.

III

Kevin was ten years old when he first saw the pretty girl from down the street. That was a year before they met the boy who wanted to kill them.

Meeting Sam two days after his birthday was his best present. Ever. His brother, Bob, who was really his cousin, had given him a yo-yo, which he really did like, but not as much as meeting Samantha. He would never tell Bob that, of course. In fact, he wasn't sure he'd tell Bob about Samantha at all. It was his secret. Bob might be eight years older than Kevin, but he was a bit slow—he'd never catch on.

The moon was full that night, and Kevin was in bed by seven o'clock. He always went to bed early. Sometimes before supper. But tonight he'd been under the covers for what seemed like an hour, and he couldn't sleep. He thought maybe it was too bright with the moonlight coming through the white shade. He liked it dark when he slept. Pitch-dark, so he couldn't even see his hand when he put it an inch from his nose.

Maybe if he put some newspapers or his blanket over the window, it would be dark enough.

He climbed out of bed, pulled off the gray wool blanket, and hefted it up to hook over the rod. Wow, it was really bright out there. He glanced back at his bedroom door. Mother was in bed.

The shade hung from a spring-loaded roll at the top, a smudged sheet of canvas that covered the small window most of the time. There was nothing to look out at but the backyard anyway. Kevin lowered the blanket and lifted the bottom edge of the shade.

A dull glow shone over the ashes in the backyard. He could see the doghouse on the left, like it was day. He could even see each board in the old fence that ran around the house. Kevin lifted his eyes to the sky. A bright moon that glowed like a light bulb smiled down at him and he smiled back. Wow!

He started to lower the shade when something else caught his eye. A bump on one of the fence boards. He blinked and looked at it. No, not a bump! A—

Kevin dropped the shade. Someone was out there, staring back at him!

He scrambled off his bed and backed to the wall. Who would be staring at him in the middle of the night? Who would be staring at him period? It was a kid, wasn't it? One of the neighborhood boys or girls.

Maybe he just thought he saw someone. He waited a few minutes, lots of time for whoever it was to move on, and then he worked up the courage for just one more peek.

This time he barely lifted the shade so that he could just see over the sill. She was still there! Kevin thought his chest might explode from the fright, but he kept looking. She couldn't see him now; the shade was too low. It was a girl; he could see that much. A young girl, maybe his age, with long blonde hair and a face that would have to be pretty, he thought, although he couldn't really see any details of her face.

And then she dropped from sight and disappeared.

Kevin could hardly sleep. The next night, Kevin couldn't resist peeking out, but the girl was gone. Gone for good.

He thought.

Three days later he was in bed again, and this time he knew he had been lying awake for at least an hour without being able to sleep. Mother had made him take a very, very long nap that afternoon and he just wasn't tired. The moon wasn't as bright tonight but he had covered up the window to make it darker anyway. After a long time he decided that he might be better off with more light. Maybe if he could trick his mind into thinking it was the next morning already, it would be tired after not sleeping all night.

He stood, tore off the wool blanket, and sent the shade flying up with a flip of his wrist.

A small, round face had its nose against the window. Kevin jumped back and rolled off the bed, terrified. He scrambled to his feet. She was there! Here! At his window! The girl from the other night was right here, spying on him.

Kevin almost screamed. The girl was smiling. She lifted a hand and waved as if she recognized him and had just stopped by to say hi.

He glanced at the door. Hopefully Mother hadn't heard. He turned back to the girl in the window. She was mouthing something to him now, motioning for him to do something.

He could only stand there and stare, frozen.

She was motioning for him to lift the window! No way! And he couldn't anyway; it was screwed shut.

She didn't look frightening, really. In fact, she was actually very nice looking. Her face was pretty and her hair was long. Why was he so scared of her? Maybe he shouldn't be. Her face was so . . . kind.

Kevin glanced again at the door and then slid back onto the end of his bed. She waved again, and this time he waved back. She was pointing at the window sill, motioning again. He followed her hands and suddenly understood. She was telling him to unscrew the window! He looked at the single screw that fastened the sash in place and for the first time realized that he could take it out. All he had to do was find something to turn the screw with. Something like a penny. He had some of those.

Suddenly energized by the idea, Kevin grabbed one of the pennies from an old tin can on his floor and placed it in the screw. It came loose. He unwound it until it was out.

The girl jumped up and down and motioned for him to lift the window. Kevin gave his bedroom door one last look and then yanked on the window. It flew up silently. He knelt on his bed, face to face with the girl.

"Hi," she whispered, smiling from ear to ear.

"H . . . hi," he said.

"Do you want to come out and play?"

Play? Fear replaced excitement. Behind him the house was quiet. "I can't come out."

"Sure you can. Just crawl out the window. It's easy."

"I don't think I'm supposed to. I . . ."

"Don't worry, your mother won't even know. You can just climb back in later and screw the window shut again. They're all sleeping anyway, right?"

"You know my mother?"

"Everyone has a mother."

So she didn't know Mother. She was just saying that she knew mothers didn't like their kids sneaking out. As if all mothers were like his mother.

"Right?" she asked.

"Right."

What if he did go out? What harm would it do? Mother had never actually told him not to climb out of the window at night, at least not in those words.

"I don't know. No, I really can't."

"Sure you can. I'm a girl and you're a boy. Girls and boys play together. Don't you know that?"

He didn't know what to say. He'd never played with a girl before, that was for sure.

"Just hop down."

"Are . . . are you sure it's safe?"

She reached out a hand. "Here, I'll help you."

He wasn't sure what made him do it; his hand just seemed to reach out for hers on its own. His fingers touched hers and they were warm. He had never touched a girl's hand before. The strange sensation filled him with a good feeling he'd never felt before. Butterflies.

Ten seconds later, Kevin was out of the window trembling under a bright moon next to a girl about his own height.

"Follow me," the girl said. She walked for the fence, lifted a loose board, stepped out, and motioned him on. With one last anxious look back at his window, he followed.

Kevin stood beyond the fence shivering in the night, but not from fear so much as from excitement again.

"My name's Samantha, but you can call me Sam. What's yours?"

"Kevin."

Sam stuck out her hand. "Glad to meet you, Kevin." He took her hand and shook it. But she didn't let go. Instead she led him away from his house.

"We moved here from San Francisco about a month ago. I didn't know any children lived in this house, but a week ago I heard my parents talking. Your parents are pretty private people, huh?"

"Yeah, I guess."

"My parents let me walk down to the park at the end of the street where a lot of kids hang out. It's lighted, you know. You want to go down there?"

"Now?"

"Sure, why not? It's safe. My dad's a policeman—if it wasn't safe, believe me, he would know."

"No. I . . . I can't. I really don't want to."

She shrugged. "Suit yourself. I was on my way down the other night when I looked over your fence and saw you. I guess I was spying. Do you mind?"

"No."

"Good, because I think you're cute."

Kevin didn't know what to say.

"Do you think I'm pretty?" She spun away from him and twirled around like a ballerina. She wore a pink dress and pink ribbons in her hair.

"Yes, I think you're pretty," he said.

She stopped her twirling, looked at him for a moment, and then giggled. "I can already tell that we're going to be wonderful friends. Would you like that?"

"Yes."

She skipped back, grabbed his hand, and dragged him into a run. Kevin laughed. He did like her. He liked her very much. More, in fact, than anyone he could ever remember liking.

"Where are we going?"

"Don't worry, no one will know. No one will even see us. I promise."

For the next hour Sam talked to him about her family and their house, which was three down from his. She went to something she called a private school and didn't get home until six every night, she said. Her dad couldn't afford it on his income, but her grandmother had left a trust fund for her and the only way they could use any of the money was if she went to a private school. The kids there weren't really her type. Neither were most of the neighborhood kids. When she grew up, she was going to be a cop like her dad. That's probably why she liked to sneak around, because cops do that to catch the bad guys. She asked Kevin some questions but then backed off when she saw that he was shy.

Sam liked him—he could tell. It was the first time Kevin had felt that kind of friendship from anyone.

At about eight o'clock Samantha told him that she had to get home or her parents would worry. They squeezed back through the fence and she helped him climb back through his window.

"This will be our secret, okay? No one will know. If you hear me tapping on your window at about seven o'clock, you'll know that I can play if you want to. Deal?"

"You mean we can do this again?"

"Why not? As long as you don't get caught, right?"

"Get caught?" Kevin looked at his window, suddenly fighting an urge to throw up. He wasn't sure why he felt sick; he only knew that if Mother found out she wouldn't be happy. Things went funny when Mother wasn't happy. How could he have done this? He never did things without asking. Never.

Sam put her hand on his shoulder. "Don't be afraid, Kevin. No one will know. I like you and I want to be your friend. Would you like that?"

"Yes."

Sam giggled and flashed her bright blue eyes. "I want to give you something." She pulled one of the pink ribbons from her hair and handed it to him. "Don't let your mom find it."

"This is for me?"

"So you don't forget me."

There was no chance of that. No way.

Sam held out her hand. "Until next time, partner. Slip me some skin."

He looked at her, confused.

"My dad says that. It's a street thing. Here, like this." She took his hand and slid her palm on his. "See ya. Don't forget to screw your window down."

Then Sam was gone.

Two nights later she was back. With more butterflies in his stomach and shrill warning bells ringing in his mind, Kevin slipped out his window.

Mother would find out. Sam took his hand and that made him feel warm, but Mother would find out. The ringing in his head wouldn't stop.

III

Kevin snapped out of the memories. A shrill bell screamed. He jerked to the sound. It took him a moment to make the transition from the past.

The black phone on the counter rang. It was a modern contraption with an old-style bell that sounded like an old desk phone. Kevin stared at it, suddenly unsure whether he wanted to pick it up. He rarely received phone calls; few people had reason to call him. Mostly telemarketers.

He'd set the answering machine for six rings. What if it was Samantha? Or Detective Milton?

The phone rang again. *Answer it, Kevin. Of course. Answer it.*

He stepped over to the counter and snatched the receiver from its cradle. "Hello?"

"Hello, Kevin. Did you find my little gift?"

Kevin went numb. Slater.

"I'll take that as a yes. We've had an eventful day, haven't we? First a little phone call and then a little boom and now a little gift. And all within four hours. Makes all the waiting worth it, don't you think?"

"Who are you?" Kevin demanded. "How do you know me?"

"Who am I? I am your worst nightmare. I promise you, you'll agree soon enough. How do I know you? Tsk, tsk, tsk. The fact that you even have to ask justifies everything I have in mind."

It had to be the boy! *God in heaven, save me!* Kevin slumped slowly to the floor. This couldn't be happening. "Oh God—"

"Not God, Kevin. Definitely not God. Now, I want you to listen carefully, because I'm going to give you a lot of information in a short time. Every single bit is critical if you want to survive this little game of ours. Do you understand?"

Kevin's mind raced through the years, searching for someone who might have sounded like this man, anyone who might have any reason at all to speak to him this way. Anyone but the boy.

"Answer me, you creep!" Slater said.

"Yes."

"Yes, what?"

"Yes, I understand."

"Yes, you understand what?"

"That I have to listen carefully," Kevin said.

"Good. From now on you answer me when I ask you a question, and you speak only when I say you speak. Do you understand?"

"Yes."

"Fine. There are only three rules to our game. Remember all of them. One, you say nothing to the cops about my riddles or my phone calls until after the time has passed. Then you may tell them all you want. This is personal—having the whole city coming unglued over a little bomb that might go off wouldn't be useful. Are we clear?"

"Yes."

"Two, you do exactly what I say, or I promise you will pay. Abundantly clear?"

"Why are you doing—"

"Answer me!"

"Yes!"

"Three, the riddles keep coming until you confess. As soon as you do, I go away. It's that simple. One, two, three. Get it through your thick skull and we'll do fine. Understand?"

"Please, if you'll just tell me what to confess, I'll confess. Why are you using riddles? Can I confess without solving riddles?"

Slater remained silent for a moment. "The answer to the riddles and the confession are the same. That's the first clue and that's the last clue. The next time you try to squeeze something out of me, I'll walk in there and cut off one of your ears, or something as interesting. What's the matter, Kevin? You're the brilliant seminary student. You're the smart little philosopher. A little riddle scares you?"

The riddles and the confession are the same. So then maybe it wasn't the boy.

"This isn't fair—"

"Did I ask you to speak?"

"You asked me a question."

"Which requires an answer, not a lecture. For that you will pay an extra little price. I've decided to kill to help you along with your understanding."

Kevin was aghast. "You . . . you just decided—"

"Maybe two killings."

"No, I'm sorry. I won't speak."

"Better. And just so we're clear, you of all people are in no position to talk about being fair. You may have that old fool at the seminary fooled, you may have all the old ladies at that church thinking you're a sweet, young fellow, but I know you, boy. I know how your mind works and I know what you're capable of. Guess what? I'm about to let the snake out of his dungeon. Before we're done here, the world is going to know the whole ugly truth, boy. Open the drawer in front of you."

The drawer? Kevin stood and looked at the utility drawer beneath the counter. "The drawer?"

"Open it and pull out the cell phone."

Kevin eased the drawer out. A small silver cell phone sat in the pencil tray. He picked it up.

"From now on you keep this phone with you at all times. It's set to vibrate—no need to wake up the neighbors every time I call.

Unfortunately, I won't be able to call you on your home phone once the cops bug it. Understand?"

"Yes."

That Slater had been in Kevin's house was no longer open to question. What else did Slater know?

"There's one other little matter that needs our attention before we continue. I have good news for you, Kevin." Slater's voice thickened and his breathing grew heavier. "You're not alone in this. I intend to bring someone else down with you. Her name is Samantha." Pause. "You do remember Samantha, don't you? You should; she called you recently."

"Yes."

"You like her, don't you, Kevin?"

"She's a friend."

"You don't have a lot of friends."

"No."

"Consider Samantha as my insurance. If you fail me, she dies."

"You can't do that!"

"Shut up! Shut up, you foul-mouthed lying punk! Listen carefully. *In life he's your friend, but death is the end.* That's your little bonus riddle for being so dense. You have exactly thirty minutes to solve it or your best friend will indeed go boom."

"What friend? I thought this was about me! How will you even know if I've solved the riddle?"

"Call Samantha. Ask for her help. The two of you can put your stinking heads together and figure it out."

"I'm not even sure I can reach Samantha. How will you know what I tell her?"

Slater's deep chuckle filled the phone. "You don't do what I'm doing without learning the tools of the trade, boy. I have ears and eyes everywhere. Did you know that with the right toys you can understand a man inside a house from over a thousand yards away? Seeing is even easier. The clock is ticking. You're down to twenty-nine minutes and thirty-two seconds. I suggest you hustle."

The line clicked.

"Slater?"

Nothing. Kevin shoved the phone into its cradle and looked at his watch. 4:15. There was going to be another explosion in thirty minutes, this time involving his best friend, which made no sense because he had no best friends. *In life he's your friend, but death is the end.* No cops.

4

F BI SPECIAL AGENT JENNIFER PETERS hurried down
the hall, her pulse hammering with an urgency she hadn't felt
for three months. The Long Beach bomb report had come in several
hours ago, but she hadn't been told. Why? She rounded the corner
and shoved the Los Angeles bureau chief's door open.

Frank Longmont sat at his desk, phone pressed to his ear. He
didn't bother looking up at her. He knew, didn't he? The weasel had
purposefully stalled.

"Sir?"

Frank held up his hand. Jennifer crossed her arms while the
chief talked on. Only then did she notice two other agents, whom
she didn't recognize, seated at the small conference table to her left.
Looked like East Coast stiffs. Their eyes lingered. She turned from
them and steadied her breathing.

Her blue business suit had only the smallest of slits up her left leg,
but she couldn't shake the certainty that what was decent, even conservative in her mind, still drew frequent glances from men. Her hair
was dark, to her shoulders, and her eyes a soft hazel. She had the kind
of face others might spend their lives trying to imitate—symmetrical
with soft skin and rich color. There was no disguising her physical
beauty. *Beauty is a gift,* her father used to say. *Just don't flaunt it.* A gift.
Jennifer had found beauty just as often a handicap. Many people of

both genders had difficulty accepting both beauty and excellence from the same person.

To compensate, she tried her best to ignore her appearance and instead focus on excellence. *Brains are also a gift,* her father used to say. And God had not been stingy. At age thirty, Jennifer Peters was regarded as one of the best forensic psychologists on the West Coast.

But in the end it hadn't mattered. Her excellence hadn't saved her brother. Which left her as what? A beautiful woman who was much more interested in being smart than beautiful, but who wasn't so smart after all. A nothing. A nothing whose failure had killed her brother. And now a nothing who was being ignored by the bureau chief.

Frank set down his phone and turned to the two men at the table. "Excuse us for a moment, gentlemen."

The two agents exchanged glances, rose, and left. Jennifer waited for the click of the door latch before speaking.

"Why wasn't I told?"

Frank spread his hands. "You obviously were."

She glared at him. "It's been five hours! I should already be in Long Beach."

"I've been on the phone with the Long Beach police chief. We'll be there first thing in the morning."

We'll? He was being cagey. She walked to his desk, hands on hips. "Okay, cut the innuendos. What's going on?"

Frank smiled. "Please, Jennifer, take a seat. Take a breath."

She didn't like the tone of his voice. *Easy, girl. Your life's in this man's hands.*

"It's him, isn't it?"

"We don't have enough yet. Sit." They locked stares. She sat in one of the large chairs facing the desk and crossed her legs.

Frank tapped his finger on the desk absently. "I was thinking of letting Craig take over the on-site investigation. Let you work here in a coordination role."

Jennifer felt her face flush. "This is my case! You can't just remove me!"

"Did I say remove? I don't remember using that word. And if you haven't noticed in your six years with the bureau, we juggle agents quite frequently for a host of reasons."

"No one knows this case like I do," she said. The chief wouldn't actually do this. She was way too valuable on the case!

"One of those reasons is the relationship between agent and critical parties, including victims."

"I've spent a year breathing down this guy's neck," Jennifer said. She let the desperation creep into her voice. "For heaven's sake, Frank. You can't do this to me."

"He killed your brother, Jennifer."

She stared at him. "This suddenly becomes germane? The way I see it, the fact that he killed Roy gives me a right to hunt him down."

"Please, I know this is hard, but you have to try to look at the situation objectively. Roy was the killer's last victim. We haven't heard a peep in the three months since. You ever ask yourself why he chose Roy?"

"It happened," she said. She had, of course. The answer was patently obvious but unspoken.

"He kills four other people in the Sacramento area before you start to close in. You come within five minutes of apprehending him. He takes offense and chooses someone close to you. Roy. He plays his little game of riddles and then kills Roy when you come up short."

Jennifer just stared at him.

The chief held up one hand. "No, that didn't come out like I—"

"You're saying the Riddle Killer killed my brother because of me? You have the audacity to sit there and accuse me of playing a part in my own brother's execution?"

"I said that's not what I meant. But he likely chose Roy because of your involvement."

"And did that fact affect my performance?"

He hesitated.

Jennifer closed her eyes and drew a careful breath.

"You're putting words in my mouth," Frank said. "Look, I'm sorry, really I am. I can only imagine how it was for you. And I can't think of anyone who is more qualified to go after this nut, but the equation changed when he killed your brother. He has it out for you. You're a critical party, and frankly your life's in danger."

She opened her eyes. "Don't patronize me with the danger nonsense, Frank. We signed on for danger. This is precisely what the Riddle Killer wants, you realize. He knows I'm his biggest threat. He also knows that you'll likely pull me for the very reasons you're citing. He *wants* me off the case."

She said it with a strong voice, but only because she'd long ago learned to stuff emotion. For the most part. The bureau did that. The better part of her wanted to scream at Frank and tell him where he could put his objectiveness.

He sighed. "We don't even know this is the same killer. Could be a copy cat; could be unrelated. We need someone here to piece this together carefully."

The Riddle Killer had started playing his little games nearly a year ago. He picked his victims for a variety of reasons and then stalked them until he knew their routines intimately. The riddle usually came out of thin air. He gave the victims a specified amount of time to solve the riddle under the threat of death. Inventive and cold-blooded.

Her brother, Roy Peters, had been a thirty-three-year-old attorney newly employed in Sacramento by Bradsworth and Bixx. A brilliant man with a wonderful wife, Sandy, who worked for the Red Cross. More importantly, Roy and Jennifer had been inseparable right up to college when they'd both pursued law. Roy had bought Jennifer her first bicycle, not because her father couldn't, but because he wanted to. Roy had taught her to drive. Roy had checked out every boy she'd ever dated, often to her feigned chagrin. Her brother had been her soul mate, the standard no other man could measure up to.

Jennifer had replayed the events leading up to his death a thousand times, knowing each time that she could have prevented it. If only she'd pieced the riddle together twenty minutes earlier. If only she'd gotten to him sooner. If only she hadn't been assigned to the case.

Until this moment, no one had even hinted at blame—to do so would be beneath the Bureau. But her own blame had beaten her raw over the last three months. The fact was, if she had not been on the case, Roy would be alive. Nothing would ever change that. In some way she *was* personally responsible for the death of her brother.

Her mission in life was now painfully simple. She would stop at nothing to remove the Riddle Killer from the face of the earth.

If Frank knew the depth of her obsession, he might have pulled her from the case long ago. Her survival depended on her ability to remain calm and reasonable.

"Sir, I'm begging you. You have to let me lead the investigation. He hasn't killed yet. He's growing bold, but if we let him think he can play the FBI, he'll grow bolder. Pulling me from the case would send the wrong message."

The thought dawned on her only as she spoke it. By the look on Frank's face, he hadn't considered that angle yet.

She pressed. "I've had three months to grieve, Frank. Last time I took inventory I was lucid. You owe it to the public to let me go. No one stands a better chance of stopping him before he kills again."

Frank looked at her in silence.

"You know I'm right."

"You've got tenacity; I'll give you that. Tell me that you have no leanings to any kind of personal vendetta."

"I want him out of circulation. If that's personally motivated, so be it."

"That's not what I mean."

"You think I would compromise justice with a quick trigger?" she said with a bite of sarcasm. "Or withhold information from other agencies to get the collar myself? Do you think so little of me?"

"None of us are exempt from strong emotional pulls. If my brother had been killed, I'm not sure I wouldn't turn in my badge and go after him outside the law."

She wasn't sure what to say. She'd considered the same a dozen times. Nothing would give her more satisfaction than pulling the trigger herself when it came right down to it.

"I'm not you," she finally said, but she wasn't so sure.

He nodded. "You don't see the kind of love you shared with your brother much these days, you know. I've always respected you for that."

"Thank you. Roy was an incredible person. No one will ever replace him."

"No, I guess not. Okay, Jennifer. You win. You'll have a half-dozen agencies climbing around; I want you to work with them. I'm not saying you have to spend all day playing footsie with them, but at least give them the respect of keeping them up to date."

Jennifer stood. "Of course."

"Detective Paul Milton will be expecting you first thing. He's not the gun-shy type if you know what I mean. Be nice."

"I'm incapable of anything less."

5

KEVIN CLEARED THE FIRST FOUR STAIRS in his first step. He tripped on the last and sprawled on the landing. "Come on!" He grunted and jumped to his feet. Samantha's phone number was on his desk—please say it was still on his desk. He crashed through the door. His best friend. Who could that possibly be?

He shuffled through papers and knocked a hermeneutics textbook off the desk. He'd left it right here on top; he could swear it! Maybe he should just call Milton. Where was that number!

Slow down, Kevin. Gather yourself. This is a thinking game, not a race. No, a race too. A thinking race.

He took a deep breath and put his hand to his face. *I can't call the cops. Slater will hear the call. He's got the house bugged or something. Okay. He wants me to call Samantha. This is about her too. I need Samantha. Only two minutes have passed. Twenty-eight left. Plenty of time. First thing, find Sam's number. Think. You wrote it down on a white piece of paper. You used it to call her last week and you put the paper somewhere safe because it was important to you.*

Under the phone.

He lifted the desk phone and saw the white slip. Thank God! He grabbed the receiver and punched in the number with an unsteady hand. It rang. It rang again.

"Please, please pick up—"

"Hello?"

"Hello, Sam?"

"Who's calling?"

"It's me."

"Kevin? What's wrong? You sound—"

"I have a problem, Sam. Oh dear God, I've got a problem! Did you hear about the bomb that went off down here today?"

"A bomb? You're kidding, right? No, I didn't hear of a bomb; I have this week off, unpacking from the move. What happened?"

"Some guy who calls himself Slater blew up my car."

Silence.

"Sam?" Kevin's voice trembled. He suddenly thought he might start to cry. His vision swam. "Sam, please, I need your help."

"Someone named Slater blew up your car," she repeated slowly. "Tell me more."

"He called me on my cell phone and gave me three minutes to confess a sin, which he said I would know by a riddle. *What falls but never breaks? What breaks but never falls?* I managed to get the car into a ditch by a Wal-Mart and it blew up."

"Holy . . . You're serious? Was anyone hurt?"

"No. I just—"

"Is the FBI investigating? Good night, you're right—I just turned on the television. It's all over the news up here."

"Samantha, listen! I just got another call from this guy. He says I have thirty minutes to solve another riddle or he's going to blow up another bomb."

Sam seemed to switch into another mode immediately. "Riddles. You've got to be kidding. How long ago?"

He glanced at his watch. "Five minutes."

"You've already reported it?"

"No. He said I can't tell the cops."

"Nonsense! Call the detective in charge right now. Get off the phone with me and call them, you hear me, Kevin? You can't let this guy play his game. Take his game away from him."

"He said that this bomb will kill my best friend, Sam. And I know he can hear me. This guy seems to know everything. For all I know he's watching me right now!"

"Okay, calm down. Slow down." She paused, reconsidering. "Okay, don't call the cops. Who's Slater talking about? Who are your friends down there?"

"I . . . That's the problem. I really don't have any."

"Sure you do. Just give me three people you would consider friends and I'll get the local authorities on them. Come on, let's go."

"Well, there's the dean at the school, Dr. John Francis. The priest at my parish—Bill Strong." He searched his mind for another, but nothing came. He had plenty of acquaintances, but really no one he'd call a true friend, much less a best friend.

"Okay. Good enough. Hold on a second."

She put the phone down.

Kevin lifted his T-shirt and wiped the sweat from his face. 4:24. He had until 4:45. *Come on, Samantha!* He stood and paced. *In life he's your friend, but death is the end. What—*

"Kevin?"

"Here."

"Okay, I put in an anonymous call to the Long Beach police warning that Francis and Strong could be in immediate danger. Enough to get them moved from wherever they are, which is all we can do."

"You talked to Milton?"

"He's the lead? No, but I'm sure he'll get the message. How sure are you that this guy will come unglued if you talk to the authorities?"

"He's already unglued! He said I could only speak when spoken to and he's doing this because I said something."

"Okay. You'll probably get a call any minute from the police, checking on this threat I've just reported. You have call waiting?"

"Yes."

"Ignore the beep. If you talk to the police when they call, Slater will know. What's the riddle?"

"There's something else, Sam. Slater knows you. In fact, he suggested I call you. I . . . I think he might be someone we both know."

The phone sounded hollow for a few breaths.

"He knows me. What's the sin he wants you to confess?"

"I don't know!"

"Okay, we can cover this later. We're running out of time. What's the riddle?"

"In life he's your friend, but death is the end."

"Opposites."

"Opposites?"

"*What falls but never breaks? What breaks but never falls?* Answer: Night and day. What in life is your friend, but death is the end, I don't know. But they're both opposites. Any ideas?"

"No. I don't have a clue." Night falls, day breaks. Clever. "This is *crazy!*" He ground the last word out between his teeth.

She was quiet for a moment. "If we knew the sin, we could infer the riddle. What sin are you hiding, Kevin?"

He stopped pacing. "None. Lots! What do you want me to do, spill my whole life of sins to the world? That seems to be what he wants."

"But there must be something you did that sent this guy to the moon. Think of that and think of this riddle. Anything connect?"

Kevin thought about the boy. But there was no connection between the riddles and the boy. Couldn't be him. Nothing else came to mind.

"No."

"Then let's go back to your best friend."

"You're my best friend, Sam."

"Sweet. But this guy wanted you to call me, right? He knows I would be warned, and if he knows me, he also knows that I have the capability of escaping his threat. I think I'm safe for now. There's another best friend you're missing. Something more obvious—"

"Wait! What if it's not a person?" *That's it!* He glanced at his watch. Fifteen minutes to go. Barely enough time to get there. Call waiting sounded in his ear. That would be the police.

"Ignore it," Sam said. "Such as—"

"I'll call you back, Sam. I don't have time to explain."

"I'm coming down. I'll be there in five hours."

"You . . . you are?"

"I'm on leave, remember?"

Kevin felt a surge of gratitude. "I have to go."

He hung up, nerves buzzing, stomach in knots. If he was right, it meant going back to the house. He hated going back to his aunt's house. He stood in the office, fists clenched by his sides. But he had to go back. Slater had blown up the car, and now he was going to do worse unless Kevin stopped him.

Slater was forcing him back to the house. Back to the past. Back to the house and back to the boy.

III

Kevin's watch read 4:39 when he passed the park at the end of Baker Street and pointed the car toward the white house. The faint sound of children playing on the swing sets faded. Then silence except for the purr of the Taurus. He blinked.

A row of twenty elms lined the left side of the dead-end avenue, one in the front yard of each house, casting a dark shadow over the entire length. Behind the homes, a narrow greenway fed into the park he'd just passed. To his right, warehouses backed up to train tracks. The street had been freshly paved, the lawns were all neatly manicured, the houses modest but clean. By all appearances it was the perfect little street on the edge of town.

He had not visited in over a year, and even then he'd refused to go inside. He needed Balinda's signature for the seminary application. After four failed attempts to secure it through the mail, he finally dragged himself to the front porch and rang the doorbell. She appeared after several minutes, and he addressed her without making eye contact and told her that he had some evidence in his old bedroom that would interest the authorities and would make the police station his next stop if she refused to sign. It was a lie, of course. She turned up her nose and scribbled her signature.

The last time he'd seen the inside of the house was five years ago, the day he'd finally worked up the courage to leave.

Rolling down the blacktop under the canopy of elms wasn't so different from driving through a tunnel. One that led to a past he had no desire to visit.

He passed the houses slowly—the green one, the yellow one, another green one, a beige one—all old, all unique in their own way despite the obvious similarities that came from having a common builder. Same gutters, same windows, same shingle roofs. Kevin locked his eyes on the white house, the fifteenth of the twenty on Baker Street.

Here resides Balinda and Eugene Parson with their thirty-six-year-old retarded son, Bob. Here is the childhood home of one Kevin Parson, adopted son, formerly known as Kevin Little until his mommy and daddy went to heaven.

Five minutes. *Okay, Kevin, time's running out.*

He parked the car across the street. A two-foot picket fence ran around the front yard and then rose to six feet for its run around the back. Here the fence was painted brilliant white, but once you stepped past that gate to the right, it wasn't painted at all, except by years of black ash. A flower bed ran the length of the front porch. Fake flowers, pretty and maintenance-free. Balinda replaced them every year—her idea of gardening.

A gray stone statue of some Greek goddess stood on a pedestal to the right of the Parsons' elm. The front yard was immaculate, the neatest on the street, always had been. Even the beige '59 Plymouth in the driveway had been recently polished so that you could actually see a reflection of the elm in its rear quarter panel. It hadn't been moved in years. When the Parsons had reason to leave the house, they favored the ancient blue Datsun parked in the garage.

The shades were drawn and the door had no windows, making it impossible to see inside, but Kevin knew the inside better than he knew his own house. Three doors down stood the smaller brown house that had once belonged to a cop named Rick Sheer, who had a daughter named Samantha. Her family had moved back to San Francisco when Sam went off to college.

Kevin wiped his palms on his jeans and climbed out. The sound of his door slamming sounded obscenely loud on the quiet street. The shade on the front window separated momentarily, and then closed. *Good. Come on out, Auntie.*

Suddenly the whole notion of coming felt absurd. Slater obviously knew his facts, but how would he have knowledge of Bob's dog? Or that the dog had indeed been Kevin's best friend until Samantha had come along? Maybe Slater was after Dr. Francis or the priest. Sam had made the call. Smart.

Kevin paused on the sidewalk and stared at the house. What now? Walk up and tell Balinda that someone was about to blow up the dog? He closed his eyes. *God, give me strength. You know how I hate this.* Maybe he should just leave. If Balinda had a phone, he would have called instead. Maybe he could call the neighbors and—

The door opened and Bob stepped out, grinning from ear to ear. "Hello, Kevin."

Bob wore a lopsided crew cut, undoubtedly Balinda's doing. His beige slacks hung a full six inches above a pair of shiny black leather wing tips. His shirt was a dirty white and sported large lapels reminiscent of the seventies.

Kevin grinned. "Hello, Bob. Can I see Damon?"

Bob lit up. "Damon wants to see you, Kevin. He's been waiting to see you."

"Is that so? Good, then. Let's—"

"Bobby, baby!" Balinda's shrill voice cut through the front door. "You get back in here!" She appeared out of the shadows wearing red high heels and white pantyhose patched up with streaks of clear fingernail polish. Her white dress was lined with age-stained lace embedded haphazardly with a couple dozen fake pearls, the surviving remnant of what had once been hundreds. A large sun hat perched on jet-black hair that looked freshly dyed. A string of gaudy jewels hung around her neck. But it was the white makeup she applied to her sagging face and her bright ruby red lipstick that planted Balinda firmly in the category of the walking dead.

She glared past heavily shadowed lids, studied Kevin for a moment, and then turned up her nose.

"Did I say you could go out? Get in. In, in, in!"

"It's Kevin, Mama."

"I don't care if it's Jesus Christ, pumpkin." She reached forward and straightened his collar. "You know how easily you catch cold, baby."

She ushered Bob toward the door.

"He wants to see—"

"Be nice for Princess." She gave him a little shove. "In."

God bless her soul, Balinda really did intend good for that boy. She was misguided and foolish, certainly, but she loved Bob.

Kevin swallowed and glanced at his watch. Two minutes. He cut for the gate while her back was still turned.

"And just where does the stranger think he's going?"

"I just want to check on the dog. I'll be gone before you know it."

He reached the gate and yanked it open.

"Gone! You've turned running away into a new art form, haven't you, college boy?"

"Not now, Balinda," he said calmly. His breathing came faster. She marched up behind him. He strode down the side of the house.

"At least show a little respect when you're on my grounds," she said.

He checked himself. Closed his eyes. Opened them. "Please, not now, Princess."

"That's better. The dog's fine. You, on the other hand, are not."

Kevin rounded the house and stopped. The familiar yard sat unchanged. Black. Balinda called it a garden, but the backyard was nothing more than one huge ash heap, albeit a fairly tidy ash heap, three feet deep at its center, tapering off to two feet along the fence. A fifty-five-gallon drum smoldered at the center of the yard—they were still burning. Burning, burning, every day burning. How many newsapers and books had been burned back here over the years? Enough for many tons of ash.

The doghouse stood as it always had, in the back left corner. A toolshed sat unused and in terrible need of paint in the other corner. The ash had piled up against its door.

Kevin stepped onto the hardened ash and then ran across the yard for the doghouse. Less than a minute. He dropped to one knee, peered into the doghouse, and was rewarded with a growl.

"Easy, Damon. It's me, Kevin." The old black lab had grown senile and testy, but he immediately recognized Kevin's voice. He whimpered and limped out. A chain was latched to his collar.

"What do you think you're doing?" Balinda demanded.

"Good boy." Kevin stuck his head into the old doghouse and squinted in the darkness. No bomb that he could see. He stood and walked around the small house.

Nothing.

"What is he doing, Princess?"

Kevin turned back to the house at the sound of his uncle's voice. Eugene stood on the back porch, staring out at him. He wore his customary English-style boots and riding pants complete with suspenders and a beret. The skinny man looked more like a jockey to Kevin, but in Balinda's eyes, he was a prince. He'd worn the same outfit for at least ten years. Before that it was a Henry V outfit, awkward and clumsy on such a petite man.

Balinda stood at the edge of the house, watching Kevin with wary eyes. The shade lifted in the window to her left—Kevin's old room. Bob peered out. The past stared at him through those three sets of eyes.

He looked down at his watch. Thirty minutes had come and gone. He reached down and patted the dog. "Good boy." He unleashed him, tossed the chain to the side, and headed back for the gate.

"What do you think you are doing with my property?" Balinda asked.

"I thought he could use some exercise."

"You came all the way out here to let that old bat off his chain? What do you take me for? An idiot?" She turned to the dog, who was following Kevin. "Damon! Back in your house. Back!"

The dog stopped.

"Don't just stand there, Eugene! Control that animal!"

Eugene immediately perked up. He took two steps toward the dog and flung out a flimsy arm. "Damon! Bad dog! Get back. Get back immediately."

The dog just stared at them.

"Try it with your horse training accent," Balinda said. "Put some authority in your voice."

Kevin stared at them. It had been a long time since he'd seen them like this. They'd slipped into their role-playing on the fly. For the moment he didn't even exist. It was hard to imagine he grew up with these two.

Eugene stood as tall as his short frame would allow and expanded his chest. "I say, dog! To the kennel or the whip it'll be. Be gone! Be thou gone *immeeediately!*"

"Don't just stand there; go after him like you mean it!" Balinda snapped. "And I really don't think *thou* is appropriate with an animal. Growl or something!"

Eugene crouched and took several long steps toward the dog, growling like a bear.

"Not like an animal, you idiot!" Balinda said. "You look foolish! He's the animal; you're the master. Act like one. Growl like a man! Like a ruler."

Eugene pulled himself up again and thrust out an arm, snarling like a villain. "Back in the cage, you foul-mouthed vermin!" he cried hoarsely.

Damon whimpered and ran back into his house.

"Ha!" Eugene stood up, triumphant.

Balinda clapped and giggled, delighted. "You see, didn't I tell you? Princess knows—"

A muffled explosion suddenly lifted the doghouse a foot into the air and dropped it back to the ground.

They stood, Balinda at the corner, Bob in the window, Eugene by the porch, and Kevin in the middle of the yard, staring with incredulity at the smoldering doghouse.

Kevin could not move. Damon?

Balinda took a step forward and stopped. "Wha . . . what was that?"

"Damon?" Kevin ran for the doghouse. "Damon!"

He knew before he arrived that the dog was dead. Blood quickly darkened the ash at the door. He looked in and immediately recoiled. Bile crept up his throat. How was it possible? Tears sprang into his eyes.

A screech filled the air. He looked back to see Balinda flying for the doghouse, face stricken, arms outstretched. He jumped back to avoid her rush. On the porch, Eugene was pacing and mumbling incoherently. Bob had his face planted on the window, wide-eyed.

Balinda took one look into Damon's smoking house and then staggered back. Eugene stopped and watched her. Kevin's mind spun. But it wasn't Damon that now made him dizzy. It was Princess. Not Princess—Mother!

No! No, not Princess, not Mother, not even Auntie! *Balinda.* The poor sick hag who'd sucked the life out of him.

She turned to Kevin, eyes black with hate. "You!" she screamed. "You did this!"

"No, Mother!" *She's not your Mother! Not Mother.*

"I—"

"Shut your lying mouth! We hate you!" She flung her arm toward the gate. "Get out!"

"You don't mean that . . ." *Stop it, Kevin! What do you care if she hates you? Get out.*

Balinda balled both hands to fists, dropped them to her sides, and tilted her head back. "Leave! Leave, leave, leave!" she screamed, eyes clenched.

Eugene joined in, chanting with her in a falsetto voice, mimicking her stance. "Leave, leave, leave, leave!"

Kevin left. Without daring to look at what Bob might be doing, he whirled around and fled for his car.

6

THE AIR IS STUFFY. Too hot for such a cool day. Richard Slater, as he has decided to call himself this time, strips out of his clothes and hangs them in the one closet beside the desk. He crosses the dark basement in his bare feet, pulls open the old chest freezer, and takes out two ice cubes. Not really cubes—they are frozen into small balls instead of squares. He found the unusual ice trays in a stranger's refrigerator once and decided to take them. They are wonderful.

Slater walks into the center of the room and sits down on the concrete. A large white clock on the wall ticks quietly. It's 4:47. He will call Kevin in three minutes, unless Kevin himself makes a phone call, in which case he'll remotely terminate the connection and then call Kevin back. Short of that, he wants to give Kevin a little time to digest things. That is the plan.

He lies back, flat on the cool cement, and places one ice ball in each eye socket. He's done a lot of things over the years—some of them horrible, some of them quite splendid. What do you call tipping a waitress a buck more than she deserves? What do you call tossing a baseball back to the kid who mistakenly throws it over the fence? Splendid, splendid.

The horrible things are too obvious to dwell on.

But really his whole life has been practice for this particular game.

Of course, he always says that. There's something about being in a contest of high stakes that makes the blood flow. Nothing quite compares. Killing is just killing unless there's a game to the killing. Unless there is an end game that results in some kind of ultimate victory. Extracting punishment involves making someone suffer, and death ends that suffering, cheating the true pain of suffering. At least this side of hell. Slater shivers with the excitement of it all. A small whimper of pleasure. The ice hurts now. Like fire in his eyes. Interesting how opposites can be so similar. Ice and fire.

He counts off the seconds, not in his conscious mind, but in the background, where it doesn't distract him from thought. They have some pretty good minds on their side, but none quite like his. Kevin is no idiot. He will have to see which FBI agent they send. And of course the real prize exudes brilliance: Samantha.

Slater opens his mouth and says the name slowly. "Samantha."

He's been planning this particular game for three years now, not because he needed the time, but because he's been waiting for the right timing. Then again, the wait has given him more than enough opportunity to learn far more than he needs to know. Kevin's every waking move. His motivations and his desires. His strengths and his weaknesses. The truth behind that delightful little family of his.

Electronic surveillance—it's amazing how technology has advanced even in the last three years. He can put a laser beam on a window at a great distance and pick up any voices inside the room. They will find his bugs, but only because he wants them to. He can talk to Kevin any moment of the day on his own phone without being detected by a third party. When the police get around to finding the transmitter he affixed to the telephone line down from Kevin's house, he will resort to alternatives. There are limits, of course, but they won't be reached before the game expires. Pun intended.

Two minutes have passed and his eyes are numb from the ice.

Water leaks down his cheeks and he reaches his tongue up to touch it. Can't. One more minute.

The fact is, he's thought of everything. Not in a criminal kind of let's-do-a-bank-robbery-and-think-of-everything-so-they-won't-catch-us way. But in a more fundamental way. Precise motivations and countermoves. Like a chess match that will be played in response to another's moves. This method is far more exhilarating than taking a club to someone else's pieces and declaring yourself the victor.

In a few days, Kevin will be a shell of himself, and Samantha . . .

He chuckles.

There is no way they can possibly win.

Time's up.

Slater sits up, catches what's left of the ice balls as they fall from his eyes, tosses them into his mouth, and stands. The clock reads 4:50. He walks across the room to an old metal desk lit by a single shade-less lamp. Thirty watts. A policeman's hat sits on the desk. He reminds himself to put it in the closet.

The black phone is connected to a box, which will prevent trac-ing. Another remote box hides at the hub that services this house. The cops can trace all they like. He is invisible.

"Are we ready, Kevin?"

Slater picks up the phone, flips a switch on the scrambler, and dials the cell phone he's instructed Kevin to keep with him.

| | |

Kevin ran to his car and started it before it occurred to him that he had nowhere to go. If he had Samantha's cell number, he would have called her. He almost called Milton but couldn't get past the thought of the cops turning this house into a crime scene. It was inevitable, though—he had to report the bomb. Not telling Milton about Slater's true demand had been one thing; covering up a second bomb was in a whole different league. He considered returning to explain the dog's death to Balinda, but he didn't have the stomach to face her, much less form an explanation that would make any sense.

The explosion had been muffled by the doghouse—none of the neighbors seemed to have heard. If they had, they weren't running around saying so.

Kevin sat in his car, running his fingers through his hair. A sudden fury spread through his bones. The phone in his pocket buzzed loudly against his leg and he jumped.

Slater!

It buzzed again. He fumbled for the cell phone, pulled it out, flipped it open.

"Hello?"

"Hello."

"You . . . you didn't have to do that," Kevin said, voice wavering. He hesitated and then continued quickly. "Are you the boy? You're the boy, aren't you? Look, I'm here. Just tell me what—"

"Shut up! What boy? Did I tell you to lecture me? Did I say, 'I feel badly in need of a lecture at this time, college Kevin?' Don't ever do that again. You've broken the don't-speak-to-me-unless-engaged rule several times now, college boy. The next time, I kill something that walks on two legs. Consider it negative reinforcement. Understand?"

"Yes."

"That's better. And I think it's best not to tell the cops about this one. I know I said you could after the fact, but this little bonus was just something I planned in the event you weren't a good listener, which you were so quick to confirm. Mum's the word on this one. Okay?"

Don't tell the cops? How could he—

"Answer me!"

"O . . . okay."

"Tell Balinda to keep her trap shut too. I'm sure she'll agree. She won't want the cops searching through the house, now, will she?"

"No." So Slater knew about Balinda.

"The games are on. I'm the bat; you're the ball. I keep slugging until you confess. Lock and load."

Kevin desperately wanted to ask him what he meant by that word: *confess.* But he couldn't. He could hear Slater breathing on the other end.

"Samantha's coming down," Slater said in a soft voice. "That's good. I can't decide whom I despise more, you or her." The line clicked and Slater was gone. Kevin sat in silent shock. Whoever Slater was, he seemed to know everything. Balinda, the dog, the house. Samantha. He exhaled and closed his fingers to a fist to steady their trembling.

This is really happening, Kevin. Someone who knows is going to blow the lid off. *What falls but never breaks? What breaks but never falls?* Night and day. *In life he's your friend, but death is the end.* In life the dog was a friend, but death was the end of him. But there was more. Something Slater wanted him to confess was night and day, and life and death. What?

Kevin slammed the steering wheel with his fist. What, *what?*

"What boy?" Slater had said. What boy? So then he wasn't the boy?

Dear God . . . Dear God . . . Dear God what? He couldn't even think straight to pray. He put his head back and took several long, calming breaths. "Samantha. Samantha." She would know what to do. Kevin closed his eyes.

III

Kevin was eleven years old when he first saw the boy who wanted to kill him.

He and Samantha had become the very best of friends. What

made their friendship most special was that their trips into the night remained a secret. He saw other kids now and then, but he never talked to them. Mother didn't like that. But as far as he knew, she never did discover his little secret about the window. Every few nights, whenever they'd planned, or sometimes when Sam would tap on his window, or even sometimes when he went out and tapped on Sam's window, he would sneak out and meet her.

He didn't tell Sam what was happening inside the house. He wanted to, of course, but he couldn't tell her the worst of it, although he wondered whether she might have guessed anyway. His time with Sam was special because it was the only part of his life that *wasn't* about the house. He wanted to keep it that way.

The private school Sam attended held classes year-round, so she was always busy during the day, but Kevin knew he could never sneak out during the day anyway. Mother would find out.

"Why don't you ever want to play at the park?" Sam asked him one night as they walked through the greenway. "You'd get along great with Tommy and Linda."

He shrugged. "I just don't want to. They might tell."

"We could make them swear not to. They like me; they'd promise not to tell. They could be part of our club."

"We have fun together without them, don't we? Why do we need them?"

"Well, you have to start meeting some other people, Kevin. You're growing up, you know. I can't understand why your mom won't let you out to play in the first place. That's kinda mean—"

"Don't talk about her that way!"

"Well, it is!"

Kevin lowered his head, suddenly feeling suffocated. They stood in the quiet for a moment.

Sam put her hand on his shoulder. "I'm sorry."

The way she said it made tears come to his eyes. She was so special.

"I'm sorry," she said again. "I guess just because she's different doesn't mean she's mean. Different strokes for different folks, right?"

He looked up at her, unsure.

"It's a saying." She wiped a tear that had leaked from his right eye. "At least your mom isn't one of those parents who abuse their kids. I've heard my dad talk about some things." She shuddered. "Some people are horrible."

"My mom is a princess," Kevin said softly.

Sam grinned politely and nodded. "She's never hit you, has she, Kevin?"

"Hit me? Why would she hit me?"

"Has she?"

"Never! She sends me to my room and makes me read my books. That's all. Why would anyone hit someone else?"

"Not everyone's as sweet as you, Kevin." Sam took his hand and they started to walk. "I think my dad might know about us."

Kevin pulled up. "What?"

"He's asked a few questions. Mom and Dad talk about your family every once in a while. He is a cop, after all."

"Did . . . did you tell him anything?"

"Of course not. Don't worry. Your secret's safe with me."

They walked for a few minutes, hand in hand.

"Do you like Tommy?" Kevin asked.

"Tommy? Sure."

"I mean, is he your . . . you know . . ."

"Boyfriend? Don't gross me out!"

Kevin flushed and giggled. They came to a large tree behind her house and Sam stopped. She faced him and took both of his hands in hers. "I don't have any boyfriends except you, Kevin. I like you."

He looked into her bright blue eyes. A gentle breeze lifted her blonde hair so that it swam around her, highlighted by the moon. She was the most beautiful thing Kevin had ever seen. He was so taken with her that he had trouble even speaking.

"I . . . I like you too, Sam."

"We're like secret lovers," she said softly, and suddenly her face softened. "I've never kissed a boy before. Could I kiss you?"

"Kiss me?" He swallowed.

"Yes."

Kevin's throat was suddenly dryer than baking powder. "Yes."

She leaned forward and touched her lips to his for a moment.

She pulled back and they stared at each other, wide-eyed. Kevin's heart throbbed in his ears. He should do something! Before he lost his nerve, he bent and returned the kiss.

The night seemed to disappear around him. He floated on a cloud. They looked at each other, suddenly awkward.

"I should go now," she said.

"Okay."

She turned and ran toward her house. Kevin spun around and tore home, and honestly he wasn't sure if his feet really were on the ground. He did like Samantha. He liked her very, very much. Maybe even more than his mother, which was pretty impossible.

The next few days floated by like a dream. He met Sam two nights later and they made no mention of the kiss. They didn't need to. They resumed their playing as if nothing at all had changed between them. They didn't kiss again, and Kevin wasn't sure he wanted to. It might somehow spoil the magic of that first kiss.

Sam didn't come to his window for three straight nights, and Kevin decided to sneak out and go to her house. He took the greenway past the two houses between his and Sam's on light feet, careful not to make the slightest sound. You could never know who might be out at night.

They had hidden from the sound of coming voices and approaching footsteps a hundred times before.

A half-moon sat in the black sky, peeking around slowly drifting clouds. Crickets chirped. Sam's house came into view and his heart thumped a little louder. He eased up to the picket fence and peered over it. Her room was on the bottom floor; he could see the faint glow of light past the tree in front of the window. *Please be there, Sam. Please.*

Kevin glanced around, saw no one, and pushed aside the board Sam had loosened long ago. Her dad might be a cop, but he'd never found this, had he? That's because Sam was smart too. He climbed through and brushed his hands. *Please be there, Sam.*

Kevin took a step. The tree in front of Sam's window moved. He froze. Sam? Slowly a dark head and then shoulders came into view. Someone was peeking into Sam's room!

Kevin jerked back, panicked. The form stood taller, angling for a better view. It was a boy! A tall boy with a sharp nose. Staring in on Sam!

A dozen thoughts screamed through Kevin's head. Who? What was the boy doing? He should run! No, he should yell. Was that Tommy? No, Tommy had longer hair.

The boy spun around, stared directly at Kevin, and then pushed his way past the tree. He stood tall in the moonlight, and a terrible smile twisted his face. He took a step toward Kevin.

Kevin didn't bother with the loose plank—he went over the fence faster than he could have ever imagined possible and ran for a large tree on the edge of the greenway. He pulled up behind it, panting.

Nothing happened. There was no sound of running or of heavy breathing other than his own. He would have run for home but was afraid the boy was waiting by the fence for the first sign of movement. It took him a full five minutes to work up the courage to peek ever so slowly around the tree.

Nothing.

Another five minutes and he was peering over the fence again. Nothing. Whoever the boy was, he'd gone.

Kevin finally worked up the courage to tap on Sam's window. She climbed out, all smiles. She was waiting for him, she said. Waiting for the dashing young man to come to the window of the maiden. That's how it was done in the movies.

He told her about the boy, but she found it funny. One of the neighborhood guys had a crush on her, and her prince charming had sent him packing! Hearing himself tell it, the story did sound funny. They had a good hoot that night. But Kevin had a hard time shaking the image of the boy's horrible smile.

Three nights went by before Kevin saw the boy again—this time in the greenway on his way home. At first he thought it was a dog or some animal running behind the trees, but after he'd climbed into bed, he began to wonder if it was the boy. What if he was going to spy on Sam again? He tossed and turned for half an hour before working up the resolve to go back and check on Sam. He would never go to sleep until he had.

For the first time in a year, he went out for a second time in the same night—prince charming to check on his damsel in distress. He didn't really expect to see anything.

Kevin poked his head over the fence in Sam's backyard and went rigid. The boy! He was there, peering into Sam's window again! He'd waited until Kevin went home and then snuck up to her window to spy on her!

Kevin ducked and tried to calm his breathing. He had to do something! But what? If he yelled and then took off running, the boy wouldn't catch him. At least then he might scare off the boy. He could throw a rock. No. What if he broke Sam's window?

He went up slowly for another peek. The boy was doing

something. He had his face planted against the window and was . . . he was moving his face around in circles. What was he doing? Kevin blinked. Was he . . . ? A chill snaked down Kevin's spine. The boy was licking Sam's window in slow circles.

Something ballooned in Kevin's head. Whether it was rage or just plain terror, he couldn't be sure, but he spoke while courage strengthened him.

"Hey!"

The boy spun around. For one long, still moment, they stared at each other. The boy stepped forward and Kevin fled. He bolted through the greenway, pumping his skinny arms and legs as fast as they would go without tearing loose. He dove through his fence, flew into his bedroom, and shut the window, surely making enough racket to wake the house.

Ten minutes later the night slept in silence. But Kevin couldn't. He felt trapped in the small room. What was the boy doing? Had he been stalking Sam every night? He had, hadn't he? Kevin had only stumbled on him twice, but there was no telling how long the boy had been stalking Sam.

An hour passed, and Kevin could hardly shut his eyes, much less sleep. That's when he heard the tap on his window. He bolted up in bed. Sam! He scrambled to his knees and lifted the shade.

The boy stood at the back fence, head and shoulders in plain view. He stared directly at Kevin, twirling something in his hand. It was a knife.

Kevin dropped the shade and flung the covers over his head. He lay trembling for two hours before peeking again, ever so carefully, just barely lifting the shade. The boy was gone.

The next three days dragged by like a slow nightmare. Each night he peeked out his window a hundred times. Each night the backyard remained vacant except for the doghouse and the toolshed. Each night he prayed desperately for Sam to come for a visit. She'd talked about going to a camp, but he couldn't remember exactly when she was supposed to go. Was it this week?

On the fourth night, Kevin couldn't wait any longer. He paced in his room for an hour, peering out of his window every few minutes, before deciding that he had to check on Sam before the anxiety killed him.

It took him half an hour to work his way up to her house, using the trees in the greenway as cover. The night was quiet. When he finally inched his head over Sam's fence, her light was out. He scanned the yard. No boy. Sam was gone and so was the boy.

He collapsed at the base of the fence with relief. She must be at that camp. Maybe the boy had followed her there. No. That was stupid. How could a boy follow a girl all the way to camp?

Kevin eased his way back to the cover of the greenway and headed home, feeling at ease for the first time in nearly a week. Maybe the boy had moved. Maybe he had found something else to occupy his sick little mind.

Maybe he had snuck into Sam's room and killed her.

He pulled up. No. Kevin would have heard about that. Her father was a cop and—

A blunt object slammed into the side of Kevin's head and he staggered. A groan broke from his throat. Something wrapped around his neck and jerked him upright.

"Listen, you little punk, I know who you are and I don't like you!" a voice snarled in his ear. The arm jerked him around and shoved him against a tree. Kevin wobbled at arm's length from his attacker. The boy.

If his head wasn't throbbing so badly, he might have panicked. Instead he just stared and tried to keep his legs from collapsing.

The boy sneered. Close up, his face reminded Kevin of a boar. He was older than Kevin and a foot taller, but still young, with pimples all over his nose and chin and a tattoo of a knife high on his forehead. He smelled like dirty socks.

The boy brought his face within a few inches of Kevin's. "I'm going to give you one warning and one warning only, squat. That girl is mine, not yours. If I ever see you so much as looking at her again, I'll kill her. If I catch you sneaking out to see her again, I may just kill the both of you. You hear me?"

Kevin just stood dumb.

The boy slapped him across the cheek. "You hear me?"

Kevin nodded.

The boy stepped back and glared at him. A slow lopsided grin split his face at a cruel angle. "You think you're in love with this little tramp? Huh? You're too stupid and too young to know what love is. And so is she. I'm going to teach her love, baby, and I don't need a squat like you messing with our little romance." He stepped back.

Kevin saw the knife in the boy's hand for the first time. His mind cleared. The boy saw his eyes on the knife and he lifted it slowly.

"You have any idea what a nine-inch bowie can do to a squat like you?" The boy twirled the blade in his hand. "Do you know how persuasive a bright shiny blade can be to a young girl?"

Kevin suddenly felt like he was going to vomit.

"Get back to your little room, squat, before I decide to cut you just for looking so stupid."

Kevin fled.

7

KEVIN SAT IN HIS RECLINER, waiting impatiently for Samantha, flipping through the channels to hear the various versions of the "car bomb," as they were calling it. He nursed a warm 7UP in his left hand and glanced up at the wall clock. Nine o'clock— nearly five hours had passed since she'd left Sacramento.

"Come on, Samantha," he muttered softly. "Where are you?" She'd called him halfway down. He told her about the dog and begged her to hurry. She was already doing eighty, she said.

Back to the television. They knew Kevin's identity, and a dozen reporters had tracked down his number. He'd ignored the calls per Milton's suggestion. Not that he had anything to add anyway—their theories were as good as his. Channel nine's suggestion that the bombing might be the work of a well-known fugitive dubbed the Riddle Killer interested him most. The killer had taken the lives of five people up in Sacramento and had vanished three months ago. No more details, but the speculation was enough to plant a knot in Kevin's throat. The pictures of the charred wreckage, taken from the sky, were stunning. Or terrifying, depending on how he thought of them. If he'd been anywhere near the thing when it blew, he'd be dead. Like the dog.

After Slater's call, he'd forced himself to return to the backyard and explain the situation to Balinda, but she wouldn't even acknowledge him. She'd already put the matter behind them by executive order. Poor Bob would somehow be convinced that Damon was alive and well, just gone. Balinda would have to explain her initial screaming flight across the ash after the explosion, of course, but she was an expert at explaining the unexplainable. The only time she even responded to Kevin was when he suggested they not call the police.

"Of course not. We've got nothing to report. The dog's fine. Do you see a dead dog?"

No, he didn't. Eugene had already dumped it in the burn barrel and set it on fire. Gone. What were a few more ashes?

His mind drifted to the call with Slater. *What boy?* Slater didn't seem to know of any boy. *What boy?* The key to his sin was found in the riddles. As far as he could see, the riddles had nothing to do with the boy. So then Slater *couldn't* be the boy. Thank God, thank God, thank God. Some secrets were best left buried forever.

The doorbell chimed. Kevin set down his 7UP and clambered out of his chair. He stopped at the hall mirror for a quick look. Haggard face. Smudged T-shirt. He scratched the top of his head. The bell chimed again.

"Coming."

He hurried to the peephole, peered out, saw that it was Samantha, and unlocked the door. It had been ten years since he'd kissed her on the cheek and wished her well in conquering the big bad world. Her hair had been blonde and long; her blue eyes sparkling like stars. She'd had one of those faces that looked airbrushed all the time, even without a speck of makeup. Smooth rounded cheeks and soft upturned lips, high arching eyebrows and a soft pointed nose. The most beautiful girl he'd ever seen. Of course, he wasn't seeing a lot of girls in those days.

Kevin fumbled with the knob and opened the door. Samantha stood under the porch light, dressed in jeans and smiling warmly. He'd thought of her a thousand times since she'd left, but his mind's eye could never have prepared him for seeing her now, in the flesh. He *had* seen a lot of girls in the last five years, and Sam was still the most beautiful girl he'd ever laid eyes on. Bar none.

"Are you going to invite me in, stranger?"

"Yes. Sorry, of course! Come in, come in."

She walked past him, set down her bag, and faced him. He shut the door.

"My, you've grown up," she said. "Put on a bit of muscle."

He grinned and ran his hand over his head. "I guess."

He was having difficulty not staring at her eyes. They were the kind of blue that seemed to swallow whatever they gazed upon—brilliant and deep and haunting. They didn't reflect the light so much as shine, as if illuminated by their own source. No man nor woman could look into Samantha's eyes and not think that there was indeed a God in heaven. She stood just up to his chin, slender and graceful. This was Samantha, his best friend. His only real friend. Looking at her now, he wondered how he'd survived the last ten years.

She stepped forward. "Give me a hug, my knight."

He chuckled at her childhood reference and hugged her tight. "It's so good to see you, Samantha."

She stood up on her toes and kissed his cheek. Beyond that one blissful kiss when they were eleven, their relationship had remained platonic. Neither of them wanted romance from the other. They were bosom buddies, best friends, almost brother and sister. Not that the thought hadn't crossed Kevin's mind; a friendship had just always been more appealing. She had always been the damsel in distress, and he the knight in shining armor, even though they both knew she had rescued him in the first place. Now, despite the fact that it was she who'd again come to his rescue, their childhood personas came naturally.

Sam turned to the living room, hands on her hips. "I see you like travel posters."

He walked with her and grinned self-consciously. *Quit rubbing your head; she'll think you're a dog.* He lowered his hands and tapped his right foot.

"I'd like to go to all those places someday. It's kinda like looking at the world. Reminds me there's more. Never did like being shut in."

"I like it! Well, you've come far. And I knew you would, didn't I? You just had to get away from that mother of yours."

"Aunt," he corrected. "She never was my mother."

"Aunt. Let's face it, dear Aunt Balinda did you more harm than good. When did you finally leave?"

He walked past her to the kitchen. "Twenty-three. Drink?"

She followed him. "Thanks. You stayed in that house five years after I left?"

"Afraid so. You should've taken me with you."

"You did it on your own—that's better. Now look at you, you have a college degree and you're in seminary. Impressive."

"And you graduated valedictorian. Very impressive." He pulled a soda from the fridge, popped the tab, and handed it to her.

"Thank you," she said. "For the compliment." She winked at him and took a sip. "The drink's nice too. How often do you go back?"

"Where? To the house? As little as possible. I'd rather not talk about that."

"I think that *that* might be tied to this, don't you?"

"Maybe."

Samantha set the can down on the counter and looked at him, suddenly dead serious. "Someone's stalking you. And by the sound of it, me. A killer who uses riddles who's selected us for his own reasons. Revenge. Hate. The baser motivations. We can't shut out the past."

"Right to the point."

"Tell me everything."

"Starting—"

"Starting with the phone call in your car." She walked to the front door.

Kevin followed. "Where are you going?"

"We. Come on, let's take a drive. He's obviously listening to everything we say in here—let's make his life a little more interesting. We'll take my car. Hopefully he hasn't gotten to it yet."

They climbed into a beige sedan and Samantha drove into the night. "That's better. He's probably using lasers."

"Actually, I think you're right," Kevin said.

"He told you that?"

"Something like that."

"Every detail, Kevin. I don't care how insignificant, I don't care what you told the cops, I don't care how embarrassing or stupid or crazy it sounds, I want everything."

Kevin did as she requested, eagerly, with passion, as if it were his first real confession. Sam drove haphazardly and stopped him frequently to ask questions.

When was the last time you left your car unlocked?

Never that I can remember.

Do you lock your car when it's in the garage?

No.

A nod. *Did the police find a timing device?*

Not that he knew about.

You found the ribbon behind the lamp?

Yes.

Did Slater call me Sam or Samantha?

Samantha.

An hour passed and they covered every conceivable detail of the day's events, including the information he'd hidden from Milton.

Everything except his speculation that Slater could be the boy. He'd never told Sam the whole truth about the boy, and he wasn't eager to do so now. If Slater wasn't the boy, which he claimed not to be, there was no need to dig up that matter. He'd never told Sam the whole truth and he wasn't eager to do so now.

"How long can you stay?" Kevin asked after a lull.

Sam glanced at him with a coy smile. "The big boy needs a girl in his court?"

Kevin grinned sheepishly. She hadn't changed a bit. "Turns out girls make or break me."

She arched her brow. "I technically have a week off to finish my move. I have boxes overflowing in my kitchen still. The case I was assigned to when I first arrived a couple months ago has been pretty quiet, but it just heated up. I wouldn't be surprised if they called me in."

"California Bureau of Investigation, huh? Big change from New York."

"Not really, other than being new. I've managed to do a couple things right and have my department head appropriately impressed at the moment, but I still have to earn my stripes with them, if you understand how law enforcement works. Same thing with the CIA before I switched to this job."

"CBI, CIA—gets a bit confusing," Kevin said. "You glad you made the move?"

She looked at him and grinned. "I'm closer to you, aren't I?"

He nodded and turned sheepishly. "You have no idea how much I appreciate this. Really."

"I wouldn't miss it for the world."

"Can't you pull some strings?" He faced her. "Convince them to let you stay down here?"

"Because I know you?"

"Because you're involved now. He *knows* you, for heaven's sake!"

"It doesn't work that way. If anything, that's reason for them to remove me from the case." She stared ahead, lost in thought. "Don't worry, I'm not going anywhere. The CBI is made of a dozen units, roughly a hundred agents in all. My unit is unique—hardly known to most agents. We work outside the system, technically part of the Bureau, but it's directed as much by the attorney general. Troubleshooting the harder cases. We have some latitude and discretion." She looked at him. "You, my dear, are definitely within the scope of the discretion. More than you know."

Kevin stared out his window. Black. Slater was out there somewhere. Maybe watching them now. A shiver ran down his spine.

"So. What do you think?"

Sam pulled the car to the curb a block from Kevin's house and shoved the stick into park. "I think that we have no choice but to follow Slater's demands. So far the demands involve no one but you. This isn't like a threat of terror, where either we release a hostage or they blow a building. This is either you confess or he blows up your car. Confession doesn't exactly pose a threat to society." She nodded to herself. "For now we don't involve the police like he wants. But we also take him at his word. He said *cops*—we avoid the cops. That excludes the FBI. We tell the FBI everything."

She cracked her window and stared at the sky. "I also think that Richard Slater is someone one or both of us knew or know. I think his motivation is revenge and I think he means to extract it in a way that will never be forgotten." She looked at him. "There has to be someone, Kevin."

He hesitated and then fed her part of the truth. "No one. The only enemy I can even remember having is that boy."

"What boy?"

"You know. Remember that boy who was spying on you when we were kids? The one who beat me up?"

She grinned. "The one you saved me from?"

"I asked Slater if he was the boy," Kevin said.

"Did you, now? You omitted that little detail."

"It was nothing."

"I said *every* detail, Kevin. I don't care if you think it's nothing or not. Okay?"

"Okay."

"What did he say?"

"He said, 'What boy?' It's not him."

She didn't respond.

A car drove by. SUV with bright taillights.

"Ever hear of the Riddle Killer?" Sam asked.

Kevin sat up. "On the news tonight."

"The Riddle Killer was given that name for a series of murders up in Sacramento over the last twelve months. It's been three months since his last victim—the brother of an FBI agent who was on his tail. I can guarantee that the FBI will be all over this. Same MO. Guy calls on the phone with a riddle and then executes his punishment if the riddle goes unsolved. Low, gravelly voice. Sophisticated surveillance. Sounds like the same guy."

"Except . . ."

"Except why would he choose you? And why me?" Sam asked. "Could be a copy cat."

"Maybe he's trying to confuse us. Guy like that's obviously into games, right? So maybe this just ups the thrill for him." Kevin lowered his head into his hands and massaged his temples. "Just this morning I had a discussion with Dr. Francis about mankind's capacity for evil. What's the average person capable of? Makes me wonder what I'd do if I met up with this guy." He took a deep breath. "It's hard to believe that people like this actually exist."

"He'll get his due. They always do." She reached over and rubbed his shoulder. "Don't worry, my dear knight. There's a reason I advanced as quickly as I did in the company. I haven't been handed a case so far I couldn't crack." She smirked playfully. "I told you I was gonna be a cop. And I didn't mean street beat either."

Kevin sighed and smiled. "Well, you have no idea how glad I am that it's you." He caught himself. "Not that I'm glad he's after—"

"I understand." She fired the car. "We'll beat this, Kevin. I'm not about to let some ghost from the past or some serial killer push either one of us around. We're smarter than this psycho. You'll see."

"What now?"

"Now we go find some bugs."

Twenty minutes later Sam held six eavesdropping devices in a gloved hand. One from the living room, one from each bathroom, one from each bedroom, and the infinity transmitter from the phone.

Her eyes twinkled like a competitive athlete who'd just scored a goal. Sam had always seemed beyond any kind of discouragement; her optimism was one of her most admirable traits. She carried it around her like a fragrance. As far as Kevin was concerned, Sam had what it took to one day run the CBI or CIA or whatever she so desired.

"Won't slow him down much, but at least it'll let him know that we're engaged. These types tend to get trigger-happy if they think the other side is slacking off."

She filled up the sink, dropped the devices into the water, and peeled off the surgical gloves. "Under normal circumstances I'd take these in, but if I'm right, the FBI has jurisdiction. They would scream bloody murder. First thing in the morning, I'll call my office, explain the situation, and then let Milton's office know of my involvement. Not that they will care—I guarantee that the town will be crawling with agencies by morning. I'd have a better shot working on my own than through them anyway." She was talking to herself as much as to him. "You said they'd be out first thing to sweep for bugs?"

"Yes."

"Tell them you found these lying around. I'll make sure they dust for prints. At this point you have nothing else to tell Milton, so let him do his job, and try to stay out of his way. When the FBI makes contact, cooperate. I've got a few other things I want to run down first thing. We tracking?"

"And if he calls?"

"If I'm not here, you call my cell immediately. We'll go from there." She started for the door and then turned back. "Slater will call. You do know that, don't you?"

He nodded slowly.

"Get some sleep. We'll get him. He's already made his first mistake."

"He has?"

"He pulled *me* into the game." She grinned. "I was born for cases like this."

Kevin walked over, took her hand, and kissed it. "Thank you."

"I think it would be better if I crashed down at the Howard Johnson. No offense, but you don't have a second bed and leather couches remind me of eels. I don't sleep with eels."

"Sure." He was disappointed only because he felt so alive around her. Secure. In his mind, she was absolutely perfect in every way. Of course, he wasn't exactly a Casanova, groomed to judge these things.

"I'll call you."

Then she was gone.

|||

Slater sits in a red pickup one block from Kevin's house and watches Sam back out of the driveway then drive south. "There you go; there you go." He clucks his tongue three times slowly, so that he can hear the full range of its sound. There are two sounds, actually—a deep popping as the tongue pulls free from the roof of the mouth, and a click as it strikes the gathered spittle in the base of the mouth. Details. The kind of details most people die without considering because most people are slobs who have no clue what living is really all about.

Living is about clucking your tongue and enjoying the sound.

They had found the bugs. Slater smiles. She has come and he is so very glad she has come quickly, flaunting her skinny little body all through the man's house, seducing him with her wicked tongue.

"Samantha," he whispers. "It is so good to see you again. Give me a kiss, baby."

The interior of the old Chevy is immaculate. He'd replaced the black plastic instrument panel with custom-fitted mahogany that shines now in the moonlight. A black case beside him carries the electronics he requires for his surveillance—mostly extras. Samantha found the six bugs he'd expected the cops to find, but there are still three, and not even the FBI will detect those.

"It's dark down here, Kevin. So very dark."

Slater waits an hour. Two. Three. The night is dead when he eases himself out of the cab and heads for Kevin's house.

8

JENNIFER CROSSED HER LEGS and stared at Paul Milton across the conference table. She'd made the trip down to Long Beach the previous evening, visited the crime scene where Kevin Parson's Mercury Sable had blown up, made a dozen phone calls, and then checked into a hotel on Long Beach Boulevard.

She spent the night tossing and turning, reliving that day three months earlier when Roy had been killed by the Riddle Killer. The killer didn't use a name, never had. Only a riddle. He'd asphyxiated his first four victims, striking once every six weeks or so. With Roy he used a bomb. She found his body in pieces five minutes after the explosion ripped it apart. Nothing could wash away the image.

After a couple final hours of sleep she'd headed for the station where she waited an hour for the rest to arrive.

With Roy's death the fundamentals of life became stunningly vivid, while virtually all of her aspirations had died with him. She'd taken her relationship with him for granted, and when he was snatched away, she became desperate for every other thing she took for granted. The sweet smell of air. A burning hot shower on a cold morning. Sleep. The touch of another human. The simple things in life sustained her. Life wasn't what it seemed, she'd learned that much, but she still wasn't sure what life really *was*. The parties and the promotions felt plastic now. People rushing around, climbing imaginary ladders of success, fighting to be noticed.

Like Milton. Milton was a walking media package, right down to the bone, complete with a beige trench coat, which now hung in the corner. He was holding a news conference, of all things, just past sunup when she'd first entered the station.

There was no new news; they all knew that. His insistence that the media had a right to know at least that much was no more than smoke blowing. He wanted the camera eye, end of case. Not exactly her kind of man.

Her thinking wasn't exactly professional; she knew that. He was a law enforcement officer with the same ultimate objective as hers. They were in this together, regardless of any personal differences. But Jennifer didn't find the process of putting all the nonsense aside as easy as she had before Roy's death. That was why the Bureau tended to distance agents in her situation from the front line, as Frank had attempted.

Never mind, she would rise above it all.

To her left sat Nancy Sterling, Long Beach's most experienced forensic scientist. Next to her, Gary Swanson from the state police and Mike Bowen from the ATF. Cliff Bransford, CBI, rounded out the gathering. She'd worked with Cliff and found him exceptionally tedious, but smart enough. For him, everything was by the book. Best to stay clear of him unless he approached her.

"I know you all have varying interests in this case, but the FBI has clear jurisdiction—this guy's rap includes kidnapping," Jennifer said.

Milton didn't bat an eye. "You may have jurisdiction, but I've got a city—"

"Don't worry, I'm here to work with you. I'm recommending that we use your offices as a clearinghouse. That puts all the information at your fingertips. We'll coordinate everything from here. I don't know what the CBI or the ATF will want to do about personnel placement, but I would like to work out of this office. Fair enough?"

Milton didn't respond.

"Sounds good to me," Bransford said. "We're fine out of our own offices. As far as I'm concerned, this is your case."

Bransford knew about Roy and was giving her his support. She gave him a slight nod.

"We'll stand off for the meantime," the ATF agent said. "But if explosives show up again, we'll want a larger role."

"Granted," Jennifer said. She faced Milton. "Sir?"

He stared her down and she knew then that her opinion of him wouldn't change. Even if he'd linked this case to the Riddle Killer, which was likely given the profile of the killings in Sacramento, Jennifer doubted he knew of her personal stake in the case. Roy's identity had not been circulated. Even so, she didn't care for his arrogance.

"What's your specialty, agent?" Milton asked.

"Forensic psychology, Detective."

"Profiler."

"Psychological profiles based on forensics," she corrected. She almost spoke the rest of the thought: *That's why they put the word* forensics *in there, for those who grew up in Backwater, Louisiana.*

"Fair enough. But I don't want you talking to the media."

"I wouldn't think of robbing you of all that airtime, sir."

"I think we have an understanding."

"Good. I reviewed your file as of an hour ago." She looked at Nancy. "You do quick work."

"We try," Nancy said. "You might want to take a look at it again. We found a timer."

"Preset?"

"No. A receiver set the timer off, but from what I can gather, there was no way to terminate the timer once it was engaged."

Jennifer glanced at Milton. "So whoever did this had no intention of terminating the detonation, regardless of his threat."

"So it seems."

"Anything else?"

Milton stood and turned to the blinds behind his chair. He parted them and looked down at the street. "So what does your crystal ball tell you on this one, Agent Peters?"

"It's early."

"Humor me."

They were undoubtedly thinking Riddle Killer, but she went with a conservative analysis.

"Best guess, we have a white male who is extremely angry, but not angry enough to compromise his precision or method. He's smart. And he knows it. He knew what kind of bomb to build, how to place it, how to detonate without detection. In fact, he knew that Mr. Parson would escape unharmed, and he knew that his riddle would go unsolved. That's why he didn't bother wasting resources on a termination switch."

"Random victim?" Nancy asked.

"Nothing with this guy is random. If the victim isn't a past acquaintance, then he was selected for specific reasons. His profession, his habits, the way he combs his hair."

"Which is why Parson's insistence that he doesn't know anyone who might hold a grudge doesn't add up," Milton said.

"Not necessarily. You're a cop who can list a hundred people who would take your head off, given the opportunity. The average citizen doesn't have those kinds of enemies. We're dealing with someone who's probably insane—a sideways look on a train could mark you as his next target." She paused. "That's what I would say based solely on what you've given me. But as it turns out, I have more."

"Riddle Killer," Nancy said.

Jennifer looked at her and wondered if she knew about Roy. "Yes. Same MO. The last killing we've attributed to this guy was three months ago in Sacramento, but from every indication, we're dealing with the same man."

"He used riddles, but did he ever *not* kill a victim?" Milton asked.

"You're right; this one's different. All five of his victims were given one riddle and then killed when they failed to solve it. Which means he's not finished with Kevin Parson. He didn't just blow up a car without hurting anyone for the fun of it. He's stretching himself. He's bored. He wants a new challenge. Stringing together multiple riddles is the logical progression, but it also takes more time. He would have to study his mark well enough to sustain continued threats. That means lots of surveillance over many days. It's one thing to pull off one stunt. This guy's planning on doing this again. That kind of planning takes time. Could explain why the Riddle Killer has been so quiet over the last three months."

"This guy gave a name," Bransford said. "Slater. The Riddle Killer remained nameless."

"Again. A progression, in my opinion." Jennifer pulled a thick file from her briefcase and set it on the desk. The tab had two capital letters on it: R. K.

"Don't let the size fool you; we don't know as much as you might think. There's a lot of psychological profile data in here. When it comes to evidence, this guy's as clean as they come. None of the bodies was abused in any way. The first four were asphyxiated; the last was killed with a bomb. All four asphyxiated bodies were reported to the police by the killer himself and left on park benches. For all practical purposes they were evidence-free. This killer finds satisfaction in the game more than the actual killing. The killing is only a prop, something that provides stakes high enough to make the game interesting."

She put her hand on the file. The green edges were worn white from use, mostly her own. She could practically recite the contents, all 234 pages. A full half of the writing was hers.

"A copy of the file is being reproduced for each of you as we speak. I'll be happy to answer any questions once you've had a chance to review it. Has there been any additional contact with the victim?"

"Not today," Milton said. "We have a team on the way to sweep his house. He found some bugs. More accurately, a friend of his found six of them throughout the house. A Samantha Sheer called us this morning. She's connected with the attorney general's office. Just happened to be with him last night and did us a favor. Do you know what falls but never breaks? What breaks but never falls?"

"No."

He grinned disingenuously. "Night and day."

"She gave you that?"

He nodded. "Pretty smart. On the other hand, there are too many fingers in this pot already, and the case is less than a day old."

"The case is a year old," Jennifer said. "She met with him without your knowing? You're not watching the house?"

He hesitated. "Not yet. Like I said—"

"You left him alone overnight?" Jennifer felt her face flush with anger. *Easy, girl.*

Milton's eyes narrowed slightly.

"Who do you think we're dealing with here, a cub scout? Do you even know if Parson's still alive?"

"We are under no standing threat," Milton said. "There is no direct evidence that this is the Riddle Killer. Kevin insisted he was—"

"The victim's in no position to know what's best for himself." Jennifer unfolded her legs and stood. "As soon as I get back, I'd like to get a firsthand look at the evidence, if you don't mind, Nancy."

"Of course."

"Where are you going?" Milton asked.

"To see Parson. As far as we know, he's the only living victim of the Riddle Killer. Our first job is to keep him that way. I'd like to spend a few minutes with him before your people start tearing up his house. An associate of mine, Bill Galager, will be here shortly. Please treat him with the same graciousness you've extended to me."

| | |

Jennifer left the station and sped for Kevin Parson's house, knowing that she had walked a thin line back in the conference room. Or maybe she was being too self-conscious about her cooperation because of the bureau chief's concerns. All things considered, except for the mistake of leaving the victim unguarded, Milton had handled the case well enough thus far. But one mistake and they would have another dead body on their hands. She wasn't in a position to accept that. Not this time.

Not after she'd led the Riddle Killer to Roy.

Why is that, Jenn? Kevin Parson is a victim, deserving life, liberty, and the pursuit of happiness like every other potential victim, but no more. That was the objective view of her situation.

But, no matter what face she tried to put on the matter, the bureau chief had pegged her. She *had* lost just a bit of objectivity, hadn't she? Regardless of Kevin Parson's makeup, he was now special. Perhaps more special to Jennifer than any other person in any other case, save her brother. He could be a total fool with a habit of running down the 405 freeway naked, and that much wouldn't change.

Fact was, in some small way, Kevin Parson offered her a glimpse of redemption. If Roy had died because of her, maybe Kevin would live because of her.

Because of her. She had to *personally* save him, didn't she? An eye for an eye. A life for a life.

"God, let him be a decent man," she muttered.

Jennifer dismissed the thoughts with a sigh and pulled onto his street shortly after eight. Old track houses, mostly two-story, modest, decent starter homes. She glanced at the file Milton had given her. Kevin Parson lived in the blue house two doors up. She pulled to the curb, shut off the engine, and glanced around. Quiet neighborhood.

"Okay, Kevin, let's see what kind of man he's chosen this time."

She left the file and walked to the front door. A morning newspaper featuring a front-page spread of the car bombing sat on the porch. She picked it up and rang the doorbell.

The man who answered was tall with messy brown hair and deep blue eyes that held hers without wavering. A white T-shirt with a "Jamaica" logo over the pocket. Faded blue jeans. He smelled of aftershave, although he obviously hadn't shaved today. The rugged look worked on him. Didn't look like the kind of man who'd run down the freeway naked. More like a man she'd expect to find featured in *Cosmopolitan*. Especially with those eyes. Ouch.

"Kevin Parson?" She flipped open her wallet to show her badge. "I'm Agent Peters with the FBI. Could I have a few words with you?"

"Sure. Sure, come in." He ran his fingers through his hair. "Sam said you'd probably be coming this morning."

She handed him the paper and walked in. "Looks like you made the news. Sam? That's your friend from the attorney general's office?"

Travel posters covered the walls. Odd.

"Actually, I think she's with the California Bureau of Investigation. But she just started. You know her?" He dropped the paper out on the porch and closed the door.

"She called the police this morning and reported the bugs. Could I see them?"

"Sure. Right over here." He led her to the kitchen. Two soda cans sat on the counter—he'd had a drink last night, presumably with Sam. Otherwise the kitchen was spotless.

"Here." He indicated the sink and placed the two cans in a small recycling bin. Four small eavesdropping devices that resembled watch batteries, one infinity transmitter she'd obviously pulled off the phone, and a device that resembled a common electrical splitter all sat in the water.

"Did Sam wear gloves when she removed these?"

"Yes."

"Good girl. Not that we'll find anything. I doubt our friend's stupid enough to leave prints on his toys." She faced him. "Anything unusual happen in the last twelve hours? Any phone calls, anything out of place?"

His eyes twitched, barely. *You're going too fast, Jennifer. The poor guy's still in shock and you're giving him the nth degree. You need him as much as he needs you.*

She held up her hand and smiled. "Sorry. Listen to me, barging in here and interrogating you. Let's start over. You can call me Jennifer." She reached out her hand.

He searched her eyes, took her hand. Like a child trying to decide whether to trust a stranger. For a moment she felt drawn into his gaze, exposed. They held their grip long enough to make Jennifer feel awkward. There was an innocence about him, she thought. Maybe more. Naiveté.

"Actually, there *is* more."

She dropped his hand. "There is? More than you told the police?"

"He called me again."

"But you didn't call the police?"

"I couldn't. He told me that if I called the police, he'd do something. Carry out his next threat prematurely." He looked around nervously, breaking eye contact for the first time. "I'm sorry, I'm a bit on edge. I didn't sleep that well. Do you want to sit down?"

"That would be nice."

Kevin pulled out a chair and seated her. Naive and chivalrous. A first-year seminary student who graduated from college with honors. Not exactly the kind of guy who wakes up in the morning thinking of ways to make enemies. He sat across from her and ran a hand haphazardly through his hair.

"When did he call you?"

"After I got home last night. He knows when I'm here; he knows when I'm gone. He can hear everything I say. He's probably listening to us right now."

"He may very well be. There'll be a team here in less than an hour. Until then there's not much we can do about surveillance. What we can do is try to get into this man's head. That's what I do, Kevin; I figure people out for a living. But to do that I need you to tell me everything he said to you. You're my link to him. Until we put this guy away, you and I are going to have to work very closely. No secrets. I don't care what he says you can or can't do—I need to hear it all."

"He said I couldn't tell the police anything. He also told me the FBI would be involved, but he didn't seem bothered by that. He doesn't want the city to come unglued every time he calls me."

She nearly broke her professional facade then. The killer expected the FBI. Did he expect Jennifer? It really had started again, hadn't it? He knew that she would come after him again—even welcomed it! The faint taste of copper washed through her mouth. She swallowed.

Kevin tapped his foot and stared at her without breaking eye contact. His gaze was neither piercing nor intimidating. Disarming perhaps, but not in a way that made her uncomfortable—his eyes held a quality she couldn't quite put a finger on. Maybe innocence. Wide, blue, tired innocence.

Not so different from Roy, really. Was there a connection?

You're staring back, Jennifer. Suddenly she was uncomfortable. She felt a strange empathy for him. How could any sane man threaten someone as innocent as this? Answer: *No* sane man.

I'm going to keep you alive, Kevin Parson. I won't let him hurt you.

"One step at a time," Jennifer said. "I want you to start from the phone call after you got home and tell me exactly what he said."

He relayed the phone call in meticulous detail while she asked questions and took notes. She covered every conceivable angle—the choice of words, the sequencing of events, the tone Slater used, the nearly unlimited ways in which Slater might have had access to his life.

"So you think he's been in here on more than one occasion. On one of those occasions he found Samantha's number. He thinks you and Samantha are romantically involved, but you're not."

"That's right."

"Have you ever been?"

"No, not really." Kevin shifted in his seat. "Although I'm not sure that wasn't a mistake on my part."

Obviously Slater had decided that Kevin and Samantha were more than friends. Who was mistaken, Slater or Kevin? She eyed the man before her. How naive was he?

"You should talk to her," Kevin said. "Maybe she could help somehow. She's not a cop."

"Sure." Jennifer dismissed the suggestion even as she spoke. She had no interest in consulting some rookie at this stage. All she needed was one more gunslinger on the case. "How long have you known her?"

"We grew up together here in Long Beach."

She made a note and changed the subject. "So actually Slater called you three times yesterday. Once on your cell phone, once at home here, and once on a cell phone he left for you? The third call just to make sure the phone worked."

"I guess. Yes, three times."

"We have three minutes, three calls, three rules, a riddle with three parts, three months. You think our guy likes threes?"

"Three months?"

She had to tell him. "You ever hear about the Riddle Killer?"

"The guy from Sacramento."

"Yes. We have reason to believe this is him. He killed his last victim three months ago."

"I heard that on the news." Kevin closed his eyes. "You really think it's him?"

"Yes, I do. But he's never let anyone live that we know of. I'm not trying to be crass—there's just no other way to deal with this. We have a chance, an excellent chance, of stopping him before he goes further."

He opened his eyes. "How?"

"He wants to play. It's not the killing that drives him; it's the game. We play."

"Play?" He stared at her desperately and then lowered his head. She wanted to put an arm around him, to comfort him, to hold this poor soul and tell him that everything was going to be okay. But that would be both untrue and unprofessional.

"You ever play chess?"

"A game or two."

"Think of this as a chess match. He's black and you're white. He's made his first move and you've made yours. You lost a pawn. As long as he's interested in the game, he'll play. Your job is to keep him playing long enough for us to find him. It's the only way to beat him."

Kevin ran both hands through his hair. "And what if he's listening right now?"

"We always assume he's listening. He's undoubtedly got the technology to hear what he wants to hear. But for him to hear what I just told you is music to his ears. He's back in some hole right now, rubbing his hands in anticipation of the game. The longer the better. He might not be sane, but he's brilliant. Probably a genius. He'll never toss a match and run scared just because some two-bit FBI agent's on to him."

I hope you are listening, you snake. She clenched her jaw.

Kevin offered an anemic smile. Apparently he understood, but he wasn't in a place to like anything about Slater's game. "The threes could be coincidental," he said. "Maybe."

"Nothing is coincidental with this guy. His mind works on a whole different plane than most. Can I see the cell phone he gave you?"

He pulled it out of his pocket and handed it to her. She flipped open and scrolled through the activity log. One call at 4:50 yesterday afternoon, as reported.

"Okay, keep this with you. Don't give it to the police, and don't tell them I told you not to give it to them."

That earned her a soft grin, and she couldn't resist returning it. They'd take a crack at tracking Slater's number and triangulating his position, but she wasn't optimistic. There were too many ways to beat the system.

"We'll bug the phone—"

"He said no cops."

"I mean we, the FBI. We'll use a local device that will attach to the cell. I doubt a conventional listening device will do us any good—too easy to scramble and limited on range. The recording device will be noticeable, a small box we'll fix to the back here." She drew her finger through an inch square on the back of the silver phone. "It'll contain a small chip we can remove for analysis later. Not exactly real-time surveillance, but it may be all that we get next time."

He took the phone back. "So I do what he says? Play his game?"

She nodded. "I don't think we have a choice. We'll take him at his word. He calls you; the second you hang up, you call me. He'll probably know about it, and then I guess we'll know what he means by no cops."

Kevin stood and paced to the kitchen counter and back. "Detective Milton grilled me on motivation. Without motivation you have nothing. I can understand that. I think I have an idea."

"Go ahead."

"Hate."

"Hate. That's pretty broad."

"Slater hates me. I can hear it in his voice. Raw contempt. There are few things left in this world that are pure, from my observation. The hate in this man's voice is one of them."

She looked up at him. "You're observant. The question is why. Why does Slater hate you?"

"Maybe not me, but my type," Kevin said. "People tend to react to other people in wholesale rather than detail, right? He's a minister, so I hate him. She's beautiful, so I like her. One month later you wake up and realize you have nothing in common with the woman."

"Do you have firsthand experience on the subject or are you just spinning this from a sociology text?"

Kevin blinked, caught off guard. Unless her intuition was misfiring, he had very little experience with women.

"Well . . ." He ran his hand over his head. "Both, sorta."

"This may qualify as new knowledge, Kevin, but there are men who judge a woman by more than her appearance." She wasn't sure why she felt obligated to say as much; she'd found no offense in his remark.

He didn't bat an eye. "Of course. I see you and you're beautiful, but my attraction to you is based on your caring. I can tell that you really do care about me." He broke eye contact again. "I mean, not in the way it sounds. As your case is what I mean. Not as a man—"

"I understand. Thank you. That was a nice thing to say."

The short exchange felt absurd. Kevin sat back down and for a moment neither spoke.

"But your point is valid," Jennifer said. "Most serial offenders choose victims based on what they represent, not on personal offenses. It's the meticulous thought that Slater has put into this case that makes me wonder if we aren't dealing with personal motivation here. Obsession comes to mind. He's taken a very personal interest in you."

Kevin looked away. "Could be that he's just a very meticulous person." He seemed particularly interested in depersonalizing the motive.

"You're a profiler—what is my profile?" Kevin asked. "Based on what you know, what is there about me that might set off someone?"

"I don't have enough to offer—"

"No, but based on what you do know?"

"My first blush? Okay. You're a seminary student. You take life seriously and have a higher intelligence than most. You're caring and kind and gentle. You live alone and have very few friends. You're attractive and carry yourself with confidence, notwithstanding a couple nervous habits." It occurred to Jennifer as she ran down the list that Kevin was an unusually good person, not merely innocent. "But it's your genuine innocence that stands out. If Slater has no personal stake in you, he hates you for your innocence."

There was more to Kevin than she could see at first glance, much more. How could anyone dislike, much less hate, Kevin Parson?

"You remind me of my brother," she said. Then she wished she hadn't.

What if the Riddle Killer wanted Jennifer to see the similarities between Roy and Kevin? What if he'd chosen Kevin because he intended to make Jennifer live through the hell once again?

Pure speculation.

Jennifer rose. "I have to get back to the lab. The police will be here shortly. If there's anything you need, or if you think of anything else, call. I'll have one of our men watch the house. Promise me you will never leave alone. This guy likes to drop his little bombs when they're least expected."

"Sure."

He looked lost. "Don't worry, Kevin. We'll make it through this."

"In one piece, hopefully." He grinned nervously.

She put her hand on top of his. "We will. Trust me." She once said those same words to Roy to calm him down. Jennifer removed her hand.

They stared at each other for a moment. *Say something, Jennifer.* "Remember, he wants a game. We're going to give him a game."

"Right."

Jennifer left him standing in his doorway looking anything but confident. *Trust me.* She considered staying until the techs arrived, but she had to get back to the evidence. She'd cornered the Riddle Killer once, before he'd gone after Roy, and she'd done it through careful analysis of the evidence. She did her best work when climbing around in criminals' minds, not holding their victims' hands.

On the other hand, Kevin was no ordinary victim.

Who are you, Kevin? Whoever he was, she decided that she liked him.

9

KEVIN HAD NEVER FELT entirely comfortable around women—because of his mother, Sam insisted—but Jennifer seemed different. As a professional it was her job to engender trust, he knew, but he'd seen more than the expected professional facade in her eyes. He'd seen a real woman who'd warmed to him beyond the demands of her job. He wasn't sure how that translated to her capability as an investigator, but he felt certain he could trust her sincerity.

Unfortunately, it did nothing for his confidence.

Kevin walked to the telephone and dialed Samantha's number. She answered on the fifth ring.

"Sam."

"Hi, Sam. The FBI was just here."

"And?"

"Nothing new, really. She thinks it's the Riddle Killer."

"She?"

"The agent. Jennifer Peters."

"I've heard of her. Listen, there's a chance I may need to fly back to Sacramento today. Actually, I have my office on the other line. Can I call you right back?"

"Everything okay?"

"Give me a few minutes and I'll explain, okay?"

He hung up and glanced at the clock. 8:47. Where were the

police? He checked the dishwasher. Half full. He dumped in some detergent and turned it on. It would take him a week to fill the thing up, and by that time it would begin to smell sour.

Slater would have his hands full; that much was good. Surely between Sam, Jennifer, and the Long Beach police he would be safe. Kevin crossed to the refrigerator.

Jennifer thinks I'm nice. I don't care if I'm nice—I want to be alive. And I wouldn't mind if Slater were dead. How nice is that? If a man gossips, is he not nice? The bishop gossips, so he's not nice. Kevin sighed. *Here I am rambling again while the world's blowing up around me. What would the psychobabblist say about that?*

I don't know why I do it, Doctor, but I think the strangest things at the oddest times.

So do all men, Kevin. So do all men. Women don't, of course. The female tends to be the more intelligent or at least the more stable of the sexes. Turn the country over to them and you'll wake up to find the potholes down your street filled in like they should have been a year ago. You're just a man finding his way in a mad world gone madder, madder hatter. We'll break that down next session if you drop another check in the pay box over there. Two hundred this time. My kids need . . .

Kevin twitched. He didn't remember opening the fridge, but now, standing in front of the open door, the milk jug filled his vision. Someone had scrawled a large 3 on the Albertsons jug with a black magic marker, and above it three words:

It's so dark

Slater!

Kevin released the door and stepped back.

When? What's so dark? The *fridge* is so dark? Was this another riddle? He had to tell Jennifer! No, Samantha. He had to tell Sam!

Dread crept into his bones. Where is it so dark? In the cellar. The boy! He stood still, unable to breathe. The world began to spin. *It's so dark.*

Dear God, it *was* the boy!

The door closed on its own. He backed to the wall. But Slater had said he wasn't the boy! *What boy?* he'd said.

The events of that night so long ago swept over him.

| | |

For a whole week after young Kevin's encounter with the bully, he waited in agony. Dark circles gathered under his eyes and he caught a cold. He made up a story about falling out of bed to explain the bruises on his face. His mother had put him to bed early in the afternoon to fight the cold. He just lay there, sweating on the sheets. His fear wasn't for himself, but for Samantha. The boy had promised to hurt her, and Kevin was sick with worry.

Six days later a tap had finally sounded on his window. He'd eased the blind up, holding his breath. Sam's smiling face stared at him from the backyard. Kevin nearly hit the ceiling in his excitement. As it turned out, Sam had been away at camp. She was horrified by his haggard features, and only after much urging did she convince him to come out to talk. No one would see them; she swore it. He made her search for the boy all around the yard, just to make sure. When he did sneak out, he went only just beyond his own fence, keeping a watchful eye on the greenway. They sat there, hidden in the shadows, and he told Sam everything.

"I'll tell my dad," she said. "You think if he licked my window we'll still be able to see it?"

Kevin shuddered. "Probably. You have to tell your dad. You should go tell him right now. But don't tell him about me sneaking out to see you. Just tell him I was walking by and saw the boy at your window and he chased me. Don't even tell him that he . . . did any-thing to me. Your dad might tell my mom."

"Okay."

"Then come back and tell me what he says."

"You mean tonight?"

"Right now. Go home by the street and watch out for the boy. He's going to kill us."

By now Sam was scared, despite her typical optimism. "Okay." She stood and brushed off her shorts. "My dad might not let me back out. In fact, he might even make me stay home for a while if I tell him."

Kevin thought about that. "That's okay. At least you'll be safe; that's the main thing. But please, come back as soon as you can."

"Okay." She held out her hand and pulled him up. "Friends for life?"

"Friends for life," he said. He gave her a hug and she ran off toward the street.

Sam didn't come back to his window that night. Or the next. Or for three weeks. They were the loneliest weeks of Kevin's life. He tried to convince his mom to let him out, but she wouldn't hear of it. He tried to sneak out during the day twice, not through the window, of course—he could never risk Mother discovering the screw or the loose board. He went over the back fence, but only got as far as the first tree on the greenway before Bob began to wail. He barely made it back onto the ash heap before Mother hurried out in a tizzy. The other time he went through the front door and made it all the way to Sam's house only to find, as he had known he would, that she was gone to school. His mom was waiting for him when he tried to sneak back in, and he spent the next two days in his room.

Then, on the twenty-second day, the tap came at his window. He peeked very carefully, terrified that it might be the boy. He would never be able to describe the warmth that flooded his heart when he saw Sam's face in the moonlight. He fumbled with the screw and yanked the window open. They threw their arms around each other before he tumbled out and ran with her through the fence.

"What happened?" he asked, breathless.

"My dad found him! He's a thirteen-year-old who lives on the other side of the warehouses. I guess the boy has caused trouble before; Dad knew him when I described him. Oh, you should have seen my dad, Kevin! I've never seen him so angry. He told the boy's parents that they had two weeks to move, or he was going to haul their boy off to jail. Guess what? They moved!"

"He's . . . he's gone?"

"Gone." She raised a palm and he absently high-fived it.

"You sure?"

"My dad let me out, didn't he? Yes, I'm sure. Come on!"

It took Kevin only two outings with Sam to lose his fear of the night again. The boy was indeed gone.

Two weeks later Kevin decided that it was about time he take the initiative to visit Sam. You could only play white knight so many times without actually flexing your muscle some.

Kevin snuck along the treelined greenway toward Sam's house, picking his way carefully. This was his first time out alone in over a month. He made it to her fence easily enough. The light from her window was a welcome sight. He bent down and pulled the loose picket aside.

"Pssst."

Kevin froze.

"Hello, squat."

The horrible sound of the boy's voice filled Kevin with images of a sick twisted smile. He suddenly felt nauseated.

"Stand up," the boy said.

Kevin stood slowly and pivoted. His muscles had turned to water, all except for his heart, which was slamming into his throat. There, ten feet away, stood the boy, grinning wickedly, turning the knife in his right hand. He wore a bandanna that covered his tattoo.

"I've decided something," the boy said. "There are three of us on this little totem pole here. But I'm at the bottom and I don't like that. I'm going to take out the top two. What do you think about that?"

Kevin couldn't think clearly about anything.

"I'll tell you what I'm going to do," the boy said. "First I'm going to cut you in a few places you'll never forget. I want you to use your imagination for me. Then I'm going to come back here and tap on Samantha's window like you do. When she opens the shade, I'm going to stick my knife right through the glass."

The boy chewed on his tongue; his eyes flashed with excitement. He lifted the knife and touched the blade with his left hand. He glanced down and fixated on the sharp edge. "I'll be through the glass and in her throat before she can . . ."

Kevin ran then, while the boy's eyes were still diverted.

"Hey!"

The boy took after him. Kevin had a twenty-foot head start—a fifth of what he needed to outrun the larger boy. At first sheer adrenaline pushed Kevin forward. But behind him the boy began to chuckle and his voice grew closer. Now terror pounded Kevin in unrelenting waves. He screamed, but nothing came out because his throat had frozen shut. The ground seemed to slope upward and then sideways and Kevin lost his sense of direction.

A hand touched his collar. If the boy caught him, he would use the knife. And then he would go after Sam. He might not kill her, but he would at least cut her face. Probably worse.

He wasn't sure where his house was, but it wasn't where he desperately needed it to be. So Kevin did the only thing he knew to do. He turned to his left and tore across the street.

The chuckling stopped for a moment. The boy grunted and doubled his efforts—Kevin could hear his feet pounding with a new determination.

The chuckling started again.

Kevin's chest ached and his breath came in huge gasps now. For a terrible moment he considered just falling down and letting the boy cut him up.

A hand swatted him on the head. "Keep running, squat. I hate it when they just lie there."

Kevin had lost his sense of direction completely. They were coming up to one of the old warehouses in the district across the street. He saw a door in the building directly ahead. Maybe . . . maybe if he could get through that door.

He veered to his right, and then broke for the building. He slammed into the old door, yanked it open, and plunged into the darkness beyond.

The stairwell five feet inside the door saved his life, or at the very least some of his body parts. He tumbled down the stairs, crying out in pain. When he came to rest at the bottom landing, his head felt as though it had come off. He struggled to his feet and turned back to the stairs.

The boy stood at the top, backlit by the moonlight, chuckling. "The end," he said and started down the steps.

Kevin spun and ran. Right into another door. A steel door. He grasped the handle and twisted, but the bulk refused to budge. He saw the deadbolt, threw it open, and plunged headlong into a pitch-black room. He stumbled forward and smacked into a concrete wall.

The boy grabbed Kevin's hair.

Kevin screamed. His voice echoed crazily about him. He screamed louder. No one would hear them; they were underground.

"Shut up! Shut up!" The boy hit him in the mouth.

Kevin summoned all of his fear and struck out blindly into the darkness. His fist connected with something that cracked. The boy hollered and let go of Kevin's hair. Kevin's legs gave way and he collapsed.

It occurred to him in that moment that whatever the boy had initially planned for him could no longer compare to what he would do now.

Kevin rolled and staggered to his feet. The door was to his right, dull gray in the faint light. The boy faced him, one hand on his nose, the other tight around the knife.

"You just lost your eyes, boy."

Kevin bolted without thought. He sprang through the open door, spun around, and slammed it shut. He threw his left hand up and rammed the deadbolt home.

Then it was just him, in the concrete staircase, breathing hard. Silence swallowed him.

A very soft yell reached beyond the steel door. Kevin held his breath and backed up slowly. He lunged up the steps, got halfway up before the sound of the boy reached him again, just barely. He was yelling and cursing and threatening him with words Kevin could barely understand because they were so quiet.

There was no way out, was there? If he left, the boy might die in there! No one would hear his screams. He couldn't leave.

Kevin turned back and slowly descended the stairs. What if he slipped the bolt open and made a break for it? He could make it, maybe.

"I swear I'm gonna kill you . . ."

Kevin knew then that he had only two options. Open the door and get cut, maybe die. Run away and let the boy die, maybe live.

"I hate you! I hate you!" The scream was eerily distant, but raspy and bitter.

Kevin whirled around and flew up the steps. He had no choice. He had no choice. For Samantha, that's what the boy got. It was his own fault anyway.

Kevin shut the outer door behind him and ran into the night. He didn't know quite how or exactly when, but sometime while it was still dark, he made it back into his bed.

III

Something rattled violently. Kevin jerked up. The tabletop reflected the morning sun at eye level. The cell phone vibrated slowly toward the edge.

Kevin scrambled to his feet. *Dear God, give me strength.* He glanced at the clock. 9:00 A.M. Where were the police?

He reached his hand for the phone, hesitated, and then snatched it off the table. Play the game, Jennifer had said. *Play the game.*

"Hello?"

"How is our chess player doing this morning?" Slater asked.

So he *had* been listening! Kevin closed his eyes and focused his mind. His life depended on what he said. Be smart. Outthink him.

"Ready to play," he said, but his voice didn't sound ready.

"You'll have to do better than that. Kevin, Kevin, Kevin. Two little challenges, two little failures, two little booms. You're beginning to bore me. Did you see my little gift?"

"Yes."

"What's three times three?"

Three times three. "Nine," he said.

"Smart boy. Nine o'clock, time to rock. Time for the third. *What takes you there but takes you nowhere?* You have sixty minutes. It'll be worse this time, Kevin."

The phone on the counter rang shrilly. He had to keep Slater on the phone.

"Can I ask a question?" he asked.

"No. But you may answer the room phone. Maybe it will be Sam. Wouldn't that be cozy? Answer the phone."

Kevin slowly lifted the room phone off the hook.

"Kevin?" Sam's familiar voice filled his ear, and despite the impossible situation, he felt a bucket of relief wash over him. He wasn't sure what to say. He held the cell phone against his right ear and the room phone against his other ear.

"Tell her hello from Slater," Slater said.

Kevin hesitated. "Slater says hello," he said.

"He called?" she asked.

"He's on the other line."

"Too bad Jennifer left so early," Slater said. "The four of us could throw a little party. Time's running out. Fifty-nine minutes and fifty-one seconds. Your move." The cell phone clicked.

Sam spoke again. "Kevin, listen to me! Is he still on—"

"He's gone."

"Don't move. I'm turning up your street now. I'll be there in ten seconds." She disconnected.

Kevin stood, immobile, a phone in each hand. Play the game. Play the game. It was the boy; it had to be the boy.

The door flew open. "Kevin?" Sam ran in.

He spun. "I have sixty minutes."

"Or what?"

"Another bomb?"

She stepped up to him and cradled her hands under his wrists. "Okay. Listen to me, we have to think this through clearly." She eased the phones out of his hands and then took him by the shoulders. "Listen to me—"

"We have to call the FBI."

"We will. But I want you to tell me first. Tell me exactly what he said."

"I know who the Riddle Killer is."

She stared, stunned. "Who?"

Kevin sat heavily in a chair. "The boy."

"I thought he told you he *wasn't* the boy."

Kevin's mind began to work faster. "He said, 'What boy?' He didn't say he *wasn't* the boy." He ran to the refrigerator, opened the door, pulled out the milk jug, and slammed it on the counter.

She stared at the thick-stroked letters. Her eyes shifted to him and then back. "When was—"

"He was in here last night."

"*It's so dark.* What's so dark?"

Kevin paced and rubbed his head.

"Tell me, Kevin. Just tell me. We're running out of time here."

"Your dad made the boy leave, but he came back."

"What do you mean? We never saw him again!"

"I did! He caught me on my way to your house two weeks later. He said he was going to hurt you. And me. I ran and somehow . . ." Emotions clogged his head. He glanced at the clock. 9:02. "Somehow we ended up in a storage basement in one of the warehouses. I don't even remember which one anymore. I locked him in and ran away."

She blinked. "What happened?"

"I had to do it, Sam!" He spoke desperately now. "He was going to kill you! And me!"

"It's okay. It's okay, Kevin. We can talk about it later, okay? Right now—"

"That's the sin he wants me to confess. I left him to die in the dark."

"But he *didn't* die, did he? Obviously he's alive. You didn't kill anyone."

He paused. Of course! The dark night flashed through his mind. Unless Slater wasn't the boy, but someone who knew about the incident, a psychopath who'd discovered the truth somehow and had decided that Kevin should pay.

"Either way, I locked a boy in a basement and left him to die. That's intent. That's as good as murder."

"You don't know that this has anything to do with the boy. We have to think this through, Kevin."

"We don't have time to think this through! It's the only thing that makes any sense. If I confess, this crazy game stops." He paced and rubbed his head, suppressing a sudden urge to cry over the thought of actually confessing after all that he'd done to rid himself of his past. "Oh God, what have I done? This can't be happening. Not after everything else."

She stared at him, digesting the new information, her eyes wrinkled with empathy. "So then confess, Kevin. That was almost twenty years ago."

"Come on, Sam!" He whirled to her, angry. "This will blow sky-high. Every American who watches the news will know about the seminary student who buried another kid alive and left him to die. This will ruin me!"

"Better ruined than dead. Besides, you had reason to lock up the boy. I'll come to your defense."

"None of that matters. If I am capable of attempted murder, I am capable of anything. That's the reputation that will follow me." He gritted his teeth. "This is nuts. We're running out of time. I have to call the newspaper and tell them. It's the only way to stop that maniac before he kills me."

"Maybe, but he's also demanding that you solve the riddle. We may be dealing with the same killer from Sacramento—"

"I know. Jennifer told me. Still, the only way to stop him is to confess. The riddle is supposed to tell me what to confess." Kevin headed for the phone. He had to call the newspaper. Slater was listening—he'd know. This was insane.

"What was the riddle?"

He stopped. "*What takes you there but takes you nowhere?* He said it would be worse this time."

"How does *that* tie in to the boy?" she asked.

The question hadn't occurred to him. *What takes you there but takes you nowhere?* "I don't know." What if Sam was right? What if his confession about the boy wasn't what Slater was looking for?

"What connection is there between the boy and the three riddles he's given?" She grabbed a piece of paper. "Sixty minutes. Yesterday it was three minutes and then thirty minutes. Today it's sixty minutes. What time did he call?"

"Nine o'clock. Three times three. That's what he said."

Her eyes studied the riddles she'd jotted down.

"Call Agent Peters. Tell her about Slater's call and the confession. Ask her to call the newspaper and tell her to get over here as fast as she can. We have to crack these riddles."

Kevin punched in the number Jennifer had left him. The clock read 9:07. They still had fifty-three minutes. Jennifer picked up.

"He called," Kevin said.

Silence.

"He called—"

"Another riddle?"

"Yes. But I think I might know who he is and what he wants."

"Tell me!"

Kevin told her the rest in a halting run-on that ate up several minutes. An urgency he hadn't expected crowded her voice. She was impatient and demanding. But her intensity reassured him.

"So you think you know who he is, and you neglect to tell me about his demand that you confess. What are you trying to do to me? This is a killer we're dealing with!"

"I'm sorry, I was scared. I'm telling you now."

"Any other secrets?"

"No. Please, I'm sorry."

"Samantha's there?"

"Yes. You have to get this confession out," Kevin said. "That's what this is about."

"We don't know that. I don't see the relationship between the riddles and the boy."

"He was here, last night, and he wrote on my milk jug," Kevin said. "It has to be him! You wanted motivation; now you have it. I tried to kill someone. He's mad. How's that? You have to get this confession on the air."

Silence stretched on the line.

"Jennifer?"

"We need more time!" she said and then took a breath. "Okay, I'll put the confession on the wire. Stay put. Do not set foot outside that house, you hear me? Work the riddles."

"Sam—"

But Jennifer had hung up. Now there was a no-nonsense girl. He found comfort in the fact.

Kevin hung up. 9:13. "She'll call the paper."

"Three," Samantha said. "Our guy's tripping over his threes. Progressions. Three, thirty, sixty. And opposites. Night and day, life and death. *What takes you there but takes you nowhere?*" She stared at her page of notes and numbers.

"She wasn't exactly thrilled about you being here," Kevin said.

Sam looked up. "What takes you there? The obvious answer is transportation. Like a car. But he did a car. He won't do a car again. He's into progressions. More."

Kevin's mind spun. "A bus. Train. Plane. But they take you somewhere, don't they?"

"Depends on where somewhere is. I don't think it matters—*there* and *nowhere* are opposites. I think he's going to blow up some kind of public transport!"

"Unless the confession—"

"We can't assume that'll stop him." She jumped to her feet, grabbed the phone from its cradle, and punched the redial.

"Agent Peters? Sam Sheer here. Listen, I think—" She paused and listened. "Yes, I do understand jurisdiction, and as far as I'm concerned, Kevin has always been *my* jurisdiction. If you want to press the matter, I'll get authorization from the attorney gen—" Another pause, and Sam was smiling now. "My thoughts exactly. But how long will it take to evacuate all public transportation in Long Beach?" She glanced at her watch. "By my watch we have forty-two minutes." Sam listened for a while. "Thank you."

She hung up. "Sharp gal. Feisty. The news already has your story. It's going out live on television as we speak."

Kevin ran to his television and flipped it on.

"The next edition of the paper won't hit the street until tomorrow morning," Sam said. "Slater didn't mention the paper this time, did he?"

"No. I'm sure television will work. God help me."

Empathy lit Sam's gentle eyes. "Jennifer doesn't think this will satisfy him. The real game's the riddle. I think she's right." She paced and put both palms on her head. "Think, Sam, think!"

"They're evacuating the public—"

"There's no way they can get them all out in time," Sam said. "It'll take them half an hour just to get the clearances! There's more here. Slater's precise. He's given us more."

The program on the television suddenly changed. The familiar face of Tom Schilling, news anchor for the ABC affiliate, filled the screen. A red "Breaking News" banner scrolled across the picture tube.

The graphic behind Tom Schilling was a shot of Kevin's charred car with the words "Riddle Killer?" superimposed in a choppy font. The anchor glanced off-camera to his right and then faced the audience.

Kevin stared, spellbound. Tom Schilling was about to drop the hammer on his life. Goose bumps rippled up his neck. Maybe confessing *had* been a mistake.

"We have a shocking new development in the case of the car explosion on Long Beach Boulevard yesterday. Kevin Parson, the driver of the car, has come forward with new information that may shed light on the investigation."

When Kevin heard his name, the room faded, the picture blurred, and the words grew garbled, as if spoken underwater. His life was over. Tom Schilling droned on.

"Kevin Parson is a seminary student at . . ."

You're dead.

" . . . the hopeful clergyman has confessed . . ."

This is it.

" . . . locked the boy in an underground . . ."

Your life is over.

He thought it odd that this exposure brought on a sense of impending death even more acutely than Slater's threats had. He'd spent five years pulling himself out of Baker Street's sea of despondency, and now, in the space of less than twenty-four hours, he found himself overboard, drowning again. Someone would start digging into the rest of his childhood. Into the truth behind Balinda and the house.

Here am I. Kevin Parson, a shell of a man who is capable of the most wicked sin conceived of by man. Here am I, a wretched pretender. I am nothing more than a slug, role-playing its way through life in human form. When you learn everything, you will know that and more.

Thank you. Thank you, Aunt Balinda, for sharing this with me. I am nothing. Thank you, you lousy, sick, twisted auntie for slamming this nugget of truth down my throat. I am nothing, nothing, nothing. Thank you, you demon from hell for gouging out my eyes and pounding me into the ground and . . .

"—vin? Kevin!"

Kevin turned. Sam sat at the table, remote in hand, staring at him. The television was off. It occurred to him that he was trembling. He exhaled and relaxed his balled hands, ran them through his hair. *Get a grip, Kevin. Hold yourself together.*

But he didn't want to hold himself together. He wanted to cry.

"What?"

"I'm sorry, Kevin. It's not as bad as it sounds. I'll get you through this, I promise."

It's not as bad as it sounds because you don't know the whole story, Sam. You don't know what really happened in that house on Baker Street. He turned away from her. *God, help me. Please help me.*

"I'll be okay," he said and cleared his throat. "We have to focus on the riddle."

A stray thought whispered to Kevin.

"It's the numbers," Sam said. "Public transportation is numbered. Slater's going to blow a bus or a train identified with the number three."

The thought raised its voice. "He said no cops!"

"What—"

"No cops!" Kevin shouted. "They're using cops to evacuate?"

The fear he felt spread through her eyes. "Dear God!"

|||

"I don't care if they have to delay every flight in the country!" Jennifer said. "We have a credible bomb threat here, sir! Get the governor on the line if you have to. Terrorist or not, this guy's going to blow something."

"Thirty-five minutes—"

"Is enough time to start."

The bureau chief hesitated.

"Look, Frank," Jennifer said, "you have to put your neck on the line with me here. The local police don't have the muscle to push this through fast enough. Milton's working on the buses, but the bureaucracy's thicker than molasses down here. I need this from the top."

"You're sure about this?"

"Meaning what? That I'm jumping the gun? We can't afford to risk—"

"Okay. But if this turns out to be a hoax . . ."

"It won't be the first."

She hung up and took a deep breath. It had already occurred to her that they'd violated one of Slater's rules. No cops. But she saw no alternatives. She needed the local police.

A junior detective, Randal Crenshaw, burst through the door. "Milton says they're tracking down the director of local transport now. He should have an answer in ten minutes."

"How long will it take them to clear the buses once they have the word?"

"Dispatch can move pretty quick." He shrugged. "Maybe ten minutes."

She stood and paced the length of the conference table. They now had the first significant lead in the case. The boy. If indeed it was this boy. He'd be how old now? Early thirties? More importantly, someone other than Kevin knew the killer: Samantha Sheer's father, a policeman named Rick Sheer, who'd caught the boy spying.

"I want you to track down a cop who worked Long Beach about twenty years ago," she told Crenshaw. "Name's Rick Sheer. Find him. I need to talk to him. Run a search on any of his logs that mention a boy who was threatening the children in his neighborhood."

The detective scribbled the name across a piece of paper and left.

She was missing something. Somewhere in the notes she'd taken this morning was the identity of the bus or the train or whatever Slater planned on blowing, if indeed they were right about the riddle referring to public transportation.

The target wasn't Kevin, and Jennifer found relief in the realization. For the moment it wasn't *his* life at risk. For now Slater was more interested in playing. Play the game, Kevin. Lead him on. She snatched up the phone and dialed his number.

He picked up on the fifth ring.

"Any thoughts?"

"Just going to call you. It could be a bus or something identified with a three," Kevin said.

That was it! Had to be. "Three. I'll have them put a priority on anything with a three in the identifier."

"How are they doing?"

"Looks good. We should know something in ten minutes."

"That's cutting it pretty close, isn't it?"

"It's the best they can do."

| | |

Sam snapped her cell phone closed and grabbed her purse. "That's it, let's go!" She ran for the door. "I'll drive."

Kevin ran after her. "How many?"

"Long Beach proper has twenty-five buses, each identified with several letters and a number. We want number twenty-three. It runs down Alamitos and then back up Atlantic. That's not far. With any luck we'll run into it."

"What about three or thirteen?"

"They started the numbering at five and skipped thirteen."

The tires on Sam's car squealed. She was certain Slater had a bus in mind. The planes were less likely targets for the simple reason that security was far tighter than it once had been. She had checked the trams—no threes. Trains were a possibility, but again, high security. It had to be a bus. The fact that there was only one with three in its designator offered at least a sliver of hope.

Twenty-nine minutes.

They flew across Willow toward Alamitos but were stopped by a red light at Walnut. Sam glanced both directions and sped through.

"Now is one time I wouldn't mind a cop on my tail," she said. "We could use their help."

"No cops," Kevin said.

She looked at him. Two more minutes passed before they hit Alamitos.

"You see a bus, it's probably number twenty-three. You yell."

But they passed no buses. They crossed Third Street through a red. Still no bus.

Ocean Boulevard, right; Atlantic, north. No bus. Horns honked at them on several occasions.

"Time?" she asked.

"Nine thirty-seven."

"Come on! Come on!"

Sam backtracked. When they hit Third again, the light was red and cars blocked the intersection. A bus numbered "6453–17" rumbled by, headed west on Third Street. Wrong bus. The car was stuffy. Sweat beaded their foreheads. The intersection cleared and Sam shoved the accelerator down. "Come on, baby. Where are you?"

She'd cleared the intersection by fifty feet when she slammed on the brakes.

"What?"

She jerked her head around and stared back toward Third Street. She frantically grabbed her cell phone, hit the redial button.

"Yes, could you tell me which bus runs down Third Street?"

Kevin heard the deep male voice from his seat. "The Third Street bus. You need—"

Sam slammed the phone shut, yanked the wheel around, and pulled directly into traffic. She pulled through a screaming U-turn, cutting off a white Volvo and a blue sedan. Horns blared.

"They call the buses by their street names, not their numbers!" Sam said.

"But you don't know if Slater—"

"We know where the Third Street bus is. Let's clear it first and then go for twenty-three." She squealed onto Third Street and honed in on the bus, not a hundred yards ahead. Obviously dispatch hadn't reached the driver yet.

Nineteen minutes.

Sam pulled directly in front of the bus and braked. The bus blasted its horn and ground to a halt behind them.

"Tell the driver to evacuate and stay clear for at least half an hour. Tell them to spread the word to the other cars on the street. Tell them there's a bomb—it works every time. I'm calling Agent Peters."

Kevin ran to the bus. He hammered on the door, but the driver, an older man who must have been three times his recommended weight, refused to open.

"There's a bomb on board!" he yelled, flinging his hands out like an explosion. "A bomb!" He wondered if any of them recognized him from the television. *The kid-killer is now downtown pulling old women off of buses.*

A young man who looked like Tom Hanks stuck his head out an open window. "A what?"

"A bomb! Get out! Clear the bus. Clear the street."

For a moment, nothing happened. Then the door hissed open, and the same young man stumbled out. He yelled back into the bus.

"Get them out, you idiot! He said there's a bomb on this bus!"

A dozen passengers—half by what Kevin could see—bolted from their seats. The driver seemed to catch the fever. "Okay, everyone out! Watch your step. Just a precaution, ladies and gentlemen. Don't shove!"

Kevin grabbed the Tom Hanks look-alike. "Clear this street and stay clear for at least thirty minutes, you hear? Get them all out of here!"

"What is it? How do you know?"

Kevin ran for Sam's car. "Trust me. Just get them clear. The police are on their way." The passengers didn't need any encouragement. Cars stopped and then sped past the bus or backed away.

He slid into the car.

"Hold on," Sam said. She sped off, took an immediate right on the next street, and headed back toward Atlantic.

"One down. Fifteen minutes left."

"This is nuts," Kevin said. "We don't even know if Slater's—"

The cell phone went berserk in his pocket. Kevin froze and stared at his right thigh.

"What?" Sam asked.

"He . . . he's calling."

The phone vibrated again and this time he grabbed it. Samantha slowed.

"Hello?"

"I said no cops, Kevin," Slater's soft voice said. "No cops means no cops."

Kevin's fingers began to shake. "You mean the FBI?"

"Policemen. From now on it's you and Sam and Jennifer and me and no one else."

End call.

Sam had slowed way down. She looked at him with wide eyes.

"What did he say?"

"He said no cops."

The ground suddenly shook. An explosion thundered. They both ducked.

"Turn around! Turn around!"

"That was the bus," Sam whispered. She spun the car around and sped back the way they'd come.

Kevin stared as they rolled onto Third. Boiling flames and thick black smoke engulfed the surreal scene. Three blackened cars parked next to the bus smoldered. God only knew if anyone was hurt, but the immediate area looked vacant. Books lay scattered among the shattered glass of a used bookstore's windows. Its "Read It Again" sign dangled over the sidewalk dangerously. The shop owner stumbled out, stunned.

Sam shoved the gearshift into park and stared at the unearthly scene.

Her cell phone screeched and Kevin started. She lifted it slowly. "Sheer."

She blinked and immediately refocused. "How long ago?" She looked at Kevin and then the bus. A siren wailed. A car Kevin immediately recognized as Jennifer's squealed around the corner and headed toward them.

"Can Rodriguez question him?" Sam asked into her phone. "I'm in a bit of a pinch here." She turned away and lowered her voice. "He just blew up a bus. I'm parked in a car, fifty feet away from it. Yes, I am pretty sure." She listened.

Jennifer roared up and stuck her head out of her car's window. "You okay?"

"Yeah," Kevin said. His fingers were numb and his mind dazed, but he was okay.

Samantha acknowledged Jennifer with a nod, turned to the side, and covered her exposed ear. "Yes, sir. Right away. I understand . . ." She glanced at her watch. "The ten-thirty flight?"

Kevin shoved his door open.

Jennifer stopped him. "No, stay put. Don't move, I'll be right back." She drove toward the bus.

Sam finished her conversation and closed the phone.

"Do you think anyone was hurt?" Kevin asked.

She looked at the bus and shook her head. "I don't know, but we were lucky to find it when we did."

Kevin groaned and ran both hands through his hair.

"I have to go," Sam said. "That was the call I thought I might get. They want me to question a witness. His attorney will have him out by midafternoon. Unfortunately, I can't miss this. I'll explain it when I get—"

"I can't believe Slater did this," Kevin said, staring around again. "He would have killed over twenty people if we hadn't stumbled onto this bus."

She shook her head. "This changes the game. Look, I'll be back on the first flight this evening, okay? I promise. But I have to leave now if I'm going to make the flight." She rubbed his shoulder and looked in Jennifer's direction. "Tell her I'll call and give her my take; she'll take care of you." Three marked police cars had arrived and surrounded the charred bus. "We'll make it, my dear knight. I swear we'll make it."

Kevin nodded. "This is insane."

10

WITHIN FIVE MINUTES OF THE EXPLOSION, a couple dozen law enforcement officials—mostly local police but including some from her own office and several from state agencies—isolated the crime scene and began the forensic investigation. They had quickly located the bomb. By all initial appearances it was the same as the bomb in Kevin's car, only larger.

Jennifer situated Kevin in a coffee shop four doors down from the bus with strict instructions not to move—she'd be back in twenty minutes.

The parameters of the investigation had just changed. Bill Galager from the Los Angeles office arrived, as well as two junior investigators, John Mathews and Brett Mickales. They would work the case from an evidence angle, freeing her to focus on the psychology of it. One conclusion required no degree in criminal psychology—when Slater said no cops, he meant absolutely no cops. And he had the means to know if cops were involved.

According to Kevin, Slater had mentioned her by name. Jennifer. The maniac was drawing her into another trap, wasn't he? By the looks of the bus, he'd graduated into a new class.

No cops. No CBI, except Samantha, who happened to be connected to Kevin by his childhood and the boy. No ATF. No sheriff or state police. Just FBI and, specifically, just Jennifer.

"Still eager to take him on?"

Jennifer turned to Milton, who'd walked up behind her. "Eager?" A touch of defiance glimmered in his eyes, but he didn't elaborate.

"Why did he blow it early?"

"He said no cops. He obviously learned that your department had been informed—"

"They always say no cops. You're not a cop?"

"According to Kevin, he said FBI only."

Milton scoffed.

Jennifer frowned. "No cops. Evidently the history he has with us figures into his game. Bottom line is, he laid down a rule; we broke it; he blew the bus early."

"And what if he said no FBI? Would you back out? I don't think so. This is my city. You don't have the right to cut me out."

"I'm not cutting you out, Milton. Your men are all over the place."

"I'm not referring to mopping up. He's going to call again and the city knows that. They have a right to know."

"The city? You mean the press. No, Milton. The press has a right to know anything that might lend to the city's safety. You're looking at a bus this time; the next time it could be a building. You willing to risk that for the sake of protocol? If you'll excuse me, I have a case to attend to."

Milton's stare grew hot. "This is my city, not yours. I have a personal stake; you don't. Unfortunately, it seems that I'm powerless to do anything about your jurisdiction, but I was assured by your bureau chief that you would cooperate. Slater so much as coughs and you withhold it, I'll have your replacement here in five minutes."

Jennifer was tempted to slap his smug mug. She'd have to call Frank and explain. In the meantime, Milton was a thorn she would have to deal with.

"I don't like you either, Detective. You're too interested in your own good for my tastes, but I suppose that's personal. I'll keep you updated through Galager and I'll expect *your* cooperation in assisting us in any way you can. We're not stupid enough to refuse all the help we can get. But you will do nothing without my authorization. If Slater suspects your involvement, he may do 'your' city more harm than you're willing to take the heat for. Agreed?"

He eyed her carefully and then relaxed. *Didn't expect that, did you, Colombo?* She had no intention of keeping him materially involved, she realized, and the thought surprised her. In fact, in more ways than one, she welcomed Slater's restrictions. This was between her and Slater and Kevin, regardless of how personal Slater wanted to get.

"I want to put a full-court press on his house," Milton said. "Complete electronic surveillance, including wiretaps. You haven't ordered them?"

"Not wiretaps. Slater's not using the landline. The cell wizards have been monitoring the frequency on the cell phone he gave Kevin for the past forty minutes—I put in the request as soon as I left his house this morning. Slater called Kevin thirty minutes ago, just before he blew the bomb. Nothing even registered with our wizards. He's not dumb enough to talk without scrambling. This isn't your typical hack. I have an order in to fix a recording device, an AP301, to his phone ASAP, but we didn't have it on this call."

Milton glared. "I'll put someone on the house."

"No. No cops, or didn't you get that part?"

"For crying out loud, woman! You just chewed me out less than three hours ago for not having someone on him last night!"

"I'll put my own agents on the house. Keep your men clear. If you want to go head-to-head, I'll leak this to the press." She hesitated. "You get anything on the officer I asked about?"

Milton looked away and answered with some reluctance. "Officer Rick Sheer. He moved back to the San Francisco area ten years ago.

Died of cancer five years ago. There's no record that we can find of any incident involving the boy you mentioned. But that doesn't surprise me. Cops routinely deal with neighbors off the record. You say he threatened the boy's father—the incident obviously blew over. No official complaint, no arrest."

Jennifer's heart sank. That left Kevin. And Samantha. Hopefully one of them would recall something that might give them a clue to the boy's identity. All they currently had was Kevin's description, which was practically useless.

"Can you have them look again? What about a personal notebook or—"

"We wouldn't have anything like that."

"Cooperation, remember? Have them look again."

He nodded slowly. "I'll see what I can do."

"Thank you. I assume you've met Agent Galager. You'll be dealing primarily with him from here out."

"And you?"

"I'm going to do what I was trained to do, try to figure out who Slater is. Excuse me, Detective."

She walked past the bus, found Galager. "What do you have?"

"Same guy who did the car." Bill Galager was a redhead with too many freckles to count. He glanced at Nancy, who knelt over fragments of twisted metal at the flash point.

"She's good."

Jennifer nodded. "Work over the evidence in her lab with her and then send it on to Quantico for more testing. Bring this to Milton's attention, and please do your best to keep him off my back."

"Will do. What about any evidence they find at his house?"

A team had arrived at Kevin's house twenty minutes earlier and was scouring the place for anything Slater might have left. She doubted they would find anything. The victims' houses in Sacramento had yielded nothing. Slater might have no scruples, but he had plenty of discipline.

"Same. Let's do our own sweep as well. If you find anything, let me know. I'll be by your office in a couple hours."

He nodded. "You think it's him?"

"Until I find evidence that contradicts it."

"There are some differences. Could be a copy cat."

"Could be. But I don't think so."

"And I'm assuming Kevin matches the victim profile?"

Jennifer searched Galager's eyes. Bill was one of the only agents who'd known Roy well enough to call him a friend.

"He could be Roy in another life," she said. Then she turned toward the coffee shop.

At least five hundred onlookers had gathered behind the police lines now. The news crews were set up, sending live feed across the country. Both Fox News and CNN were undoubtedly running alerts. How many times had the American public seen pictures from Israel of twisted bus wreckage? But this was California. Here, you could count the incidents over the past ten years on one hand.

Milton was giving the vultures an update. Good for him.

11

JENNIFER'S VOICE JARRED KEVIN from his thoughts. "Hey, cowboy, you want a ride out of here?"

He looked up from the corner table and blinked. "Sure."

"Let's go."

She didn't take him home. Detectives were still searching the place for anything Slater might have left. It would take them a few hours.

"They're not going to dump my underwear drawers, are they?"

Jennifer laughed. "Not unless Slater left his shorts."

"Probably just as well I'm gone."

"You like things neat, don't you?"

"Clean, sure."

"That's good. A man should know how to do laundry."

"Where're we going?"

"You have the phone with you?"

He instinctively felt his pocket. Amazing how small phones could be. He pulled it out and flipped it open. It fit in his palm, open.

"Just checking," she said, turning onto Willow.

"You think he'll call again?" he asked.

"Yes, the confession wasn't what he was looking for."

"I guess not."

"But he does want a confession. You're sure about that, right?"

"That's what he said. When I confess, he goes away. But confess what?"

"That's the million-dollar question, isn't it? What does Slater want you to confess? You have no inkling whatsoever?"

"I just ruined my career and only God knows what else by telling the world that I tried to kill a boy—believe me, if I'd thought of any alternative to that confession, I'd have spilled my guts."

She nodded and frowned. "The demand for a confession's the only part of this puzzle that doesn't fit the Riddle Killer profile. Somehow he dug something up on you that he thinks is significant."

"Like what? How many sins have you committed, Agent Peters? Can you remember them all?"

"Please, call me Jennifer. No, I guess I can't."

"So what does Slater consider significant? You want me to go on television and list every sin I can ever remember committing?"

"No."

"The only thing that makes sense is the boy," Kevin said. "But then the confession should have gotten a response, right?"

"With Slater, yes. I think so. Unless, of course, he *is* the boy, but he wants you to confess something besides your attempt to kill him."

"It wasn't an attempt to kill him. It was more like self-defense. The kid was about to kill *me!*"

"I can accept that. Why did he want to kill you?"

The question took Kevin off guard. "He . . . he was after Samantha."

"Samantha. She just keeps cropping up, doesn't she?"

Jennifer looked out her window and for a few minutes the car remained silent.

III

Kevin was only eleven when he trapped the boy in the cellar and nearly died of fear. He'd left the boy to die—no matter how badly he tried to tell himself otherwise, he knew he had locked the boy in a tomb.

He couldn't tell Sam, of course. If she knew, she would surely tell her father, who would set the boy free and maybe send him to jail, and then he would get out, probably within a couple months, and come back and kill Sam. He couldn't ever tell her.

But he couldn't *not* tell her either. She was his bosom buddy. She was his best, best friend, whom he loved more than he loved his mother. Maybe.

On the third night he meant to go in search of the warehouse, just to take a peek; just to see if it had really, really happened. But after an hour pacing outside his window, he climbed back into his house.

"You're different," Sam told him the next night. "You're not looking me in the eyes like you used to. You keep looking off at the trees. What's wrong?"

"I am not looking off. I'm just enjoying the night."

"Don't try to fool me. You think I don't have a woman's intuition? I'm almost a teenager, you know. I can tell if a boy's bothered."

"Well, I'm not bothered by anything except your insistence that I'm bothered," he said.

"So then you *are* bothered. See? But you were bothered before I said you were bothered, so I think you're not telling me something."

He felt suddenly angry. "I am not!" he said.

She looked at him for a few seconds and then gazed up into the trees herself. "You are bothered by something, but I can see that you're not telling me because you think it might hurt me. That's sweet, so I'm going to pretend you're not bothered." She took his arm.

She was giving him a way out. What kind of friend would ever do that? Sam would do that because she was the sweetest girl in the whole world, no exceptions.

It took Kevin four months of agony to finally work up the courage to go in search of the boy's fate.

Part of him wanted to find the boy's bones in a rotting pile. But most of him didn't want to find the boy at all, didn't want to confirm that the whole thing had really happened.

The first challenge was to find the right warehouse. Guarding a flashlight as closely as he could, he looked through the warehouses for an hour, sneaking from door to door. He began to wonder if he'd ever find it again. But then he opened an old wooden door and there, five feet away, was the dark stairway.

Kevin jerked back and very nearly ran for his life.

But it was only a stairway. What if the boy wasn't there anymore? He could see the latch on the steel door in the shadows below. Seemed safe enough. *You have to do this, Kevin. If you're anything like a knight or a man or even a boy who's already eleven, you have to at least find out if he's in there.*

Kevin played his light down the stairwell and forced his feet down the stairs, one step at a time.

No sound. Of course not—it had been four months. The steel door latch was still closed as if he'd thrown it closed yesterday. He stopped in front of the door and stared, unwilling to actually open it. Visions of pirates and dungeons full of skeletons clattered through his mind.

Behind him the moonlight glowed pale gray. He could always run up the stairs if a skeleton took after him, which was incredibly stupid anyway. What would Sam think of him now?

"Hello?" he called.

Nothing.

The sound of his voice helped. He walked forward and knocked. "Hello?" Still nothing.

Slowly, heart thumping in his ears, palms wet with sweat, Kevin eased the latch open. He pushed the door. It creaked open.

Black. Musty. Kevin held his breath and gave the door a shove. He saw the splotches of blood immediately. But no body.

His bones shook from head to toe. It was real. That was blood all over the floor. Dried and darkened, but exactly where he remembered it should be. He pushed the door again, to make sure no one was behind it. He was alone.

Kevin stepped into the room. A bandanna lay in the corner. The boy's bandanna. He had definitely locked the boy in this cellar, and there was no way out that he could see. That meant one of two things had happened. Either the boy had died in here and someone had found him, or someone had found him before he'd died.

His mind ran through the possibilities. If he'd been found alive, it would have been in the first couple weeks. Which meant he'd been free for over three months and said nothing to the police. If he'd been found dead, of course, he couldn't say anything. Either way, he was probably gone for good. Maybe even alive and gone for good.

Kevin hurried out, slammed the door closed, latched it, and ran into the night, determined never, ever to even think about the boy again. He'd saved Sam, hadn't he? Yes, he had! And he hadn't been arrested or sent to the gas chamber or even accused of doing anything wrong. Because he had done what was right!

Elated and overcome with relief, he ran straight to Sam's house, even though it was past her bedtime. It took him fifteen minutes to wake her and convince her to climb out.

"What is it? My father will kill us if he finds us, you know."

He grabbed her hand and ran for the fence.

"Kevin Parson, I am in my pajamas! What is this all about?"

Yes, what's this about, Kevin? You're acting like a maniac!

But he couldn't help himself. He'd never felt so wonderful in all his life. He loved Sam so much!

He stepped past the fence and she followed him. "Kevin, this is . . ."

He threw his arms around her and hugged her tight, squeezing off her words. "I love you, Sam! I love you so much!"

She stood still in his arms, unmoving. It didn't matter; he was so overwhelmed with joy. "You are the best friend a boy could ever, ever have," he said.

She finally put her arms around him and patted his shoulder. It felt a bit polite, but Kevin didn't care. He pulled back and brushed blonde strands of hair from her face. "I won't ever let anyone hurt you. Ever. Not if I have to die first. You know that, don't you?"

She laughed, caught up in his show of affection. "What's gotten into you? Of course I do."

He looked away, wishing for a response as enthusiastic as he felt. It didn't matter; he was a man now.

Her hand touched his chin and turned his face toward her. "Listen to me," Sam said. "I love you more than anything I can imagine. You really are my knight in shining armor." She smiled. "And I think that it's incredibly sweet of you to drag me out here in my pajamas to make sure I know how much you love me."

Kevin smiled wide, stupidly, but it didn't matter. He didn't have to pretend with Sam.

They hugged tight then, tighter than they had ever hugged before.

"Promise to never leave me," Kevin said.

"I promise," Sam said. "And if you ever need me, all you have to do is knock on my window and I'll come flying out in my pajamas."

Kevin laughed. Then Sam laughed, and Kevin laughed at Sam's laughing. It might have been the best night of Kevin's life.

|||

"—Samantha?"

Kevin faced Jennifer. "Pardon?"

She looked at him. "Why was the boy after Samantha?"

"Because he was a demented wacko who found pleasure in cutting up animals and terrorizing the neighborhood. I didn't exactly have the time or the presence of mind to sit him down and run a psychological profile on him. I was scared to death."

Jennifer chuckled. "Touché. Too bad, though. Now we're sitting twenty years beyond that night, and I have the formidable task of trying to do it myself. Whether you like it or not, you may be my best hope of understanding him. Assuming the boy and Slater are one and the same, you're the only person we know who's had any meaningful contact with him, then or now."

As much as the thought of going back to the past made Kevin nauseated, he knew that she was right. He sighed. "I'll do whatever I can." He looked out the side window. "I should have made sure he was dead then."

"You would have done society a favor. In self-defense, of course."

"And what if Slater does show up on my doorstep one of these days? Do I have the right to kill him?"

"We have law enforcement for a reason." She paused. "On the other hand, I might."

"You might what?"

"Take him out. If I knew for sure it was Slater."

"What evil is man capable of?" Kevin said absently.

"What?"

"Nothing." But it was something. It struck Kevin for the first time that he had not only had the capacity to kill Slater, but also the *desire* to do so, self-defense or not. What would Dr. John Francis say to that?

"So. The boy was taller than you, about thirteen, blond and ugly," Jennifer said. "Nothing else?"

The sensation that there was something else nagged at Kevin, but he couldn't remember. "I can't think of anything."

They passed a store that Kevin recognized. "Where are we going?"

Suddenly he knew. His foot began to tap. They drove around a deserted park filled with elm trees.

"I thought I'd take you to your aunt's home. See if we can jog loose a few memories. Visual association can do wonders . . ."

He didn't hear the rest. A buzz lit through his mind and he felt claustrophobic in her car.

Jennifer looked at him but said nothing. He was sweating; she could surely see that. She turned onto Baker Street and drove under the elms toward his childhood house. Could she hear his thumping heart too?

"So this is where it all happened," she said absently.

"I . . . I don't want to go to the house," he said.

She looked at him again. "We're not going to the house. Just down the street. Is that okay?"

He couldn't say no—might as well wave a red flag in front of her. "Sure. I'm sorry. I'm not on the best terms with my aunt. My mother died when I was young and my aunt raised me. We've had our differences. Mostly over college."

"Okay. That's not uncommon."

But she saw more in him, didn't she? And so what if she did? Why did he feel so compelled to hide his upbringing? It was weird but not demented. Samantha said otherwise, but she was biased. It wasn't like he was a victim of physical abuse or anything so horrifying.

He took a slow breath and tried to relax.

"You think the boy chased you into one of those old warehouses across the tracks, that's what you said?"

He looked to his right. The memory of that night came back fresh and raw. "Yes, but I was scared out of my mind, and it was dark. I can't remember which one."

"Have you ever checked any of them? To see if there even is one with a basement?"

Kevin fought a wave of panic. He couldn't let her into the past. He shook his head. "No."

"Why not?"

"It was a long time ago."

She nodded. "There are only a few possibilities. Hopefully nothing's changed. You know we'll have to search."

He nodded. "And what if you find him?"

"Then we know he's obviously not Slater."

"And what about me?"

"We'll know that you killed him. In self-defense."

They drove past the white house. "This is where your aunt lives?"

"Yes."

"And that's the old Sheer residence?"

"Yes."

"None of this jogs your memory of any details?"

"No."

She remained silent to the end of the street, where she turned around and headed back.

Kevin's world felt like it was crumbling around him. Coming here alone was hard enough, but doing it with Jennifer somehow seemed profane. He wanted to tell her what Balinda had really done. He wanted her to comfort him, the little boy who had grown old in this world of madness. Waves of sorrow swept through his mind. His eyes went misty.

"I'm sorry, Kevin," Jennifer said softly. "I don't know what happened here, but I can see it left its mark on you. Believe me, if we weren't up against a clock, I wouldn't have brought you back here in your present state."

She cared for him, didn't she? She really did. A tear slipped from his eye and ran down his cheek. The emotion was suddenly beyond him. He began to cry, and then immediately tried to swallow it, which only made the condition worse. He hid his face in his left hand and started to sob, horribly aware of the foolishness of it all.

She drove out of the neighborhood and then stopped. He looked up through blurred eyes and saw that they were by the park. Jennifer sat still, looking at him with soft eyes.

"I'm . . . sorry," he managed past a tight throat. "It's just . . . my life's falling apart . . ."

"Shh, shh, shh. It's okay." Her hand touched his shoulder. "It's okay, really. You've been through hell these last two days. I had no right."

Kevin put his hands over his face and took a deep breath. "Man. This is crazy. Nothing like making a fool of yourself."

Her hand rubbed his arm again. "Don't be silly. You don't think I've seen a grown man cry before? I could tell you some stories. There's nothing quite like watching a three-hundred-pound, heavily tattooed gorilla sob uncontrollably for an hour. I don't know any decent man who could go through what you've gone through without a good cry."

He smiled, embarrassed. "Is that so?"

"That's so."

Jennifer's smile softened and she looked away. "The Riddle Killer's last victim was my brother. His name was Roy. That was three months ago. He was chosen because I was closing in on the killer."

Kevin wasn't sure what to say. "Your brother?"

"You remind me of him, you know." She faced him. "I won't let this maniac kill you, Kevin. I'm not sure I could survive that."

"I'm so sorry. I had no idea."

"Now you do. Want to go for a walk? I think we could both use some fresh air."

"Okay."

They walked side by side over an emerald green lawn, past a pond with ducks and two large geese. She was laughing and telling him about a goose that had once chased her for the sandwich she held. Next to the horror that had swept over him not five minutes earlier, Kevin felt unusually peaceful, as if he were walking with his guardian angel. He wondered about Jennifer's true intentions. She was a professional, doing her job. All FBI agents talked and laughed like this— it was their way of making someone in his shoes feel comfortable enough to work with them.

The thought made him feel suddenly awkward. Clumsy. Like a three-hundred-pound gorilla. On the other hand, she'd lost her brother.

He stopped.

She touched his arm. "Kevin? What is it?"

"Like a three-hundred-pound, heavily tattooed gorilla."

"That's what he—"

"The boy had a tattoo," Kevin blurted.

"The boy you locked in the cellar? Where?"

"On his forehead! A tattoo of a knife."

"You're sure?"

"Yes! He had it covered with a bandanna that last night, but I saw it the first night."

They exchanged stares. "How many men have a tattoo on their foreheads? Not many." A smile nudged her lips. "That's good," she said. "That's very good."

12

S AMANTHA WAS THE LAST PASSENGER to board the flight to Sacramento. An hour and a half later she entered a little-known conference room at the attorney general's headquarters, the office of the California Bureau of Investigation's "Alpha Division," as it was known by some. A bulldog of a man named Chris Barston, who was up on suspicion of aiding terrorists by promulgating bomb-construction methods on the Internet, sat across the table. They'd hauled him in last night. His Internet dealings were not her concern, but the information he had to share evidently was, or Roland, her boss, wouldn't have insisted she come. Roland sat at the head of the table, leaning back in his chair. She'd liked the chief from the moment they were introduced, and when she came to him two days after her orientation and asked to be assigned to the Riddle Killer case, he'd agreed. The FBI and the CBI were both active in the case, but Samantha suggested that the killer had inside connections, and the possibility had intrigued Roland.

The call from Kevin had blindsided her. She hadn't expected the Riddle Killer to surface in Southern California at all. She wasn't nec-essarily convinced that the Riddle Killer and Slater were the same. If Slater was the Riddle Killer and he was also the boy, it would explain his ties to her, Kevin, and Jennifer. But certain details about Slater's calls to Kevin nagged at her.

"Thanks for coming, Sam. Enjoy your holiday?"

"I wasn't aware I *was* on a holiday."

"You're not. Your witness." Roland looked at Chris, who stared past him.

Sam pulled up her chair and opened a blue file Rodriguez had brought to her at the airport. She'd read the contents on the way in.

"Hello, Mr. Barston. My name's Samantha Sheer."

He ignored her and kept his eyes in Roland's direction.

"You may look this way, Chris. I'm going to be asking the questions. Have you ever been questioned by a woman before?"

The man stared at her. Roland grinned. "Answer the woman, Chris."

"I agreed to tell you what I know about Salman. That'll take thirty seconds."

"Great," Sam said. "Then we can limit our exposure to each other so we don't . . . you know, rub off on each other. I think we can stomach thirty seconds, don't you?"

The man's face darkened.

"Tell us about Salman."

He cleared his throat. "I met him in Houston about a month ago. Pakistani. You know, India and all. Speaks with an accent."

"Pakistanis live in Pakistan, not India. That's why they call it Pakistan. Go on."

"You going to mock me for the full thirty seconds here?"

"I'll try to control myself."

He shifted. "Anyway, Salman and I had a mutual interest in . . . you know, bombs. He's clean; I can swear that. He had this tattoo of a bomb on his shoulder. I got one here of a knife." He showed them a small blue knife on his right forearm. "Then he showed me one on his back, a huge dagger. Said he wanted to have it removed because the chicks didn't dig it back in wherever."

"Pakistan."

"Pakistan. He told me he knew a guy who had a tattoo of a knife on his forehead. He didn't tell me nothing about this guy except that his name was Slater and he was into explosive devices. That's it. That's all I know."

"And you think the name Slater interests us why?"

"The news of Long Beach. They said it could be a man named Slater."

"When did your friend know this Slater?"

"I said that's it. That's all I know. That's the deal. If I knew more, I would tell you more. I already wrote down where this Salman guy works last I knew. He's straight up. Talk to him."

Sam looked at Roland. He nodded.

"Okay, Chris. I guess your thirty seconds are up. You're free to go."

Chris stood, glared at her one last time, and left.

"What do you think?" Roland asked.

"I'm not sure what our man would be doing all the way down in Houston, but I think I'm going to Texas. I want to make contact first. For all we know, Salman doesn't even exist. It may take a day or two to track him down. Until then I want to go back to Long Beach."

"Fine. Just keep a low profile down there. If the Riddle Killer's working with someone inside, we don't want him suddenly running scared."

"I'm limiting direct contact to the FBI agent in charge. Jennifer Peters."

"Just watch what you say. For all we know, Agent Peters is Slater."

"Unlikely."

"Just tread lightly."

|||

The prior twenty-four hours had produced more evidence than the entire year combined, but the leads weren't pointing to any quick answers. Meticulous lab work took time, a commodity Jennifer wasn't sure they had enough of. Slater would strike again, and sooner or later they would have bodies to contend with. A car, a bus—what was next?

The city was reeling from news of the bus. Milton had spent half the day preparing and issuing statements to hungry reporters. At least it kept him out of her hair.

She sat at the corner desk Milton had graciously given her and stared at the loose sheets of paper spread before her. It was 4:30, and for the moment she was stuck. A Subway veggie sandwich she'd ordered two hours ago sat on the edge of the desk, and she considered unwrapping it.

Her eyes dropped to the pad under her fingertips. She'd split the page horizontally and then vertically, creating four quadrants, an old technique she used to visually compartmentalize data. Kevin's house, the warehouse search, the knife tattoo, and forensics from the bus.

"Who are you, Slater?" she mumbled. "You're here, aren't you, staring up at me, chuckling behind these words somewhere?"

First quadrant. They'd swept and dusted Kevin's house and turned up exactly nothing. Hundreds of prints, of course—it would take time to work through all of them. But in the high-probability contact points—the phone, the doorknobs, the window latches, the desk, the wood dinette chairs—they had found only Jennifer's and Kevin's prints, and some partials that were unidentifiable. Probably Sam's. She'd been in the house, but according to Kevin she hadn't stayed long or handled anything except for the phone, where they'd found the partials. Either way, the chances that Slater had walked around the place pressing uncovered fingers against dense surfaces had been absurd from the beginning.

No eavesdropping devices turned up either, again not surprising. Slater had used the six bugs they'd uncovered because they were convenient at the time. He had other means of listening in—remote laser transmitters, relayed audio scopes—all of which they would eventually track down, but not likely soon enough. They'd found disturbed ground at the oil rig's base, two hundred yards from Kevin's house, and taken casts of four different shoe prints. Again, the evidence might help them incriminate Slater, but it wasn't identifying him— at least not quickly enough.

The writing on the milk jug was in for analysis at Quantico. Same story. Comparisons could and one day would be made, but not before they actually had Slater in their sights.

They'd affixed the AP301 recording device to Slater's cell phone and were monitoring the house using an IR laser.

Let the games begin.

Jennifer had left Kevin in his house at noon, pleading that he get some sleep. She watched him wander around his living room like a zombie. He'd been pushed beyond himself.

You like him, don't you, Jenn?

Don't be stupid! I hardly know him! I feel empathy for him. I'm attributing Roy's goodness to him.

But you like him. He's handsome, caring, and as innocent as a butter-fly. He has magical eyes and a smile that swallows the room. He's . . .

Naive and damaged. His reaction to driving through his old neighborhood had been in part precipitated by the stress of Slater's threats, granted. But there had to be more.

He was similar to Roy in many ways, but the more she thought about it, the more she saw the dissimilarities between this case and the ones in Sacramento. Slater seemed to have a specific, personally motivated agenda with Kevin. He wasn't a random victim. Neither was Jennifer nor Samantha. What if Kevin had been the Riddle Killer's prime mark all along? What if the others were just a kind of practice? Warmup?

Jennifer closed her eyes and stretched her neck. She'd made an appointment to see the dean at Kevin's seminary, Dr. John Francis, first thing tomorrow morning. He attended one of those huge churches that held a service on Saturday evening. Jennifer picked up the sandwich and peeled back the wax paper.

Second quadrant. The warehouse. Milton had somehow convinced the bureau chief to speak to her about his involvement. The man was starting to become a major irritant. She'd reluctantly agreed to give him the warehouse search. The fact was, she could use the manpower and they knew the territory. She made it clear that if he breathed one word of his involvement to the media, she'd personally see to it that he took full responsibility for whatever negative consequences resulted. He'd taken four uniformed officers and a search warrant to the warehouse district. The likelihood that Slater was watching the neighborhood was minimal. He might be a surveillance crackerjack, but he couldn't have eyes everywhere.

Based on Kevin's story, he might have stumbled into any of a couple dozen warehouses that night. Milton's team was searching each one now, looking for any that might have a subterranean storage room, an oil pit, a garbage dump—anything similar. Most warehouses today were built on slabs, but some of the older buildings featured underground units that were cheaper to cool.

She could understand Kevin's subconscious erasure of such a traumatic location. It would either be stamped indelibly on his brain or gone, and there was no reason for him to hide any knowledge at this point. Discovery of the basement would be a windfall. If indeed the boy was Slater.

Third quadrant. The knife tattoo. Jennifer took a bite out of the sandwich. Hunger swarmed her with the first taste of tomato. She'd missed breakfast, hadn't she? Seemed like a week ago.

She stared at the third quadrant. Again, assuming the boy was Slater, and assuming he hadn't removed the tattoo, they now had their first bona fide identifier. A tattoo of a knife on the forehead—not exactly something you see on every corner. Twenty-three agents and policemen were quietly working the search. Tattoo parlors that had existed twenty years earlier in the immediate vicinity were first to be scrutinized, but finding one that had any records was near impossible. They were working in concentric circles. More likely was finding a tattoo parlor that remembered a man with a knife tattoo on his forehead. Not all tattoo bearers frequented parlors, but ones with Slater's profile might. For all they knew, he was now covered in tattoos. All he needed was one—a knife in the center of his forehead.

Fourth quadrant. The bus. Another bite. The sandwich was like a slice of heaven.

Same guy, no doubt. Same device: a suitcase bolted behind the gas tank, loaded with enough dynamite to shred a bus, detonated using tungsten leads stripped from an incandescent bulb on a simple five-dollar, battery-operated alarm clock. A mechanical servo could override the clock and either terminate or trigger the detonation. The bomb had been planted days, even weeks ago, based on the dust they'd lifted off one of its bolts. If they could ID what was left of the servo, they might have a shot of tracing its origins. Unlikely.

How long had Slater been planning this?

The phone chirped. Jennifer wiped her mouth, took a quick swallow from a bottle of Evian, and picked up the phone. "Jennifer."

"We think we found it."

Milton. She sat up. "The warehouse."

"We have some blood here."

She tossed the rest of the sandwich in the waste bin and grabbed her keys. "I'm on my way."

|||

Kevin looked out between the blinds for the fourth time in two hours. They'd decided to place one unmarked car a block up the street—FBI. Slater seemed ambiguous about the FBI. Either way, the agent behind the wheel would watch only. He would not follow if or when Kevin left at Slater's next beckoning. Static surveillance only.

Kevin released the slats and paced back into the kitchen. In the park, Jennifer had reached out to him and he'd let her. He found her fierce nature compelling. It reminded him of Samantha.

Where was Samantha? He'd called her twice and gotten only her voice mail. He desperately wanted to talk to her about the visit to Baker Street with Jennifer. She would understand. Not that Jennifer didn't, but Sam might be able to help him sort out these new feelings.

He walked to the refrigerator, opened it, and pulled out a liter of 7UP. Feelings. Extremes. The hatred toward Slater that had begun to swell in his gut wasn't so strange. How was he supposed to feel toward someone who had come within a few seconds of taking not only his life, but countless others for undisclosed reasons? If Slater would just quit being so idiotic and tell him what the deal was, Kevin could handle the man. As it was, the imbecile was hiding behind these stupid games, and Kevin was losing patience. Yesterday he'd been too shocked to process his anger. A common form of denial, Jennifer had said. Shock breeds denial, which in turn tempers anger. But now the denial was giving way to this bitterness toward an enemy who refused to show his hand.

Kevin poured half a glass, swallowed the 7UP in several long drafts, and slammed the empty glass on the counter.

He ran his hand through his hair, grunted, and walked to the living room. How could one man wreak so much havoc in the space of one day? Slater was nothing less than a terrorist. If Kevin owned a gun and Slater worked up the stomach to confront him face to face, he was pretty sure he'd have no compunction about putting a slug or two in the man's face. Especially if he was the boy. Kevin shivered involuntarily. Shoulda gone back and made sure the stinking rat was dead. He would have been within his rights, if not according to the law, then in the eyes of God. Turn the other cheek shouldn't apply to sick sewer rats with knives in their hands who licked neighborhood girls' windows.

Slater was listening now, right? Kevin looked around the room and settled on the window.

"Slater?" His voice bounced back at him.

"You hear me, Slater? Listen, you sick scab, I don't know why you're stalking me or why you're too terrified to show your face, but you're only proving one thing. You're toilet water. You're a punk without the guts to face your adversary. Come on, baby! Come and get me!"

"Kevin?"

He whirled around. Sam stood in the rear sliding-glass doorway, staring at him. He hadn't heard the door slide open.

"You okay?" she whispered.

"Sure. Sorry, I was just having a word with our friend, in case he was listening."

Sam shut the door and lifted a finger to her lips. She walked to the front window and pulled the drapes.

"What . . ."

She motioned him quiet again and led him to the garage. "If we talk quietly here, we won't be heard."

"Slater? The car up the street's FBI."

"I know. Which is why I parked two blocks up and came in the back. You don't think Slater's going to see them?"

"He didn't say no FBI."

"Maybe because he is FBI," she said.

"What?"

"We haven't ruled it out."

"We? Who's we?"

She held his gaze for a moment. "Just an expression. They find anything else here?"

"No. Some footprints by the oil rig up the hill. They took a bunch of fingerprints, the milk jug. Jennifer didn't think any of it would help them much."

Sam nodded. "She told me about the tattoo. You never told me about the tattoo."

"I didn't tell you anything about him after that night, remember? He was gone. End of story."

"Not anymore. They'll find the warehouse, and when they do, they'll find more—who knows, maybe the boy."

"Actually, I went back four months later."

"What?"

"He was gone. There was blood on the floor and his bandanna, but he was gone. They won't find him."

Sam looked at him for a few moments. He wasn't sure what she was thinking, but something wasn't quite right.

"You said, *we* haven't ruled it out," he said. "You've always been straight with me, Sam. Who is we?"

She looked into his eyes and put a hand on his cheek. "I'm sorry, Kevin, I can't tell you everything—not now, not yet. Soon. You're right, I have always been straight with you. I've been more than a friend. I've loved you like a brother. A day hasn't gone by these past ten years that I haven't thought about you at least once. You're part of me. And now I need you to trust me. Can you do that?"

The revelation made his head spin. She was somehow involved, wasn't she? She'd been onto Slater before yesterday. It was why Slater knew her!

"What . . . what's going on?"

Her hand slid down his arm and took his fingers. "Nothing's changed. Slater's the same person he was yesterday, and I'm going to do my best to get to him before he hurts anyone. I'm just not at liberty to tell you what we know. Not yet. It wouldn't make any difference to you anyway. Trust me. For old time's sake."

He nodded. Actually, this was better, wasn't it? The fact that she had some inside track and wasn't just blindly feeling her way around this case—that was good.

"But you think the FBI is involved?"

She put her finger on his lips to seal them. "I can't talk about it. Forget I said it. Nothing's changed." She reached up, kissed him on the cheek, and released his hand.

"Can I trust Jennifer?"

She turned. "Sure—trust Jennifer. But trust me first."

"What do you mean, first?"

"I mean if you have to choose between me and Jennifer, choose me."

He felt his pulse thicken. What was she saying? *Choose me.* Did she think he would ever choose Jennifer over her? He wasn't even sure what he felt for Jennifer. She had offered to ease his pain and confusion in a time of vulnerability and he had let her. That was all.

"I would always choose you. I owe my life to you."

She smiled and for a moment he imagined that they were kids again, sitting under an elm with a full moon on their faces, laughing at a squirrel's inquisitive head poking through the branches.

"Actually, I think it's the other way around. I owe you *my* life," she said. "Literally. You saved me from Slater once, didn't you? Now it's my turn to return the favor."

In a strange way, it all made perfect sense.

"Okay," she said. "I have a plan. I mean to flush the snake from his hole." She winked at him and glanced at her watch. "The sooner we get out of here the better. Grab your toothbrush, a change of clothes, and some deodorant if you want. We're taking a trip."

"We are? Where? We can't just leave. Jennifer told me to stay here."

"Until what? Did Slater tell you not to leave?"

"No."

"Let me see the phone."

He fished out the cell phone Slater had left him and handed it to her.

"Did Slater tell you to keep this on?"

Kevin considered the question. "He said to keep it with me at all times."

Sam pushed the power off button. "Then we'll take it."

"Jennifer will have a cow. This wasn't the plan."

"Change of plans, my dear knight. It's time for a little cat and mouse of our own."

13

THE WAREHOUSE was less than a hundred yards from Kevin's old house, two rows back from the road, an old wooden storage facility that had been white before flaking paint revealed its gray underbelly. From the side entrance, none of the houses on Baker Street was visible.

"This it?"

"It's abandoned. Looks like it has been for a while," Milton said.

"Show me."

Two uniforms stood by the door, watching her. One of them handed her a flashlight. "You'll need this."

She took it and turned it on.

The warehouse smelled of a decade's worth of undisturbed dust. Beyond the side door was a single stairwell descending into blackness. The rest of the three-thousand-or-so square feet of concrete sat vacant in dim light filtered by a dozen cracks in the walls.

"Don't they tear these things down?" she asked.

"They used to hold all kinds of goods in these warehouses before the navy moved in just south of here. The government bought this land and hasn't seen fit to rebuild yet. I'm sure they'll get around to it."

A lone cop stood at the bottom of the stairs, shining his flashlight on the threshold. "The door was locked from the outside—took some jarring to get it loose."

Jennifer descended. A steel door led into a ten-by-ten room, concrete, empty. She played her torch over the pitted walls. Exposed floor joists held the ceiling. Most of it. One small section had rotted through.

"The blood's over here," Milton said.

Jennifer directed her light to where he stood looking down at two large dark stains on the concrete. She squatted and studied each.

"The splatter's consistent with blood." The basic position of the stains also matched Kevin's story—both he and the boy had bled. "At this age we probably won't get any reliable DNA evidence, but we can at least verify species. I knew Kevin was hiding something the first time I talked to him."

She glanced at Milton, surprised by his tone.

"And this isn't the last of it. I guarantee he's hiding more," he said.

Milton was a first-class pig. She stood and walked over to a small, almost unnoticeable hole in the ceiling. "The boy's way out?"

"Could be."

So, assuming this read as fact, what would it mean? That Kevin hadn't killed the boy? That they had fought and that Kevin had locked the door from the outside, but then the boy had managed to crawl out through the rotting ceiling? Who knew why he hadn't come back to terrorize Kevin until now?

Or it could mean that the boy actually had died in here, only to be discovered by some passerby years later, body disposed of. Unlikely. Unless a drifter or anyone else had reason to hide the body, it would have been investigated. She'd already run a search for reports and found none.

"Okay, we need to do a bloodstain distribution analysis. I want to know what happened down here. Assuming it is blood, did anyone lie in it? Any blood on the walls or up through the ceiling? I want species identification and, if possible, blood type. Send a sample to the FBI lab immediately. And this stays out of the press."

Milton said nothing. He looked up at the corner and frowned. A shadow passed over his face. It occurred to her that she might actually hate the man.

"Don't get any ideas, Detective. Everything goes through me."

He looked at her for a moment and then walked for the door. "Sure."

|||

Kevin drove them along Palos Verdes Drive, west toward Palos Verdes. Slater's bugged phone sat on the dash, turned off.

Sam stared ahead, eyes sparkling. "If Slater can't make contact, how can he play the game? He's driven by the riddles, but if we neutralize his ability to communicate a riddle, then there *is* no riddle, is there? At the least he has to rethink his strategy."

"Or blow up another bomb," Kevin said.

"We're not technically breaking one of his rules. He detonates a bomb and *he's* breaking the rules of engagement. I don't think Slater will do that."

Kevin thought about Sam's plan. On one hand, it felt good to be doing something—anything—besides waiting. The idea made sense on its surface. On the other hand, he didn't trust Slater to follow his own rules. Sam knew him better, maybe, but it was his life they were messing with.

"Why not just turn off the phone and stick around?"

"He'd find a way to communicate."

"He still might."

"Possible. But this way we also get you out of there. The one thing we need now is time. A dozen new leads have surfaced in the last twenty-four hours, but we need time."

There was the *we* word again.

"We should at least tell Jennifer, don't you think?"

"Think of this as a test. We cut off all contact and then we gradually resume contact. Unless Slater's following us now, he'll be lost. His opponent will have disappeared. He may rant and rave, but he won't play the game without you. We add some people to the loop and see if Slater suddenly knows more than he should. Follow?"

"What if he has the car bugged?"

"Then he did it today under the noses of the FBI. They swept it this morning, remember?"

Kevin nodded. The idea was growing on him. "Just like that we're gone, huh?"

She grinned. "Just like that."

"Like sneaking out at night."

It took them half an hour to reach the quaint hotel—an old Victorian mansion that had been converted and expanded to accommodate forty rooms. They pulled into its parking lot at ten after six. A cool, salty breeze drifted off the Pacific, half a mile down green sloping hills. Sam grinned and pulled out her overnight bag.

"Do they have rooms available?" Kevin asked.

"We have reservations. A suite with two bedrooms."

He looked up at the hotel and then back toward the sea. A Conoco station with a Taco Bell stood a hundred yards to the north. Outback Steakhouse, fifty yards south. Cars drifted by, a Lexus, a Mercedes. The madness in Long Beach seemed distant.

"Come on," Sam said. "Let's settle in and get something to eat."

Half an hour later they sat across from each other in a cozy café on the hotel's ground floor, overlooking a dimming horizon. They'd left their cell phones, turned off, in the room. She still wore her office pager, but Slater had no way to reach either of them. It seemed that Sam's simple plan wasn't such a bad idea.

"What would happen if I just disappeared?" Kevin asked, cutting into a thick New York strip.

She forked a small bite of cheese-smothered chicken into her mouth and dabbed her lips with her napkin. "Just up and leave until we find him?"

"Why not?"

"Why not. Leave him high and dry." She took a drink of iced tea and cut another piece. "You could move up to San Francisco."

"He's ruined my life down here anyway. I don't see how I can continue in seminary."

"I doubt you're the first seminary student to have his sins exposed."

"Murder isn't exactly your typical confession."

"Self-defense. And as far as we know, he lived."

"The confession sounded pretty ominous. I think I'm finished."

"And how's murder so different from gossip? Wasn't that your point to the dean? You're no more capable of evil than the bishop, remember? Murder, gossip—what's the difference? Evil is evil."

"Evil is evil as long as you keep it in the classroom. Out here in the real world, gossip doesn't even feel evil."

"Which is why any good detective learns to trust the facts over feelings." She went back to her food. "Either way, I don't think you can run. He'll track you down. That's how his kind works. You raise the stakes and he's likely to come back with higher stakes."

Kevin looked out the window. Darkness had all but swallowed the horizon. Jennifer's words came back to him. Take him out, she'd said.

"Like a hunted animal," he said.

"Except that you're not an animal. You have the same capacities he does."

"Jennifer told me that if I had the opportunity I should blow him away." Anger boiled through his chest. He'd come so far, worked so hard, pulled himself out of the deepest despair, only to be hijacked by some ghost from the past.

He slammed the table with his fist, rattling the dishes.

He met the stares from an older couple two tables down. "I'm sorry, Kevin," Samantha said. "I know this is hard."

"What's to prevent *me* from being the hunter?" he asked. "He wants a game; I'll give him a game! Why don't I throw out a challenge and force *him* to respond to me? Would you do anything different?"

"Fight terror with terror."

"Exactly!"

"No," she said.

"What do you mean, no? Maybe the only way to corner him is to play the game his way."

"You don't fight evil with evil; it just leads to anarchy. We have rules and we have scruples, unlike Slater. What are you going to do, threaten to blow up the convention center unless he gives himself up? Somehow I don't think he'd do anything but laugh. Besides, we have no way of contacting him."

The maître d' approached from Kevin's right. "Excuse me, sir, is everything all right?"

Someone had complained. "Yes. I'm sorry, I'll try to control myself." Kevin flashed him an embarrassed smile. The man dipped his head and left.

Kevin took a deep breath and picked up his fork, but his appetite was suddenly gone. The fact was, when he thought about what Slater was doing to him, he could hardly think of anything but killing him. Destroy the destroyer.

"I know it sounds a bit pretentious right now, but Slater doesn't scare me," Sam said, staring off into the darkness outside, wearing a coy smile. "You'll see, Kevin. His days are numbered."

"And mine might be as well."

"Not a chance. I won't let that happen."

He wasn't brimming with her confidence, but he couldn't resist her infectious smile. This was his Samantha. G.I. Jane.

"Jennifer said that, huh?" Sam asked. "Blow him away."

"Actually, I think she said 'take him out.' Makes sense to me."

"Maybe." She stared at him across the candle flame. "You like her, don't you?"

"Who, Jennifer?" He shrugged. "She seems like a good person."

"I don't mean in a 'good person' kind of way."

"Come on, Sam. I hardly know her. I haven't dated anyone for years." He smiled sheepishly. "Good night, the last girl I kissed was you."

"Is that so? When we were eleven?"

"How could you forget?"

"I haven't. But you do like her. I can see it in your eyes when you say her name."

Kevin felt his face flush. "She's an FBI agent who's trying to save my neck. What's there not to like?" He looked to his right and caught the continuing stare of the older couple. They looked away. "She reminds me of you."

"Really? How so?"

"Kind. No-nonsense. Pretty . . ."

"Like I said, you like her."

"Please—"

"It's okay, Kevin," she said softly. "I want you to like her."

"You do?"

"Yes. I approve." She grinned and placed the last small bite of chicken in her mouth. Even the way she chewed her food was nothing less than spectacular, he thought. Her chin and cheeks were so smooth in motion.

"What about . . ." He trailed off, suddenly self-conscious.

"What about us? That's very sweet, my knight, but I'm not sure we could ever be romantically involved. Don't get me wrong, I love you dearly. I'm just not sure we want to risk what we have for romance."

"Great things always come at great risk," he said.

She stared at him with those intoxicating eyes, caught off guard by his forward statement.

"Isn't that right?" he asked.

"Yes."

"So then don't say we could never be romantically involved. I kissed you once and you sent me to heaven. Didn't you feel something?"

"When you kissed me?"

"Yes."

"I was floating for a week."

"You never told me that."

She grinned, and if he wasn't mistaken, now she was embarrassed. "Maybe I wanted you to make the next move. Isn't that what a knight does for his damsel in distress?"

"I guess I never was a very good knight."

"You've turned into quite a dashing one," Sam said with a twinkle in her eye. "I think she likes you."

"Jennifer? She told you that?"

"Woman's intuition. Remember?"

Sam set down her napkin and stood. "Would you like to dance?"

He glanced around. No one else was dancing, but several colored lights turned slowly on the tiny dance floor. Michael Bolton crooned over the speakers.

"I . . . I'm not sure I know how to—"

"Sure you do. Just like when we were kids. Under the moonlight. Don't tell me you've never danced since then."

"No, not really."

She looked at him gently. "Then we definitely should. Will you?"

He smiled and dipped his head. "It would be my pleasure."

They held each other gently and danced for several long minutes. It wasn't a sensual dance or even romantic. It was just the right thing to do after ten years of separation.

Slater did not call that night.

14

Sunday
Morning

THE WALL IS DARK BROWN, almost black, and pitted. Slightly damp in spots, leaking an odor of mold and mildew and something else he never has been able to place. A single incandescent bulb glows in the bathroom, casting just enough light into the main basement for Slater to see the darkness of the wall.

These are the things he likes: cold, dark, wetness, mildew, and chocolate sundaes with equal portions of ice cream and fudge. Oh, yes, and he likes fascination. In fact, he likes to be fascinating above everything else, and really, in order to be properly fascinating, he has to dispense with the expected and deliver only what they don't expect. This is why confused teenage boys pierce their eyelids and tattoo their foreheads, and why girls out to impress them shave their heads. It is all a pathetic, hopeless attempt to be fascinating.

The problem with doing something so senseless as piercing an eyelid is that it reveals your intentions. *Here am I, a poor teenage slug who requires your attention. Look at me, see how I resemble a puddle of dog vomit? Won't you please throw your fingers to your teeth and be wildly fascinated by me?*

The pitiful first gropings of the dark man.

But Slater knows what they do not. He knows that the dark man is most fascinating when he moves in complete obscurity. Hidden. Unknown. That's why he is called the *dark* man. That's why he has started in the dark. That's why he does all of his best work at night. That's why he loves this basement. Because for all practical purposes, Slater *is* the Dark Man.

Someone famous should write a comic book based on him.

Slater stands from his stool. He's been looking at the pitted wall for over an hour without moving. He finds it fascinating. Darkness is always fascinating. He's never quite sure what he's looking at, unlike a piece of white paper, which only grows fascinating if he puts a black pen to it.

It's light outside—he knows this because of the single crack in the corner. Samantha has taken Kevin and gone into hiding. Which means that after all these months, she's learned something new.

Slater hums softly and walks toward a small vanity. The secret of being the Dark Man is not looking like a dark man at all. That is why the world looks at stupid little teenagers with rings in their noses as idiots. It's like walking around school, stripped to the waist in a Charles Atlas pose all day. Please. Too obvious. Too stupid. Too boring.

Now the angel of light routine—those who pile on the white to obscure the Dark Man, like Sunday school teachers and clergy, like priests—not a bad instinct really. But these days, a white collar is no longer the best disguise.

The best disguise is simply obscurity.

Slater sits and tilts the mirror so that it catches enough light from the bathroom to cast his reflection. You see, now there is a Nobody. A strongly built man with blond hair and grayish eyes. A wedding band on his left hand, a closet full of pressed shirts and Dockers and a silver Honda Accord out on the street.

He could walk up to any Betty in the mall and say, "Excuse me, do I look like the Dark Man to you?"

"What on earth are you talking about?" she would say. Because she wouldn't associate him with a name like Dark Man. She, along with ten thousand other mall flies, would be fooled. Blind. Shrouded by darkness.

That is his secret. He can walk under their noses without the slightest hint of guilt. He is virtually transparent, for the very reason that he is so much like them. They see him every day and don't know who he is.

Slater frowns at himself and wags his head in mockery. "I like you, Kevin. I love you, Kevin." Sam can be such a cockroach. He should have killed her when he had the chance, long ago.

Now she's in the thick of things again, which is good because he can finish the job, once and for all. But her audacity makes him nauseated.

"Let's run away and play hide-and-seek," he mocks again. "What do you take me for?"

The fact is, Sam knows more about him than any of the others. True, her little disappearing act will gain them nothing, but at least she's made a move, which is more than he can say for the rest. She's trying to flush him out. She might even know that he's been under their noses all along.

But the Dark Man isn't that stupid. They can't hide forever. Kevin will eventually stick his slimy head out of his hole, and when he does, Slater will be there to bite it off.

He leans the mirror against the wall and crosses to the room he's prepared for his guest. It is slightly larger than a closet, encased in concrete. A steel door. Leather restraints lay on the floor, but he doubts he'll need them. The game will end here, where it's been designed to end. The rest of this cat-and-mouse foolishness is only a smoke screen to keep them in the dark, where all good games are played. If the newspapers think they have a hot story now, they are about to be reeducated. The occasional destruction of a car or bus by way of explosion a story hardly makes. What he plans will be worthy of a book.

"I despise you," he says softly. "I loathe the way you walk and the way you speak. Your heart is vile. I will kill you."

|||

The anger had worked its way up to a seething through the night. Kevin tossed and turned in a fitful attempt at sleep. Sam's optimism sat like a light on the horizon of his mind, but as the night wore on, the light grew dim until it faded altogether, obscured by bitterness toward the man who had stomped into his life uninvited.

Fury was a good word for it. Rage. Indignation. They all worked. He relived that night twenty years ago a hundred times. The boy sneering at him as he turned the knife in his hands, threatening to shove the blade through Sam's chest. The boy's name was Slater—had to be. How he'd escaped was beyond Kevin. Why he'd waited so long to come after him made no sense either. He should have killed Slater then.

His pillow felt like a wet sponge. His sheets clung to his legs like mildewed leaves. He couldn't remember a time when he was so upset, so distraught, since the boy had first threatened him so many years ago.

Sam's plan was brilliant, except for the obvious fact that it only delayed the inevitable. Slater wasn't going away—he would wait out there in the dark, biding his time while Kevin slowly dehydrated beneath the sheets. He couldn't do this. He couldn't just wait and waste away while Slater chuckled under his rock.

The idea ignited in his mind with the sky's first graying. *Buy a gun.* His eyes sprang open. Of course! Why not? Become the hunter.

Don't be absurd. He closed his eyes. *You aren't a killer.* The discussion with Dr. Francis was one thing—all that talk about gossip and killing being the same thing. But when it came right down to it, he could never kill another human. He couldn't line up a man in the gun's sights and send a slug through his head. *POW!* Surprise, creep.

Kevin slowly opened his eyes. Where would he get a gun anyway? A pawnshop? Not with today's laws. Not legally, anyway. On the other hand, for the right price . . .

Forget it. What was he going to do, shoot the phone if Slater called again? The man was too good to walk into danger. How could he lure Slater into a confrontation?

Kevin rolled over and tried to put the idea from his mind. But now the notion began to grow, fed by his own loathing. In the end Slater would kill him—nothing else made any sense. So why not take the fight to him first? Why not demand a meeting? Face me, you slime bucket. Come out of the shadows and look me in the eyes. You want a game?

Suddenly the thought of anything less seemed weak. He had to at least try.

He wrestled off the sheets and slid to the floor. Sam wouldn't agree. He would do this without her, now, before she awakened and stopped him. He quickly pulled on his jeans and a T-shirt. The details didn't seem so critical at the moment—where he'd find a gun, how he'd hide it, how he'd use it. With enough money . . .

Kevin grabbed his wallet off the nightstand and fumbled through it. It would have to be cash. He'd stuffed his emergency cash, the four hundred dollars from under his mattress, into his wallet before leaving the house. Still there. Surely with that much he could buy a gun on the black market.

Kevin eased out of his room, saw that Sam's door was still closed, and walked for the door before pulling up. He should at least leave a note. *Couldn't sleep, went to put a slug in Slater's head, be back soon.*

He found a pad of paper with the hotel's insignia stenciled across the top and scribbled a note. *Couldn't sleep, went for a drive, be back soon.*

The morning air felt cool on his clammy skin. Six o'clock. The underworld was undoubtedly still stirring. He had to get out before Sam awoke or he wouldn't be going anywhere. She would worry if he didn't return quickly. As soon as the night crawlers made their appearance, he would pull over and ask one of them the dreaded question: Where can I buy a gun to blow away the man who's after me?

He started the car and headed south.

And what if the night crawler recognized him? His face had been plastered on the news. The jarring thought made Kevin flinch. He swerved. A white sedan on his tail flashed its lights. He quickly pulled over, as if it had been his intention all along. The car sped by.

Maybe he should have brought a sock to pull over his head. Kmart special over here—one bad man with a stocking over his head, holding up a night crawler with a wallet. Give me your gun, buster.

Twenty minutes later he emerged from a 7-Eleven with a pair of dark glasses and an orange Broncos baseball cap. With a day's stubble, he looked nothing like the man he'd seen on television the previous day. But he decided to take the drive up to Inglewood just to be sure. Probably more guns to be had up there anyway.

An accident on 405 stretched the hour trip into two hours. It was eight-thirty before he'd pulled onto Western Avenue in Inglewood. He had no idea where to begin looking. Sam would be up now.

He drove aimlessly, palms sweaty on the steering wheel, telling himself he had no business asking anyone where to buy a gun, much less buying one. If he headed back over to Hawthorn and headed south, he could be back in Palos Verdes in under an hour.

But Palos Verdes was within spitting distance of Long Beach. And Slater was waiting in Long Beach. He had to find himself a gun. Maybe a knife would be better. Definitely easier to find. Then again, killing with a knife somehow felt more evil than killing with a gun, and harder, assuming he could do either.

What would Jennifer say to this sudden madness that had overtaken him? *Take him out.* No, that was figurative, Kevin. He swallowed, suddenly swamped with the foolishness of what he was doing. He didn't even have a plan! *God, help me.*

For someone studying to be a priest, he sure hadn't prayed much in the past two days. He'd been too busy confessing his sin to the world. He wasn't sure he even believed that God *could* save him. Could God really reach in and save his people? He imagined a huge finger flicking the head off Slater's shoulders. For that matter, what did it take to become one of God's people? How was the soul truly regenerated? Through the sinner's prayer? *Take my heart, take my soul; wash my mind as white as snow. And if anyone comes after me with a gun, please put him in a place where there is no sun—preferably six feet under in a concrete tomb.*

He'd never really prayed like that. Oh, he'd prayed plenty in church. He'd committed himself to vocation and to ministry. He'd said what he needed to say to become who he was trying to become, and he was doing what he needed to do to help others become like him. But he was no longer sure what he'd become. He'd broken with his past and started fresh.

Or had he?

Sure he had. Out with the old, in with the new, yippee-kie-ay, yabba dabba doo. *Are you regenerated, Kevin? Are you saved? Are you worthy of feeding at the trough with the others in the flock? Are you fit to shepherd the sheep grazing in God's green pastures?*

I was three days ago. At least I thought I was. At least I was successfully pretending to think I was.

Praying to a heavenly Father filled his mind with images of Eugene, dressed in his riding boots, issuing commands in a phony

English accent. Fathers were silly men who went about pretending they were important.

Kevin cleared his throat. "God, if anyone ever needed your help, I do. However you do it, you have to save me. I may not be a priest, but I do want to be your . . . your child."

Tears filled his eyes. *Why the sudden emotion?*

It's coming because you never were anyone's child. Just like Father Strong used to say. God's waiting with outstretched hands. You never really took that seriously, but that's what becoming a child is all about. Trust him at his Word, as the good reverend would say.

Kevin pulled into a Burger King. Three young men walked out in baggy jeans with chains that hung from their belt loops to their knees.

A gun. Right now he didn't need God's Word. Right now he needed a gun.

|||

Jennifer picked up her phone, dialed Kevin's number, and let it ring a dozen times. Still no answer. He'd been gone since five o'clock last evening, and she had hardly slept.

They had set up audio surveillance with a single laser beam, which when placed on any one of Kevin's windows could turn the glass into an effective diaphragm for sounds beyond. Slater had probably used a similar device. The problem with the laser technology was that it picked up sounds indiscriminately. A digital-signal processor decoded the sounds and filtered voice, but the settings had to be adjusted whenever the operator changed windows, or when conditions—such as the closing of drapes—changed sufficiently to interfere with the acoustics of the room. For some reason Kevin had decided to close the drapes just before his departure.

A young agent named McConnel was resetting the laser receiver when Kevin had come out. McConnel said he heard a barrage of static in his earphone and looked up to see the garage door open and the rented Ford Taurus pull out. He'd reported the incident immediately, but his hands were tied. No following.

The fact that McConnel had heard nothing resembling a phone call before Kevin's departure was somewhat comforting, but the call could have come while the agent was adjusting the receiver.

Jennifer had tried to reach Sam at the Howard Johnson hotel, on the whim that she might know Kevin's whereabouts. No luck. The agent wasn't picking up her cell and the hotel clerk said that she'd checked out yesterday morning. She remembered Sam because she'd been tipped twenty dollars. Any agent who'd leave a tip for a desk clerk was unusual at the least.

Jennifer only hoped that Slater would have as much difficulty reaching Kevin as she did. If so, the disappearing act might actually offer some benefits. No bombs. So far. Hopefully the statewide bulletin on the Taurus wouldn't trigger one. She wasn't sure why Kevin had left—most probably a reaction to the stress—but in doing so he may have inadvertently stalled Slater.

Jennifer called the agent on duty by the house and learned, as expected, nothing new. She decided to try the dean a few minutes early.

Dr. John Francis lived in an old brick house on the edge of Long Beach, two blocks west of Los Alamitos. She knew that he was a widower with doctorates in both psychology and philosophy who'd lived in the same house for twenty-three years. Other than that all she knew was that he had taken Kevin under his wing at the seminary. And that he liked to drive fast, judging by the black Porsche 911 in his driveway.

Five minutes after pulling up to his house, Jennifer sat in a cozy living room, listening to quiet strains of Bach, nursing a hot cup of green tea. Dr. Francis sat opposite her in an armchair, legs crossed, smiling without trying to. He was quite distressed over all the news he'd heard about his student, but she would never guess it with a glance. The professor had one of those faces that couldn't help but reflect God's goodness, regardless of what might be happening.

"How well do you know Kevin?" she asked.

"Quite well as far as students go. But you must understand, that doesn't qualify me to pass any judgment on his past."

"His past. We'll come back to that. This may sound like a simple case of revenge based on what the media is pumping over the air, but I think it's more complicated than that. I think whoever's after Kevin sees his life as it is now and takes exception to it. That's where you come in. It appears that Kevin's a quiet man. Not a lot of friends. In fact, he evidently considers you his best. Maybe his only, other than Sam."

"Sam? You mean his childhood friend, Samantha? Yes, he's spoken of her. He seems quite taken with her."

"Tell me about him."

"You're looking for something in his life today that might elicit anger in someone from his past?"

She smiled. The psychologist in him was speaking. "Exactly."

"Unless Kevin comes forward with his confession, which he did, the man will extract a price."

"That's the basic story."

"But the confession missed the mark. So now you dig deeper, in search of that which so offends this Slater."

She nodded. Dr. Francis was a quick study. She decided to deal straight with the man. "On the surface it seems obvious. We have a student pursuing a holy vocation. As it turns out, his past is filled with mystery and murder. Someone takes exception to that dichotomy."

"We all have pasts filled with mystery and murder," Dr. Francis said.

Interesting way to put it.

"In fact, it's one of the aspects of the human condition Kevin and I have discussed before."

"Oh?"

"It's one of the first things an intelligent man like Kevin, who comes to the church later in life, notices. There is a pervasive incongruity between the church's theology and the way most of us in the church live."

"Hypocrisy."

"One of its faces, yes. Hypocrisy. Saying one thing but doing another. Studying to be a priest while hiding a small cocaine addiction, for example. The world flushes this out and cries scandal. But the more ominous face isn't nearly so obvious. This is what interested Kevin the most. He was quite astute, really."

"I'm not sure I follow. What's not so obvious?"

"The evil that lies in all of us," the professor said. "Not blatant hypocrisy, but deception. Not even realizing that the sin we regularly commit is sin at all. Going about life honestly believing that we are pure when all along we are riddled with sin."

She looked at his gentle smile, taken by the simplicity of his words.

"A preacher stands against the immorality of adultery, but all the while he harbors anger toward the third parishioner from the left because the parishioner challenged one of his teachings three months ago. Is anger not as evil as adultery? Or a woman who scorns the man across the aisle for alcoholic indiscretions, while she routinely gossips about him after services. Is gossip not as evil as any vice? What's especially damaging in both cases is that neither the man who harbors anger nor the woman who gossips seriously considers the evil of their own actions. Their sins remain hidden. This is the true cancer in the church."

"Sounds like the same cancer that eats away at the rest of society."

"Exactly. Although in the church it makes every attempt to

remain hidden, where it is left alone to grow in the dark. You ever wonder why incidences of divorce and gluttony and virtually all of evil's fruits are as high in the church as in society at large?"

"Actually, I didn't know that."

"Though being freed from sin, most remain slaves, blinded and gagged by their own deception. 'The good that I would, that I do not do and that which I would not, that I do.' Welcome to the church in America."

"And you're saying you've discussed this with Kevin?"

"I discuss this with every class I teach on the subject. Kevin, more than most students, understood it."

"Based on what you're saying, what Slater's doing isn't so different from what every old lady in the church does when she gossips?" *And killing Roy was no different either,* she almost said.

"Assuming that old ladies have a proclivity for gossip, a false assumption, actually. On the other hand, Saint Paul drew a distinction between some sins and others. Although he did place gossip in the most vile category."

Jennifer set down her cup on a cherry wood end table. "So you're suggesting that the Riddle Killer is interested in Kevin confessing his true nature, not necessarily some particular sin. Seems like a stretch. To what end? Why would Slater single out Kevin, unless Kevin somehow wronged him?"

"Now you're out of my league, I'm afraid."

"You're pushing theory way beyond what feels reasonable, Doctor. My brother was murdered. I hardly see any similarities between his killer and an old lady in a church."

"I'm so sorry. I didn't know." His compassion appeared thoroughly genuine.

"Even naysayers accept the brilliance of the teachings of Jesus," he said. "You do know what he said on the matter?"

"Tell me."

"That to hate a man is the same as killing him. Perhaps the gossipers are murderers after all."

The notion struck her as absurd. Jennifer sighed. "So Slater, who was once wronged by Kevin, studies him today and sees this great inconsistency—that Kevin lives a life of minor sins—anger, resentment, gossip. But Slater believes, as you seem to, that minor sins are no less evil than the greater sins. Kevin decides to become a priest. This upsets Slater and he decides to teach Kevin a lesson. That the gist of it?"

"Who's to say how a demented mind works?" The professor smiled. "Really, it's beyond me how anyone could do this to another man, especially a man like Kevin. Regardless of his past sins, Kevin is a walking testimony of God's grace. You'd think he's been through his share of difficulties. To have become the man he is today is nothing short of amazing."

She studied Dr. Francis. "He is quite unusual, isn't he? I didn't know his type still lived on the West Coast."

"His type?" the professor asked. "You mean his innocence?"

"Innocent, genuine. Maybe even naive, in a nonoffensive way."

"You're aware of his past?"

"Sketchy. I haven't exactly had the time to dig past his file these last two days."

The doctor's brow went up. "Perhaps you would do well to pay a visit to the home of his childhood. I don't know the entire story, but from what Father Strong told me, Kevin's childhood was anything but normal. Not necessarily terrible, mind you, but I wouldn't be surprised to find more there than Father Strong or any of the rest of us suspects, particularly in light of these recent events."

"So you don't know the details of his past. Still, you say he's been through his share of difficulties."

"His parents died when he was one. He was raised by an aunt who despises his pursuit of higher education. As you say, he acts like a man who has recently walked off an island to discover that there is a rest-of-the-world. Naive. I think there's something in Kevin's past that haunts him. It may shed some light on this man you call Slater."

"The boy," she said.

"I'm afraid I don't know about any boy."

She would take a trip to Baker Street as soon as she left. "Nothing else comes to mind? No other students or faculty might have any motive to hurt Kevin?"

"Heavens, no. Not unless all of our gossiping students are becoming murderers to flush out the truth." He grinned.

"You sound like a wonderful teacher, Dr. Francis. Do you mind if I call on you again?"

"Please." He tapped his chest. "There's a special place in here for Kevin. I can't place it or explain why I am so taken by the boy, but I think we all have something to learn from his story."

She stood. "I pray you're right."

"I didn't know you were a religious woman."

"I'm not."

15

THE YOUNG MEN WITH THE CHAINS didn't look like they were carrying any weapons. Not that criminals made a habit of hanging guns around their necks from shoestrings for all to see. Either way, Kevin gave them a pass and pulled back onto Western.

Maybe looking in less obvious spots would fare better. Side streets. Any beer-drinking slug wearing a wife-beater would be packing one, right? Or at least have a piece tucked under the mattress nearby. The fact was, Kevin had no clue what he was doing and the growing realization pushed his nerves into overdrive.

He drove several neighborhoods before working up the courage to park in one particularly seedy-looking lane and take to foot. Wouldn't it be ironic if he were held up at gunpoint minding his own business? Why play games with a serial killer when you could take a stroll down misery lane and get offed any day of the week? Just like in the movies. Or was the other more like a movie?

He walked down the street, past houses with prying eyes. Maybe now would be a good time to pray. On the other hand, considering his intentions, praying felt inappropriate. A ball rolled out on the sidewalk three feet in front of him. He glanced at the house to his right and saw a boy, maybe three feet tall, staring at him with wide brown eyes. A large, shirtless man covered in tattoos, bald except for a black goatee, stood in the doorway behind the boy, watching him from under bushy eyebrows. Kevin picked up the ball and tossed it awkwardly back into the brown lawn.

"You lost?" the man asked.

That obvious? "No," he said and turned away.

"You look lost to me, boy."

Kevin was suddenly too terrified to respond. He walked on, not daring to look back. The man humphed, but made no other comment. Half a block later he glanced back. The man had retreated into his house.

Now, that wasn't so bad. You go, boy. Kevin the player.

Kevin the fool. Here he was, wandering a strange neighborhood, pretending to have a clue, scheming nondescript plans, while the real game awaited its star player twenty miles south. What if Slater had called in the last couple hours? What if he'd called Jennifer or the police with the next threat? Or what if Sam had awakened, found him gone, turned on the phone, and received a call?

Kevin stopped walking. What on earth did he think he was doing? Sam. Sam had a gun. She'd never shown it to him, but he knew she carried it in her purse. Why not just take her gun? What was she going to do, throw him in jail for—

"Excuse me."

Kevin spun around. The man from the doorway stood five feet away. He'd pulled on a white T-shirt that barely managed to contain his bulging shoulders.

"I asked you a question."

Kevin's heart pounded. "I'm . . . I'm not lost."

"I don't believe you. I see a Wall Street punk walking down the sidewalk at ten in the morning and I know he's lost. You trying to score?"

"Score? No. Gosh, no."

"Gosh?" The man grinned and savored the word. "Gosh, no. Then what are you doing so far from home?"

"I'm . . . just walking."

"This look like Central Park to you? Not even the right state, boy. I can hook you up."

A cool sweat ran down Kevin's back. Ask him. Just ask him.

He glanced around. "Actually, I'm looking for a weapon."

The man's eyebrows went up. "And you think this is where weapons grow on trees, is that it?"

"No."

The man studied him. "You a cop?"

"Do I look like a cop?"

"You look like a fool. Is there a difference? What kind of idiot walks around a strange neighborhood looking for a piece?"

"I'm sorry. I should probably leave."

"I guess so."

The man was blocking the sidewalk, so Kevin sidestepped to the street. He took three steps before the man spoke again.

"How much you got?"

He stopped and faced the man. "Four hundred dollars."

"Let me see it."

What if the man robbed him? Too late now. He pulled out his wallet and spread it open.

"Follow me." The man turned and walked back toward his house without checking to see if Kevin followed.

He did. Like a puppy. How many prying eyes watched the sucker from Wall Street slinking along behind Biff?

He followed the man up to his porch. "Wait here." He left Kevin with his hands in his pockets.

Thirty seconds later he was back with something wrapped in an old white T-shirt. "Give me the money."

"What is it?"

"It's a thirty-eight. Cleaned and loaded." Biff glanced up the street. "Worth six, but it's your lucky day. I need the cash."

Kevin fished out his wallet with a trembling hand and handed the contents to the man. He took the bundle. Where was he going to put it? He couldn't just walk down the street with a bundle that had *gun* written all over it. He started to shove it down his pants— too bulky.

The man finished flipping through the bills and saw Kevin's dilemma. He grinned. "Boy, you are a case, aren't you? What're you gonna do, hold up your dog? Give me the shirt."

Kevin unwrapped a shiny silver pistol with a black handle. He gripped the butt with his fingertips and handed the shirt to the man.

The man looked at the gun and smirked. "What do you think you have there? A pastry? Hold it like a man."

Kevin snugged the gun in his palm.

"In your belt. Pull your shirt over it."

Kevin shoved the cold steel barrel past his bellybutton and covered it with his shirt. Still looked pretty obvious to him.

"Suck your gut in. For another hundred I'll show you how to pull the trigger." Grin.

"No thanks."

He turned and walked back out to the sidewalk. He had a gun. What on earth he was going to do with it, he still had no idea. But he had the piece. It was okay to pray now, maybe.

God, help me.

III

Baker Street. It was the third time in two days Jennifer had driven down the narrow lane under the elms. The warehouse where they'd found the blood couldn't be seen from the street itself—it was in the second row of buildings. She imagined a young boy racing across the street toward the clustered warehouses with a bully at his heels. Kevin and the boy.

"What is here that you want to hide, Kevin?" she murmured. "Hmm?" The white house loomed to her left, immaculate, with the shiny beige Plymouth in its driveway. "What did Aunt Balinda do to you?"

Jennifer parked her car on the street and walked up to the porch. A slight breeze rustled through the leaves. The green lawn appeared freshly mowed and trimmed around the edges. She didn't notice until she stepped up on the porch that the red roses in the flower beds were imitation. For that matter, so were all the flowers. It seemed Aunt Balinda was too tidy a person to mess with the natural flaws of nature. Everything about the house was perfectly finished.

She rang the bell and stepped back. A curtain to her left parted; a middle-aged man with a crew cut looked out. Bob. Kevin's retarded older cousin. The face stared, smiled, and disappeared. Then nothing.

Jennifer rang the bell again. What were they doing in there? Bob had seen her . . .

The door cracked and filled with an old, heavily painted, saggy face. "What do you want?"

Jennifer flipped open her badge. "Agent Peters, FBI. Just wondered if I could come in and ask you a few questions."

"Certainly not."

"Just a few—"

"Do you have a search warrant?"

"No. I didn't think I would need one."

"We all make mistakes, dear. Come back with a search warrant." The woman started to close the door.

"Balinda, I presume?"

She turned back. "Yeah? So what?"

"I will be back, Balinda, and I'll bring the police with me. We'll turn the place inside out. Is that what you want?"

Balinda hesitated. Her eyelashes flapped several times. Ruby red lipstick glistened on her lips, like glossy putty. She smelled of too much talcum powder.

"What do you want?" Balinda asked again.

"I told you. Just a few questions."

"Then ask them." She made no move from the door.

The woman was begging to be properly engaged. "I don't think you understand me. When I come back in an hour, I'll have a half-dozen blue suits with me. We'll have guns and microphones. We'll strip-search you if we have to."

Balinda just stared.

"Or you can let me in now, just me. Are you aware that your son Kevin is in trouble?"

"Doesn't surprise me. I told him he'd end up in trouble if he went off."

"Well, it seems that your warning had some merit."

The woman made no move.

Jennifer nodded and stepped back. "Okay. I'll be back."

"You won't touch anything?"

"Not a thing." She lifted both hands.

"Fine. But I don't like people invading our privacy, you understand?"

"I understand."

Balinda walked inside and Jennifer pushed the door open. A single glance into the dimly lit house washed away her understanding.

She entered a hallway of sorts, formed by stacks of newspapers that ran nearly to the ceiling, leaving a passage just wide enough for a slight man to walk through without getting newsprint on his shoulders. Two faces peered at her from the end of the makeshift hallway—Bob's and another man's—both craning for a view.

Jennifer stepped in and closed the door behind her. Balinda whispered urgently to the two men and they retreated like mice. Grayed carpet had been worn to the wood subfloor. The edge of a newspaper to Jennifer's right stuck out far enough for her to read the headline. *London Herald.* June 24, 1972. Over thirty years old.

"Ask your questions," Balinda snapped from the end of the hall.

Jennifer walked toward her, mind swimming. Why had they stacked all these papers in tall neat stacks like this? The display gave eccentricity a whole new meaning. What kind of woman would do this?

Aunt Balinda wore a white dress, high heels, and enough costume jewelry to sink a battleship. Behind her, backlit by a window that overlooked a dirt yard, Eugene stood in riding boots and what appeared to be a jockey's outfit. Bob wore plaid knickers that revealed the tops of knee-high socks. A polo shirt hugged his thin frame.

The hall directed her into what appeared to be the living room, but again, its dimensions had been altered by floor-to-ceiling stacks of paper. Newspapers alternated with books and magazines and the occasional box. A foot-wide crack between two of the stacks allowed light in from what had once been a window. For all of its mess, the room had an order to it, like a bird's nest. The stacks stood several rows deep, allowing just enough room for old Victorian furniture placed just so between smaller mounds of paper in the middle of the floor. These appeared to be in the process of being sorted.

To Jennifer's right, a small kitchen table was piled high with dishes, some clean, most dirty. A collection of empty TV dinner packages sat on one of the chairs. The boxes had been cut with a pair of blue-handled scissors, which rested on the top box.

"Are you going to ask your questions?"

"I'm . . . I'm sorry, I just didn't expect this. What are you doing here?"

"We live here. What do you think we're doing here?"

"You like newspapers." They weren't complete papers, but sections and clippings from newspapers, she saw, categorized according to subject by placards set into the stacks. People. World. Food. Play. Religion.

Bob stepped away from where he'd cornered himself in the kitchen. "Do you like to play?" He held out an old Game Boy in his hand, a monochrome model that looked like it might play Pong with enough persuasion. "This is my computer."

"Hush, Bobby, honey," Balinda said. "Go to your room and read your books."

"It's a real computer."

"I'm sure the lady isn't interested. She's not from our world. Go to your room."

"She's pretty, Mom."

"She's a dog! Do you like dog hair, Bobby? If you play with her, you'll get dog hair all over you. Is that what you want?"

Bob's eyes widened. "The dog is gone."

"Yes, she will be. Now go to your room and sleep."

The boy started to walk away.

"What do you say?" Eugene said.

Bob turned back and dipped his head at Balinda. "Thank you, Princess." He flashed a grin, hurried off through the kitchen, and shuffled down another hall, this one stacked with books.

"I'm sorry, but you know children," Balinda said. "Minds full of mush. They only understand certain things."

"Do you mind if we sit?"

"Eugene, get our guest a chair."

"Yes, Princess." He grabbed two chairs from the table, set one beside Jennifer, and held the other for Balinda to sit. When she did, he lowered his head with the respect of an eighteenth-century butler. Jennifer stared. They had created a world out of their newspapers and all of this paraphernalia—shaped to fit their lives.

"Thank you."

"You're welcome, madam," Eugene said, dipping his head again.

It wasn't unheard of for adults to create their own realities and then protect them—most people clung to some form of illusion, whether it be found in an extension of entertainment or in religion or simply in a self-propagated lifestyle. The lines between reality and fantasy blurred for every human at some level, but this—this was a case study to be sure.

Jennifer decided to slip into their world. When in Rome . . .

"You've created your own world here, haven't you? Ingenious." She looked around, awed. Beyond the living room stood another doorway, maybe leading to the master bedroom. A stair banister ran along one wall. The same Sunday *Times* Jennifer had read earlier was spread out on the coffee table. The cover story, an article on George W. Bush, had been neatly cut out. The picture of Bush was at the bottom of a discard box. A stack two feet deep sat untouched next to the *Times,* topped by the *Miami Herald.* How many papers did they receive each day?

"You cut away what you don't like and keep the rest," Jennifer said. "What do you do with the clippings?" She turned to Balinda.

The old woman wasn't sure what to think of her sudden change. "What clippings?"

"The ones you don't like."

She knew with one look at Eugene that she'd guessed right. The man glanced nervously at his princess.

"What a brilliant idea!" Jennifer said. "You create your own world by clipping out only those stories that fit your idyllic world and then you discard the rest."

Balinda was speechless.

"Who's the president, Eugene?"

"Eisenhower," the man said without hesitation.

"Of course. Eisenhower. None of the others are worthy to be president. Any news of Reagan or the Bushes or Clinton just gets cut out."

"Don't be silly," Balinda said. "Everyone knows that Eisenhower is our president. We don't go along with the pretenders."

"And who won the World Series this year, Eugene?"

"Baseball isn't played anymore."

"No, of course not. Trick question. What do you do with all the baseball stories?"

"Baseball isn't played—"

"Shut up, Eugene!" Balinda snapped. "Don't repeat yourself like a fool in a lady's presence! Go cut something up."

He saluted and stood at attention. "Yes, sir!"

"Sir? What has gotten into you? You're losing your mind just because we have a visitor? Do I look like a general to you?"

He lowered his hand. "Forgive me, my princess. Perhaps I should save us some coin by cutting some coupons. I should love to take the carriage to the shop for stores as soon as I do."

She glared at him. He did an about-face and walked for the stack of fresh newspapers.

"Don't mind him," Balinda said. "He gets a bit strange when he's excited."

Jennifer glanced out the window. A thin ribbon of smoke drifted skyward from a barrel. The yard was black . . .

They burned them! Whatever didn't fit neatly into the world Balinda wanted went up in smoke. Newspaper stories, books, even pictures on TV dinner boxes. She looked around for a television. An old black and white sat dusty in the living room.

Jennifer stood and walked toward it. "I have to hand it to you, Balinda; you take the cake."

"We do what we are entitled to in the privacy of our home," she said.

"Of course. You have every right. Frankly, it would take tremendous strength and resolve to sustain the world you've managed to build around yourself."

"Thank you. We've given our lives to it. One has to find a way in this chaotic world."

"I can see that." She eased through the living room and peered over the banister. The staircase was filled in with reams of old papers. "Where does this lead?"

"The basement. We don't use it anymore. Not for a long time."

"How long?"

"Thirty years. Maybe longer. It frightened Bob, so we nailed it shut."

Jennifer faced the hall Bob had disappeared down. Kevin's room was down there somewhere, hidden behind piles of books—probably butchered—and magazines. She walked down the hall.

Balinda stood and followed. "Now wait a minute. Where—"

"I just want to see, Balinda. I just want to see how you managed it."

"Questions, you said. You're walking, not talking."

"I won't touch a thing. That's what I said. And I won't."

She passed a bathroom on her right, cluttered and filthy. The hall ended at the doorways of two rooms. The door on the right was shut—presumably Bob's room. The door on the left was open a crack. She pushed it open. A small bed sat in one corner, strewn with loose clippings from children's books. Hundreds of books stood against one wall—half with their covers torn off, altered, or trimmed to meet Balinda's approval. A small window with a pull-down shade looked into the backyard.

"Kevin's old room?" she asked.

"Until he abandoned us. I told him that if he left he'd end up in trouble. I tried to warn him."

"Do you even want to know what kind of trouble he's in?"

Balinda turned away. "What happens out of this house is not my concern. I told him he had no business running off with the serpent. Sss, sss, sss. It's lies, lies, all lies out there. They say we came from monkeys. You're all fools."

"You're right, the world is full of fools. But I can assure you, Kevin isn't one of them."

Balinda's eyes flashed. "Oh, he's not, is he? He was always too smart for us! Bob was the dumb one and Kevin was God himself, come to enlighten the rest of us poor idiots!" She took a breath through her nostrils.

She'd hit a button in the old hag. The adopted nephew wasn't retarded like her own son and Balinda had taken exception to the fact.

Jennifer swallowed and walked to the window. It was fastened down with one screw. What kind of mother would raise a boy in an environment like this? The thought of Kevin crying as they passed by the house yesterday came with new understanding. *Dear Kevin, what did she do to you? Who was the small boy who lived in this room?* The screw was loose in its hole.

Balinda followed Jennifer's stare.

"He used to crawl out of that window. He didn't know that I knew, but I did. Nothing happens around here without my knowing."

Jennifer turned back and brushed past Balinda. Nausea swept through her stomach. In a twisted way, Balinda had probably raised

Kevin with noble intentions. She'd protected him from a terrible world full of evil and death. But at what price?

Slow down, Jennifer. You don't know what happened here. You don't even know that this wasn't a wonderful environment for a child to be raised in.

She stepped into the living room and calmed herself.

"I knew he was sneaking out," Balinda was saying. "But I just couldn't stop him. Not without beating him raw. Never did believe in that kind of discipline. It may have been a mistake. Look at where it got him. Maybe I should have beaten him."

Jennifer took a shallow breath. "What kind of discipline *did* you use?"

"You don't need discipline when your house is in order. Life is discipline enough. Anything more is an admission of weakness." She said it all with her chest puffed, proud. "Isolate them with the truth and they will shine like the stars."

The revelation came like a cool balm. She looked around. So Kevin's rearing had been weird and distorted, but maybe not terrible.

"A man has been threatening Kevin," she said. "We believe it's someone your son—"

"He's my nephew."

"Sorry. Nephew. Someone Kevin might have known when he was ten or eleven. A boy who threatened Kevin. He had a fight with this boy. Maybe you remember something that might help us identify him."

"It must have been the time he came home all bloody. I do remember that. Yes, we found him in bed in the morning and his nose was a mess. He refused to talk about it, but I knew he'd been out. I knew everything."

"What kind of friends did Kevin have at that age?"

Balinda hesitated. "His family was his friend. Bob was his friend."

"But he must have had other friends in the neighborhood. How about Samantha?"

"That fool girl? They sneaked around. Don't think I didn't know. He let it slip a few times. She was the one who may have ruined him in the first place! No, we tried to discourage him from keeping friends outside the house. This is an evil world. You don't just let your children play with anyone!"

"You didn't know *any* of his friends?"

Balinda stared at her for a long time and then walked for the door. "You're starting to repeat your questions. I don't think we can help you more than we have." She opened the door.

Jennifer took a last look around the house. She pitied the poor boy who grew up in this distorted world. He would enter the real world . . . naive.

Like Kevin.

But Balinda was probably right. There was nothing more to learn here.

16

S AMANTHA PACED THE FLOOR of the hotel room for the hundredth time. She'd anticipated almost every eventuality, but not Kevin's disappearance.

Roland had paged her and she'd called him from the room phone. He wasn't thrilled about her having turned off her cell but agreed that her plan had some merit. Meanwhile they had set up a meeting with the Pakistani, Salman, in Houston. This evening. Removing Kevin from the game by pulling him out of Slater's reach might have been the best way to stall the killer until her return tomorrow. But she hadn't considered the possibility that Kevin would disappear. Now she was due to catch a flight in a few hours, and Kevin was gone.

Jennifer Peters would be burning up the phone lines by now, trying to find them, but Sam couldn't bring herself to tip her hand—not yet. Something about the whole investigation bothered her, but she couldn't put a finger on it. Something wasn't right.

She reviewed the facts as she knew them.

One. Someone, probably a white male, had terrorized Sacramento over the last twelve months by selecting seemingly random victims, giving them a riddle to solve, and then killing them when they failed. He'd been dubbed the Riddle Killer by the media and the name had stuck with law enforcement. Jennifer's brother, Roy, had been his last victim.

Two. She had opened an undercover CBI investigation under the premise that the killer had or was an inside man. Nothing indicated that the killer knew of her investigation.

Three. Someone with almost the same MO as the Riddle Killer was now stalking both Kevin and her in a game of riddles.

Four. A concrete connection had been established between this same killer and a boy who'd threatened both her and Kevin twenty years earlier.

On the surface, it all made perfect sense: A boy named Slater takes to torturing animals and terrorizing other children. He's nearly killed by one of those children, Kevin, when Kevin locks him in a cellar to protect a young girl Slater intends to harm. But Slater escapes the cellar and grows up to become one of society's worst nightmares—a man void of conscience with a lust for blood. Now, twenty years later, Slater learns that the two children who tormented him so long ago are alive. He stalks them and devises a game to deal with both in one fell swoop. Obvious, right?

No. Not in Sam's mind. For starters, why had Slater waited so long to go after both her and Kevin? Did the small incident in the cellar just skip his mind for twenty years? And what was the likelihood that she, employed by the CBI, just happened to be assigned to a case involving the same person who tried to kill her twenty years ago?

And now, in the eleventh hour, this new lead from Sacramento—someone in Houston who claimed to know Slater. Or more accurately, the Riddle Killer. If she was right, they were all barking up the wrong tree.

Sam glanced at her watch. Two-thirty and still nothing. She had a plane to catch for Dallas at five. "Come on, Kevin. You're forcing my hand here."

She sighed and picked up her cell phone. She reluctantly switched it on and dialed Jennifer Peters's number.

"Peters."

"Hello, Agent Peters. Samantha Sheer—"

"Samantha! Where are you? Kevin's gone. We've been trying to track him down all morning."

"Slow down. I know Kevin's gone. He's with me. Or was with me, I should say."

"With *you?* This isn't your investigation. You have no right this side of hell to act without our approval! You trying to get him killed?"

Wrong, Jennifer, I don't need your approval. "Don't insult me."

"Do you have any idea how crazy things are down here? The media's gotten wind, presumably through that deadhead Milton, that Kevin's disappeared, and they're already suggesting Slater kidnapped him. They've got cameras on rooftops, waiting for the next bomb, for heaven's sake! A killer's loose out there, and the only man who may be able to lead us to him has gone AWOL. Why didn't you call? Where is he now?"

"Take a breath, Jennifer. I have called, against my better judgment. I've put in a request to share what we know with you, but only you, do you understand? What I share with you, no one else hears. Not Milton, not the FBI, no one."

"Put in a request with whom?"

"With the attorney general. We've been working this case from a new angle, you might say. Now you know, but no one else does."

Silence.

"Agreed?"

"I swear, the way these bureaucracies work, you'd think we still lived in caves. I've been busting my butt for a year on this case, and now I learn that some crackpot agency is doing an end run? Do you have any information that might be useful, or is that a secret too?"

"We have reason to suspect an inside link."

"Inside. As in law enforcement?"

"Maybe. We would have shared files a long time ago if we didn't suspect that someone inside may be tracking with Slater."

"Meaning?"

"Meaning we're not sure who we can trust. For reasons I can't go into today, I don't think Slater is who you think he is."

"You mean the boy? *I* don't even know who I think he is!"

"That's not what I mean. He probably is the boy. But who's the boy?"

"You tell us. He threatened you, didn't he?"

"That was a long time ago, and we have no ID. For all we know, he's the director of the FBI now."

"Please, don't patronize me."

"You're right. He's not the director of the FBI. All I'm saying is that we can't eliminate the possibility that he's someone on the inside. I'll know more tomorrow."

"This is ridiculous. Where are you now?"

Sam paused. She had no choice now. Withholding information from Jennifer would only hamper her investigation at this point. She needed the FBI to focus on their own investigation, not meddle in hers. And there was this little fact that Kevin was missing.

She explained her rationale for taking Kevin, and Jennifer listened patiently, interrupting occasionally with pointed questions. Sam's reasoning finally won her a grunt of approval. The news of Kevin's disappearance didn't.

"So as far as we know, Slater does have him," Jennifer said.

"I doubt it. But it does look like I've made a mistake. I didn't expect this."

Jennifer let the apology go, which from Sam was as good as an acceptance. The FBI agent sighed.

"Let's hope he comes in. Soon. How well did you know him when he was a boy?"

"We were close. I didn't have a better friend."

"I visited his aunt's house this morning."

Sam sat on the bed. How much did Jennifer know? Kevin had never shared the details of his life in the house with Sam, but she knew much more than he suspected.

"I never did see the inside of the house," Sam said. "His aunt wouldn't allow it. It was hard enough sneaking around the way we did."

"Was there abuse?"

"Physical, no. Not that I saw. But in my book Kevin suffered severe, systematic psychological abuse from the day he entered that twisted house. You talked to Balinda?"

"Yes. She's created a sanctuary for herself in there. The only realities that make it past the cutting floor are the ones she decides are real. God only knows what the house was like twenty years ago. Manipulation of a child's learning process isn't unheard of—it's even broadly accepted in some arenas. Military school comes to mind. But I've never heard of anything like Balinda's little kingdom. Judging by Kevin's reaction to the place, I would tend to agree. He suffered abuse in that house."

Sam let the phone line remain silent for a while.

"Be careful, Jennifer. This is a case about a hurting man as much as it is a hunt for a killer."

Jennifer hesitated. "Meaning?"

"There's more. There are secrets behind the walls of that house."

"Secrets he hasn't shared with you, his childhood sweetheart?"

"Yes."

By the sound of Jennifer's breathing, Sam knew she felt uncomfortable with the tone of the conversation. She decided to expand the agent's mind a little.

"I want you to consider something that's nagged me for the last two days, Jennifer. No one hears, understand? This is between us. Agreed?"

"Go on."

"I would like you to consider the possibility that Kevin and Slater are really the same person." She dropped the bomb and let Jennifer respond.

"I . . . I don't think that's possible." Jennifer chuckled nervously. "I mean that would be . . . the evidence doesn't support that! How could he pull off such a crazy stunt?"

"He's not pulling anything off. Please, understand me, I'm not suggesting it's true, and God knows even considering the idea terrifies me, but there are elements to this case that just don't sit right. I think the possibility is at least worth some thought."

"He would have to be calling himself. You're suggesting he was in Sacramento, blowing up victims three months ago?"

"If he is the Riddle Killer. I'm working on that."

"And if he is Slater, who's the boy? We found blood in the warehouse, consistent with this story. There was a boy."

"Unless the boy was really Kevin. Or there was no boy."

"You were there—"

"I never actually saw the boy, Jennifer."

"Your father forced the family to leave! What do you mean you never *saw* the boy?"

"I mean I told my father the boy was there—there was plenty of evidence at my window and I believed Kevin for the rest. Call it a white lie. Regardless, I actually never saw the boy. We forced the family of a bully to move, but thinking back on it, the boy ran off before my dad could apprehend him. He accused a local bully based on my testimony, and I based my testimony on Kevin's. But there was no definitive evidence that it was someone *other* than Kevin. I didn't even know Kevin had locked the boy in the warehouse until yesterday."

"The physical evidence for Kevin being Slater doesn't add up. He blew up his own car?"

"I'm not saying that he *is* Slater. I'm only positing a possibility. Considering his childhood, Multiple Personality Disorder may not be out of the question—the Kevin we know wouldn't necessarily even know that he's Slater. Everything that we have so far could fit the scenario; that's all I'm saying. There are no inconsistencies. Think about it."

"Neither is there any evidence to support it. Highly unlikely. MPD results only in very limited cases of severe childhood abuse. Almost always physical abuse. Balinda might be a witch, but she doesn't fit the profile for physical abuse. You said so yourself."

"You're right, there wasn't physical abuse. But there are exceptions."

"Not any that fit this scenario. At least not that I know of, and it is my field of study."

Probably right. Highly unlikely, but in cases like this every possibility had to be considered. Something was not what it seemed, and as disturbing as her suggestion was, Sam couldn't just discard it. If Kevin was Slater, exposing the fact would be the greatest favor she could do for her childhood friend.

On the other hand, hearing herself say it out loud, the notion sounded absurd. A simple voice or handwriting analysis would settle the matter.

"Have the lab run a handwriting comparison from the jug."

"We already have. Standard procedure. It was negative."

"It's technically possible for multiple personalities to have varying motor characteristics."

"In this case, I don't think so."

"Then start comparing it with everyone else connected to the case. Someone on the inside's working this, Jennifer. Someone's not who we think they are."

"Then get me your file."

"It's on the way."

"And if Kevin contacts you, call me. Immediately." To say that the agent sounded agitated would be like saying the sky was big.

"You have my word."

"As much as your plan to isolate Kevin may have made sense, having Slater's voice on tape could be invaluable. Particularly in light of your suggestion. Turn it on and leave it on."

Sam picked up Slater's silver phone and switched it on. "Done."

"The recording device is still active?"

"Yes."

A knock sounded on the door. Sam started.

"What is it?" Jennifer asked.

"Someone's at the door." She walked for the door.

"Who?"

She turned the deadbolt and pulled it open. Kevin stood in the hallway, blinking and haggard.

"Kevin," Sam said. "It's Kevin."

, | | |

Jennifer lowered the phone and sat hard. The notion that Kevin and the Riddle Killer might be the same man wasn't only absurd; it was . . . wrong. Sick. Deeply disturbing.

Galager walked by her desk, headed for the lab. She couldn't bring herself to look at him. Was it possible?

Her mind spun back to the scene of Roy's death. Was it possible that Kevin—

No! It made no sense.

And why is this such an infuriating prospect, Jennifer? You can't imagine Kevin killing Roy because you like Kevin. He reminds you of Roy, for heaven's sake.

Jennifer rehearsed the facts quickly. If Kevin was Slater, then he would have to be calling himself, possible but unlikely. He would also have to have an alter ego of which he was clueless. She had interviewed enough witnesses over the years to recognize sincerity, and Kevin had it in spades. He would have had to plant the bombs long ago, possible, but in both cases he would have had to detonate them without his own knowing.

No. No, this was too much. She began to relax. The man she had comforted in the park yesterday was no killer. The boy, whose blood they'd found in the cellar, on the other hand, could be.

Point was, she had panicked at the thought that Kevin might be the killer, hadn't she? She should have been ecstatic at the mere prospect of uncovering the killer's true identity. Which said that she cared far too much for Kevin, an absurdity in itself given the fact that she hardly knew him!

On the other hand, she was bound to him in a way few people ever are. They shared the death of her brother in common—she as the victim's survivor, he as the next victim.

Jennifer sighed and stood. She was too emotionally wrapped up in this whole thing. The bureau chief was right.

"Galager!"

The man paused at the door across the room. She motioned him back.

"What's up?"

"We found Kevin."

Galager pulled up. "Where?"

"Palos Verdes. He's okay."

"Should I get Milton?"

He was the last person she wanted to bring in. But she had her marching orders, didn't she? At least she didn't have to deal with him directly. She scribbled the information on a notepad, ripped the page off, and handed it to Galager.

"Fill him in. Tell him I'm tied up."

It was the truth. She was tied up, in knots that refused to loosen.

| | |

They sat on the bed in a stalemate. Kevin was hiding something; that much Sam had known since she'd first talked to him. Friday night. Now his lying was more blatant, but try as she may, she could not coax the truth out of him. His story that he'd been wandering through his old neighborhood, thinking, for the past eight hours was simply unbelievable. True, given his circumstances, almost any behavior was possible. But she knew Kevin too well; she could read those clear blue eyes, and they were shifting. Something else was bothering him.

"Okay, Kevin, but I still don't think you're telling me everything. I have a plane to catch in a couple hours. With any luck, Slater will take the day to revel in his little victory yesterday. God knows we need the time."

"When will you be back?"

"Tomorrow morning." She stood, walked to the window, and pulled back the curtain. "We're closing in, Kevin. We're right on this guy's tail; I can feel it in my bones."

"I wish you weren't going."

Sam turned back. "Jennifer will be here. She'll want to talk to you."

He looked past her out the window. "Yeah."

Dark circles hung under his eyes. He seemed distracted.

"I need a drink," he said. "You want one?"

"I'm fine. You're not going to run off again, are you?"

He grinned. "Come on. I'm here, aren't I?"

"Yes, you are. Hurry back."

He opened the door to leave.

The beige phone on the nightstand rang shrilly. She glanced at the clock beside it—3 P.M. They had overstayed their checkout.

"Go ahead," she told Kevin. "It's probably the front desk."

Kevin left and she picked up the phone.

"Hello?"

"Hello, Samantha."

Slater! She whirled to the door. So Kevin *couldn't* be Slater! He'd been in the room when the killer had called.

"Kevin!" He was gone.

"Not Kevin. It's your other lover, dear."

How had Slater gotten their number? The only person who knew where they were was Jennifer. *Jennifer* . . .

"They want my voice, Samantha. I want to give them my voice. Have you turned the cell phone back on, or are you still playing your idiotic cat-and-mouse game?"

"It's on."

The line clicked. Slater's cell began to ring. She grabbed it and answered.

"There, that's better, don't you think? The game won't last forever; we might as well make this more interesting."

It was the first time she'd actually heard his voice. Low and gravelly.

"What good is a game that you can't lose?" she asked. "It proves nothing."

"Oh, but I can lose, Sam. The fact that I haven't proves that I'm smarter than you." Short heavy breath. "I came within a single pane of glass of killing you once. This time I won't fail."

The boy. She turned and sat on the bed. "So that was you."

"Do you know why I wanted to kill you?"

"No." Keep him talking. "Tell me."

"Because all nice people deserve to die. Especially the pretty ones with bright blue eyes. I despise beauty almost as much as I despise nice little boys. I'm not sure who I hate more, you or that imbecile you call your lover."

"You make me sick!" Samantha said. "You prey on innocence because you're too stupid to realize it's far more fascinating than evil."

Silence. Only heavy breathing. She'd struck a nerve.

"Kevin confessed, as you demanded," she said. "He told the whole world about that night. But you can't live by your own rules, can you?"

"Yes, of course. The boy. Was that me? Maybe it was, maybe it wasn't. Kevin still hasn't confessed his sin. He hasn't even hinted at it. The secret's much too dark, even for him, I think."

"What? *What* sin?"

He chuckled.

"The sin, Samantha. *The* sin. Riddle time. *What wants to be filled but will always be empty?* I'll give you a clue: It's not your head. It has a number: 36933. You have ninety minutes before the fireworks begin. And please remember, no cops."

"Why are you so afraid of the cops?"

"It's not who I'm afraid of; it's who I want to play with." The line clicked.

He was gone.

Sam stood still, mind reeling. He'd called on the hotel room phone. Could he have tracked them down so quickly? Or the phone— could he have a way of tracking it once she turned it on? Unlikely. She paced to the end of the bed and back. Think, Sam! Think! Where was Kevin? They had to—

"Sam?" Kevin's muffled voice sounded beyond the door. He knocked.

She ran for the door. Opened it.

"He called," she said.

"Slater?" His face went white.

"Yes."

Kevin stepped in, can of 7UP in his hand. "What did he say?"

"Another riddle. *What wants to be filled but will always be empty?* With some numbers. 36933." The most obvious solution had already run through her mind. She ran to the coffee table and grabbed the telephone book.

"Call Jennifer."

"How much time?"

"Ninety minutes. Threes. This guy's obsessed with threes and progressions of threes. Call her!"

Kevin set his drink down, jumped for the phone, and punched in her number. He relayed the information quickly.

"On the room phone," he said.

"No, he called back on the cell," Sam corrected him.

"He called back on the cell," Kevin relayed.

Sam spread the phone directory map open and searched the streets. Thirty-third. A warehouse district.

"No cops. Remind her no cops. If she has any ideas, call, but keep the others out of it. He was very clear."

She closed her eyes and took a deep breath. It was the only answer that made immediate sense. But why would Slater choose such an obvious riddle?

She looked up at Kevin. "Tell Jennifer that I was wrong about Slater. You were in the room when Slater called."

Kevin looked at her with a raised eyebrow, passed on the message, listened for a moment, and then addressed Sam. "She says she's on her way. Don't move."

Only Jennifer could know specifically where they were. She would have picked up the caller ID when Sam called her on the room phone. How had Slater tracked them down so quickly?

Sam stepped forward and took the phone from Kevin. "Don't bother coming, Jennifer. We'll be gone. Work the riddle. I'll call you as soon as we have something."

"How will leaving help you? I want Kevin back in my sights where I can work with him. You hear me?"

"I hear you. We're out of time now. Just work the riddle. I'll call you."

"Sam—"

She hung up. She had to think this through.

"Okay, Kevin. Here we go. Slater's into threes; we know that. He's also into progressions. Every target is larger than the one before. He gives you three minutes, then thirty minutes, then sixty minutes, and now ninety minutes. And he gives this number, 36933. The 369 follows the natural progression, but the 33 doesn't. Unless they're not part of the 369. I think we have an address: 369 Thirty-third Street. It's in a warehouse district in Long Beach, about ten miles from here. *What wants to be filled but will always be empty?* A vacant warehouse."

"That's it?"

"Unless you can think of anything better. Opposites, remember? All of his riddles have been about opposites. Things that aren't what they want or seem to be. Night and day. Buses that go around in circles. A warehouse that is designed to hold things but is empty."

"Maybe."

They stared at each other for a few seconds. They had no choice. She grabbed his hand.

"Come on, let's go."

17

THE WAREHOUSE IDENTIFIED AS 369 on Thirty-third Street stood among a dozen others in northern Long Beach, all constructed from the same corrugated tin, all two stories high, all addressed with the same large black numbers above the doors. Years of neglect had worn most of them down to a dull gray. The 369 was hardly more than a shadow. No sign identifying a business name. Looked vacant.

Kevin slowed the car and peered ahead at the looming structure. Dust blew across the sidewalk. A faded Mountain Dew bottle, the two-liter plastic variety, bumped up against a single-entry door to the right of the loading bay.

He stopped the car thirty yards from the corner and eased the gearshift into park. He could hear several sounds—the purring of the engine, the blower blasting air over their feet, the thumping in his chest. They all sounded too loud.

He glanced at Sam, who stared at the structure, searching.

"What now?"

He had to get the gun out of the trunk; that was what now. Not because he thought Slater would be here, but because he wasn't going anywhere without his new purchase.

"Now we go in," she said. "Unless the fire codes were nonexistent twenty years ago, the building will have a rear entrance."

"You take the back," Kevin said. "I'll take the front."

Sam's right eyebrow lifted. "I think you should wait here."

"No. I'm going in."

"I really don't think—"

"I can't sit around and play dumb, Sam!" The aggression in his tone surprised him. "I have to do something."

She faced 369 Thirty-third Street again. Time was ticking. Sixty-two minutes. Kevin wiped a trickling line of sweat from his temple with the back of his hand.

"Doesn't seem right," Sam said.

"Too easy."

She didn't respond.

"We don't have a key—how are we getting in?" he asked.

"Depends. Getting in isn't the concern. What if he's rigged it to blow upon entry?"

"That's not his game," Kevin said. "He said ninety minutes. Wouldn't he stick to his own rules?"

She nodded. "Has so far. Blew the bus ahead of schedule but only because we broke the rules. Still doesn't seem right." She cracked her door. "Okay, let's see what we have here."

Kevin got out and followed Sam toward the building. As far as he could see in both directions, the street was empty. A warm late afternoon breeze lifted dust from the pavement in a small dust devil twenty feet to his right. The plastic Mountain Dew bottle thumped quietly against the entry door. Somewhere a crow cawed. If Jennifer had figured out the riddle, at least she wasn't making the mistake of swarming in with the cops. They walked up to a steel door with a corroded deadbolt.

"So how *are* we getting in?" Kevin whispered.

Sam eased the plastic bottle aside with her foot, put a hand on the doorknob, and twisted. The door swung in with a creak. "Like that."

They exchanged stares. Sam stuck her head into the black opening, looked around briefly, and pulled back. "You sure you're up to
this?"

"Do I have a choice?"

"I could go in alone."

Kevin looked at the dark gap and squinted. Black. The gun was
still back in the trunk.

"Okay, I'm going around back to see what we have," Sam said.
"Wait for me to signal you. When you go in, find lights and turn
them on, but otherwise touch nothing. Look for anything out of the
ordinary. Could be a suitcase, a box, anything not covered in dust. I'll
work my way through the warehouse in the dark just in case someone's in there. Unlikely, but we'll take the precaution. Clear?"

"Yes." Kevin wasn't sure how clear it was. His mind was still on
the gun in the trunk.

"Go easy." She edged to the corner, looked around, and then disappeared.

Kevin ran for the car on his tiptoes. He found the shiny silver pistol where he'd hidden it under the carpet behind the spare tire. He
shoved it into his belt, closed the trunk as quietly as he could, and
hurried back to the warehouse.

The gun handle stuck out from his belly like a black horn. He
pulled his shirt over the butt and flattened it as best he could.

Darkness shrouded the warehouse interior. Still no signal from
Sam. Kevin poked his head in and peered through the oil-thick blackness. He reached in and felt for a light switch along the wall. His fingers touched a cool metal box with a plastic switch on its face. He
flipped the switch.

A loud hum. Light flooded the warehouse. He grabbed at his
midsection and withdrew the gun. Nothing stirred.

He peeked again. A vacant foyer with a receiving desk. Lots of dust. The smell of mildewing rags filled his nostrils. But nothing like a bomb that he could see. Beyond the receiving area, stairs led up to a second floor. Offices. A panel of switches was mounted to the wall at the foot of the stairs. Marks broke the dust directly up the middle of the steps. Footprints.

He instinctively pulled his head from the door. Slater! Had to be. Sam was right; this was it!

Still no signal from her. Unless she'd called him and he'd missed it. With all these walls it was possible.

Kevin held his breath and slipped through the door. He stood still for a moment and then walked on the balls of his feet toward the receiving desk. Behind the desk—could be a place for a bomb. No, the footprints went up . . .

Clunk!

Kevin whirled around. The door had swung shut! The wind? Yes, the wind had—

Click. The lights went out.

Kevin started in the direction of the door, blinded by darkness. He took several quick steps, stuck out a hand, and groped for the door. His knuckles smashed into steel. He fumbled for the handle, found it, and twisted.

But it refused to turn. He gripped hard and jerked the handle first to the left and then to the right. Locked.

Okay, Kevin, stay calm. It's one of those doors that stays locked. Except that it had opened for Sam. Because she was on the outside.

Wasn't it normally the other way around?

He turned and yelled. "Sam?" His voice sounded muted.

"Sam!" This time the word echoed from beyond the stairs.

He'd seen a light panel by the stairs. Maybe they operated other lights? Kevin turned and walked toward the stairs, but his knees found the reception desk first. The crash sent a bolt of electricity through his nerves and he nearly dropped the gun. He stepped to the side and shuffled up to where he remembered the light switches.

"Samantha!"

He slapped the wall, found the switches, and palmed them on. No lights.

The floor above him creaked. "Sam?"

"Kevin!" Sam! Her voice sounded distant, from the back, as if she was still outside the building.

"Sam, I'm in here!"

His eyes had adjusted to the darkness. Light glowed from the upper level. Kevin glanced back toward the door, saw only darkness, and mounted the stairs. Light glowed faintly above him, a window maybe.

"Sam?"

She didn't respond.

He had to get to some light! Another floorboard creaked and he whipped around, gun extended. Was the weapon cocked? He snugged his thumb over the hammer and pulled it back. *Click.* Easy, Kevin. You've never shot a gun in your life. You shoot at a shadow and it might be Sam. And what if the gun doesn't even work?

He headed up the stairs on weak legs.

"Kevin!"

Sam's voice came from his right and forward, definitely outside. He paused halfway up the steps, tried to still his breathing so that he could hear better, but finally gave up and hurried toward the light at the top.

The glow came from a doorway at the end of a barely visible hallway. His breathing came hushed and low now. Something thumped down the hall. He held his breath. There it was again, a step. Boots. Directly ahead and to his right. From one of the other rooms along the hall. Sam? No, Sam was still outside! *Dear God, give me strength.*

He felt exposed standing in the hall. What was he thinking, waltzing up the stairs as if he were some kind of gunslinger?

Frantic, Kevin stepped to the faint outline of a doorway on his right. The floorboards protested under his feet. He cleared the doorway and slid back against the wall on his left.

Boots. There was definitely someone else on the upper floor with him. Could be Sam if the acoustics had misdirected her voice. Could it be her? Sure it could.

It is, Kevin. It's Sam. She's in the next room, and she's found the bomb. No, her voice had been distant. And she didn't walk like that. No way.

Her voice suddenly came again, faint. "Kevin!"

This time there was no mistake, Sam was yelling at him from below, out near the front door now. Her fist pounded on the steel door.

"Kevin, are you in there?"

He took one step back toward the doorway. The boot again. Thumping in the next room.

Someone was in there! Slater. He gripped the pistol tightly. Slater had lured him in. That's why the riddle was so simple. A dread spread through his bones.

Sam was at the front door. The deadbolt wasn't engaged—she should be able to either break it or pick it.

Another thought occurred to him. The bomb was probably set to go off—what if he was trapped in here when it did? What if the cops came and Slater detonated the bomb early? But Sam would never allow the cops anywhere near the warehouse now.

But what if she couldn't get the door open?

Panicked, Kevin slid along the wall, met a corner, and felt his way along the back wall. He put his ear on the plaster.

Breathing. Slow and deep. Not his. Slow shuffling.

A low voice reached through the wall. "Kevinnnn . . ."

He froze.

"Forty-six minutesss . . . Kevinnnn."

|| |

The difference between innocence and naiveté has never registered in Slater's mind. The two are synonymous. In fact, there is no such animal as innocence. They are all as guilty as hell. But he can't deny that some are more naive than others, and watching Kevin creep up the stairs like a mouse has reminded Slater of how utterly naive his nemesis really is.

He'd been sorely tempted to kick the man in the head then, while Kevin was still four steps from the top. Watching him tumble and break would have held its appeal. But place-kicking has always struck him as one of sport's more boring moments.

Welcome to my house, Kevin.

The man has gone and gotten himself a gun. He holds it like he might hold a vial of the Ebola virus and probably hasn't thought to cock it, but he's at least gathered the resolve to arm himself. And he is undoubtedly packing without Samantha's knowledge. She would never allow a civilian to stumble around with a loaded weapon. Kevin has found a sliver of manhood. How fun! The man may actually try to kill him, as if he's become the stalker instead of the victim.

In ways not even Kevin can yet know, this isn't such a new thing. Kevin has tried to kill him before. Their lives are inseparably intertwined, each bent on killing the other. To think that this man who's crept up the stairs holding his big shiny pistol has the stomach to pull the trigger, much less kill, is absurd.

Now the fool has wedged himself in the next room down and is undoubtedly wetting himself. If he only knew what lay in store for him in the hours to come, he might be lying in a puddle of his own vomit.

Here, kitty, kitty.

"Forty-six minutesss . . . Kevinnnn . . ."

| | |

Kevin nearly pulled the trigger then. Not with calculated aim, but out of sheer terror.

"Sam?" His voice sounded like a wounded lamb's bleating. He was briefly revolted by his weakness. If this was Slater, he was getting exactly what he wanted. A face to face. A chance to blow him away.

The doorway stood opposite him, its gaping hole darker than the black surrounding it. If he were to run now, he could bound down the stairs and reach the front door, right?

A new sound reached into the room—the sound of something sharp scraping along the wall outside. Down the hall toward his door.

Kevin gripped the pistol in both hands, pointed it at the doorway, and slid down to his seat. If Slater stepped through that space, he'd do it. He'd see the dark form and start pulling the trigger.

The scraping continued, closer, closer. Closer.

"Kevinnn," a voice whispered.

God, help me! His mind started to go fuzzy.

Take him out, Kevin. Jennifer's voice echoed through his mind. Blow the scumbag away!

He could hardly see the gun in front of him to aim it, but he could point. And whoever walked through that door wouldn't be able to see him, right? Not in this darkness. Kevin would only see a shadow, but he had that advantage.

The scraping closed in on the door.

Sweat slipped into Kevin's eyes. He held his breath.

Sam's voice yelled distant. "Kevin, you stay put! You hear me?"

He couldn't respond.

"Stay right there."

She was going to get something to force the door. Pick the lock. A brick, a crowbar, a gun. A gun! She had a gun in her purse. *Hurry!*

The whisper came again. "Kevinnnn . . ."

The doorway suddenly filled with the dark shape of a man. Kevin's finger tightened on the trigger. What . . . what if it wasn't Slater? A bum, maybe.

The form stood still, as if staring at him. If it moved . . . If it even flinched, Kevin would pull the trigger.

Blood pounded through his head as if pumps had been shoved in his ears and were trying to suck him dry. *Whoosh, whoosh.* He couldn't move other than to tremble slightly in the dark. He was eleven years old again, facing the boy in the cellar. Trapped. *That'll cost you your eyeballs, punk.*

A metal object clanged against the front door. Sam!

The figure didn't flinch.

Now, Kevin! Now! Before he runs. Pull the trigger!

Clang!

"Why would I do something so senseless as blow up an old abandoned warehouse?" Slater's voice asked.

"It's so nice to meet you again face to face, Kevin. I like the dark, don't you? I thought about bringing candles for the occasion, but I like this better."

Shoot! Shoot, shoot, SHOOT!

"We've only been at this three days and I'm already tired of it. Practice is over. We start the real game tonight," Slater said.

The sound of steel against steel echoed from the front door.

"We'll be seeing you."

The figure moved.

The pressure Kevin had exerted on the trigger finally sprang the hammer at the same instant. The room ignited with a brilliant flash chased by a horrendous thunder. He saw Slater's black coat as he cleared the doorway.

"Aaaahhhh!" He fired again. A third time. He scrambled to his feet, leapt for the opening, and spun into the hallway. A door at the end of the hall swung closed. The man was gone. Darkness surrounded Kevin.

He whirled around, grabbed the railing, and stumbled down the stairs.

"Kevin!"

The door burst open to daylight before Kevin reached it. Sam jumped clear and he spilled out onto the sidewalk.

Sam had her weapon drawn. She took one look at Kevin and spun into the doorway, gun extended.

"He's gone," Kevin panted. "Out back. A window or something."

"Wait here." Sam ran to the corner, shoved her head around, and then disappeared.

The ground felt uneven under Kevin's feet. He gripped a telephone pole and steadied himself. Why had he waited? He could have ended the whole thing with one shot, right there in the room. On the other hand, he had no proof that the figure was Slater. Could've been an idiot playing . . .

No, it was Slater. Definitely. You spineless punk! *You let him walk. He was right there and you whimpered like a dog!* Kevin grunted and closed his eyes, furious.

Sam reappeared thirty seconds later.

"He's gone."

"He was just there! Are you sure?"

"There's a fire escape with a ladder. He could be anywhere by now. I doubt he's hanging around for an encore." She glanced back, considering.

"There's no bomb, Sam. He wanted to meet me. That's why the riddle was so easy. I saw him."

She stepped up to the door, looked inside, and flipped the switches. Nothing happened.

"How did the door lock?"

"I don't know. I was just in there and it slammed behind me."

She stepped just beyond the door and looked up. "It's rigged. He used a pulley with a string . . ." She followed the string with her eyes.

"What is it?"

"The string ends by the counter. He was down here when he pulled the door closed."

The revelation struck Kevin as absurd. "In the lobby?"

"Yes, I think so. String's pretty well hidden, but he was here. I don't want to contaminate the scene—we need to get some light in there." She walked back out and opened her cell phone. "You sure it was him?"

"He spoke to me. He stood right there and asked me why he'd be so senseless as to blow up an abandoned building." Kevin's legs felt like putty. He abruptly sat on the sidewalk. The gun hung from his right hand.

Sam eyed it. "This is what you found wandering your old neighborhood this morning?"

Kevin set the gun down. "Sorry. I can't just let him push me around anymore."

She nodded. "Put it back in the trunk or wherever you had it stashed, and please, don't use it again."

"I shot at him. You think maybe I hit him?"

"I didn't see any blood. But they'll find evidence of the shots." She paused. "They may want you to surrender the gun. I don't suppose it's legal."

He shook his head.

"Just get it out of sight before the others get here. I'll talk to Jennifer."

"Others?"

She glanced at her watch. "It's time for her to take over here. I have a plane to catch."

18

THERE WAS NO BOMB and Slater had met his objective forty minutes early. They had solved their first riddle within the allotted time, but it still had served the killer. He'd made contact with Kevin in person and escaped without a trace.

Sam had called Jennifer with the details while waiting for her cab to arrive. She was still unsettled about something—was even a little reluctant to call Jennifer, but she said that she had no choice. Of all the authorities, she trusted Jennifer the most. No cops until the ninety-minute mark had passed; that much she'd insisted on.

Jennifer was on her way with an FBI team to begin the investigation. Sam would be lucky to catch her flight; Kevin watched the cab's taillights as it sped down the street and around the corner.

Yes indeed, they had solved the riddle. Or had they? He should be swimming in relief about now—he'd come nose to nose with a madman and survived. Chased him away with a few shots to boot. Sort of.

But his head still felt like it was caught in a vise. He agreed with Sam; something wasn't right.

What was it about this appointment in Houston that was so important to her? And why wasn't she forthcoming on the actual nature of the meeting? She knew the Riddle Killer was here. What was there in Houston?

And why wouldn't she just tell him? Here in Long Beach the city was terrorized by the man the media had dubbed the Riddle Killer, but Sam was off on a tangent in another city. Made no sense.

A black car swung onto the street and roared toward him. Jennifer.

Two other agents climbed out with her, one with weapon drawn, both armed with flashlights. Jennifer spoke quickly to them, sending one around back and the other for the front door, which still stood open in a splintered frame. Sam had taken the car jack to it.

Jennifer approached him, dressed in a blue suit, hair flowing around her shoulders in the warm breeze. "Are you okay?" she asked.

She glanced at the warehouse, and for a brief moment Kevin imagined that her question was only a courtesy—her real interest lay in whatever awaited her prying eyes beyond the door. A new crime scene. Like all of them, she loved the crime scenes. As well she should—the crime scene led to the criminal, in this case Slater.

She turned her attention back to him.

"As okay as I can be, I suppose," he said.

She walked up to him and looked into his eyes. "I thought we understood each other."

He ran a hand through his hair. "What do you mean?"

"I mean we're on the same side here. I mean you tell me everything, or did our conversation yesterday not make an impression on you?"

He suddenly felt like a silly schoolboy standing in the principal's office. "Of course we're on the same side."

"Then make me a promise you can live by. You don't disappear unless we agree for you to disappear. In fact, you do *nothing* unless we agree you do it. I can't do this without you, and I certainly don't need you following someone else's lead."

An unreasonable sorrow swept over Kevin. He felt a knot in his throat, as if he might cry, right here in front of her. Again. Nothing would be so humiliating.

"I'm sorry. Sam said—"

"I don't care what Sam tells you. You're my responsibility, not hers. Heaven knows I need all the help I can get, but until you hear differently from someone besides Sam, you follow my lead. Regardless of whose idea it is, you talk to me. Okay?"

"Okay."

She sighed and closed her eyes momentarily. "Now what did Sam suggest?"

"That I should do everything you say."

Jennifer blinked. "She's right." She looked past him at the warehouse. "I want this creep as much as you do. You're our best shot . . ." She stopped.

"I know. You need me to get him. Who gives a rip about Kevin as long as we get what we need out of him; is that it?"

She stared at him, whether angered or embarrassed, he couldn't tell. Her face softened.

"No, that isn't it. I'm sorry you're living through this hell, Kevin. It's beyond me why innocent people have to suffer, but try as I have, changing the fact is beyond me." She held his eyes with her own. "I didn't mean to sound so harsh. I just . . . I'm not going to let him get to you. He killed my brother, remember? I lost Roy, but I'm not going to lose you."

Kevin suddenly understood. It explained her anger. Maybe more.

"And yes, as a matter of fact, I do need you," she said. "You're our best hope of apprehending a very demented nut case who happens to be after you."

Now Kevin felt more like a clumsy freshman than anyone who might be hauled into the school office for discipline. *Stupid, Kevin. Stupid, stupid.*

"I'm sorry. I'm so sorry."

"Apology accepted. Just don't run off again, okay?"

"Guaranteed." He lifted his eyes and saw the same strange look he'd seen in Sam's eyes at times. A cross between concern and empathy. *Stupid, stupid, Kevin.*

Jennifer dropped her eyes to his mouth and took a deep breath. "So. You saw him."

He nodded.

She glanced back at the door. "He's progressing."

"Progressing?"

"He wants more. More contact, more danger. Resolution."

"Then why doesn't he just come out and ask me for whatever it is he wants?"

She held a flashlight in her hand. "Are you up to walking through it with me? We'll wait until my men come out—I don't want to compromise any evidence. I realize you're frazzled, but the sooner I know how this went down, the greater our chances of using any information we come up with."

He nodded. "The cops know yet?"

"Not yet. Milton can't seem to keep his trap shut. He knows we found you and so does the media. As far as the public is concerned, this didn't happen. Tensions are high enough as it is."

She looked at her watch. "We still have eighteen minutes left in his ninety-minute window. Somehow that doesn't add up. Honestly, we were thinking library rather than warehouse."

"Library. *What wants to be filled but will always be empty?* As in empty knowledge."

"Yes."

"Hmm."

"We're getting evidence; that's what counts. We have his voice on tape; we have his presence in this building; we have more background. He's had several chances to hurt you and he hasn't. Sam told me that you spoke with him. I need to know exactly what he said."

"More background?" Kevin asked. "What background?"

An FBI agent walked toward them. "Excuse me, just wanted to let you know that the lights are back on. Fuse was pulled."

"No explosives?"

"Not that we can find. There's something here I think you should see."

She looked up at Kevin. "I'll be right back."

"Do you want me to show you what happened?"

"As soon as they're finished securing the scene. We don't want any more footprints or trace evidence than necessary. Hold tight." She hurried for the door and disappeared into the warehouse.

Kevin shoved his hands into his pockets and ran his fingers over Slater's cell phone. He was a klutz, no doubt about it. Maybe that was the sin Slater wanted him to confess. Kevin Parson is a fool and a klutz, a man incapable of entering society in any normal way because his Aunt Balinda beat his intellect against an imaginary wall for the first twenty-three years of his life. His mind is scarred beyond recognition.

He glanced back at the building, and the image of Jennifer walking for the door replayed itself. Sam was right; she liked him, didn't she?

Liked him? How could he know whether she liked him? *You see, Kevin. That's the way first-class losers think. They have no shame. They find themselves pinned down by an assassin's knife and their mind is drawn to the FBI agent they've known for all of three days.* Two days if he subtracted the day he ran off with Sam, the stunning CBI agent.

The cell phone vibrated at his fingertips and he jumped.

It went off again. Slater was calling and that was a problem, wasn't it? Why would Slater call now?

The phone rang a third time before he managed to unfold it. "H . . . hello?"

"H . . . hello? You sound like an imbecile, Kevin. I thought I said no cops."

Kevin spun to the warehouse. The agents were inside. There was a bomb in there after all, wasn't there? "Cops? We didn't call cops. I thought FBI were okay."

"Cops, Kevin. They're all pigs. Pigs in the parlor. I'm watching the news and the news says the cops know where you are. Maybe I should count to three and blow their guts to kingdom come."

"You said no *cops!*" Kevin shouted. There was a bomb in the warehouse and Jennifer was in there. He had to get her out. He ran for the door. "We didn't *use* the cops."

"Are you running, Kevin? Quick, quick get them out. But don't get too close. The bomb might go boom and they'll find your entrails on the walls with the others'."

Kevin shoved his head in the door. "Out!" he screamed. "Get out! There's a bomb!"

He ran for the street.

"You're right, there is a bomb," Slater said. "You have thirteen minutes left, Kevin. If I decide not to punish you. *What wants to be filled but will always be empty?*"

He slid to a stop. "Slater! Come out and face me, you . . ."

But Slater was gone. Kevin snapped the phone shut and whirled to the warehouse just in time to see Jennifer emerge, followed by both agents.

Jennifer saw the look on his face and stopped. "What is it?"

"Slater," he said dumbly.

"Slater called," Jennifer said. She rushed up to him. "We're wrong, aren't we? This isn't it!"

Kevin's head began to spin. He placed his hands on his temples and closed his eyes. "Think, Jennifer. Think! *What wants to be filled but will always be empty?* He knew we would come here so he waited for us, but this isn't it! What wants to be filled? What!"

"A library," the agent named Bill said.

"Did he say how much time?" Jennifer asked.

"Thirteen minutes. He said he may blow it early because the cops talked to the press."

"Milton," Jennifer said. "I swear I could wring his neck. God help us." She yanked a notepad from her hip pocket, stared at the page filled with writing, and began to pace. "36933, what else could have a number associated—"

"A reference number," Kevin blurted.

"But from which library?" Jennifer asked. "There's got to be a thousand—"

"The school of divinity," Kevin said. "Augustine Memorial. He's going to blow up the Augustine Memorial Library."

They stared at each other for a moment frozen in time. As one, the three FBI agents ran for the car. "Call Milton!" Bill said. "Evacuate the library."

"No cops," Jennifer said. "Call the school."

"What if we can't get through to the right people fast enough? We need a squad car over there."

"That's why we're going. What's the fastest way to the school?"

Kevin ran for his car across the street. "Down Willow. Follow me."

He slid behind the wheel, fired the engine, and squealed away from the curb. Eleven minutes. Could they reach the library in eleven minutes? Depended on traffic. But could they find a bomb in eleven minutes?

A horrifying thought strung through his mind. Even if they did reach the library, they would have no time to search without risking being caught inside when the bomb blew. There was this matter of seconds again. They could be forty seconds off and not know it.

A car was one thing. A bus was worse. But the library—God forbid that they were wrong. "You sick coward!"

They roared down Willow, horns blaring, ignoring the lights

completely. This was becoming a bad habit. He swerved out of the path of a blue Corvette and swung onto a smaller surface street to avoid the sea of traffic. Jennifer followed in the big black car. At each intersection the street dips pounded his suspension. He would make Anaheim Street and cut east.

Seven minutes. They were going to make it. He considered the gun in the trunk. Running into the library waving a gun would accomplish nothing but the confiscation of his hard-earned prize. He only had three bullets left. One for Slater's gut, one for his heart, and one for his head. *Pow, pow, pow. I'm gonna put a slug in your filthy heart, you lying sack of maggot meat. Two can play this game, baby. You picked the wrong kid to tick off. I bloodied your nose once; this time I'm gonna put you down. Six feet under, where the worms live. You make me sick, sick . . .*

Kevin saw the white sedan in the intersection ahead at the last possible moment. He threw his weight back into the seat and shoved the brake pedal to the floor. Tires screeching, his car slid sideways, barely missed the taillight of an ancient Chevy, and miraculously straightened. Hands white on the wheel, he punched the accelerator and sped on. Jennifer followed.

Focus! There was nothing he could do about Slater now. He had to get to the library in one piece. Interesting how bitter he'd become toward the man in the space of three days. *I'm gonna put a slug in your filthy heart, you lying sack of maggot meat?* What was that?

The moment Kevin saw the arched, glass face of Augustine Memorial Library, he knew that Jennifer's attempts to clear the place had failed. An Asian student ambled by the double doors, lost in thought. They had between three and four minutes. Maybe.

Kevin crammed the gearshift into park while the car was still rolling. The car bucked and stopped. He burst out and tore for the front doors. Jennifer was already on his heels.

"No panic, Kevin! We have time. Just get them out as quickly as possible. You hear?"

He slowed to a jog. She pulled up beside him, then took the lead.

"How many study rooms are there?" she asked.

"A few upstairs. There's a basement."

"PA system?"

"Yes."

"Okay, point the way to the office. I'll make an announcement; you clear the basement."

Kevin pointed out the office, ran for the stairs, and took them in twos. How long? Three minutes? "Get out! Everyone out!" He ran down the hall, spun into the first room. "Out! Get out now!"

"What's up, partner?" a middle-aged man asked lazily.

He couldn't think of a nonpanicky way to tell the man. "There's a bomb in the building."

The man stared for a second, then bolted to his feet.

"Clear the hall!" Kevin shouted, breaking for the next room. "Get everyone out!"

Jennifer's voice came over the PA, edgy. "This is the FBI. We have reason to suspect that there may be a bomb in the library. Evacuate the building calmly and immediately." She began to repeat the message, but yells echoed through the basement, drowning out her voice.

Feet pounded; voices cried out; panic set in. Maybe it was just as well. They didn't have enough time for order.

It took a full minute, at least, for Kevin to satisfy himself that the basement was clear. He was putting himself in danger, he realized, but this was his library, his school, his fault. He gritted his teeth, ran for the stairs, and was halfway up when he remembered the supply room. Unlikely anyone would be in there. Unless . . .

He stopped four paces from the top. Carl. The janitor liked to listen to his Discman while he worked. He liked to joke about how there was more than one way to fill the mind. Books were fine, he said, but music was the higher culture. He took his breaks in the supply room.

You're cutting it close, Kevin.

He whirled and ran back down. The supply closet was to his right, in the back. The building lay in silence now except for the urgent padding of his feet. What was it like to be caught in an explosion? And where would Slater have planted the charges?

He threw the door open. "Carl!"

The janitor stood by a stack of boxes with the words *New Books* written on pink sheets of paper.

"Carl! Thank God!"

Carl smiled at him and nodded his head to whatever music pumped into his ears. Kevin ran over to him and pulled the headphones off. "Get out of here! They've evacuated the building. Hurry, man! Hurry!"

The man's eyes widened.

Kevin grabbed his hand and shoved him toward the door. "Run! Everyone else is out."

"What is it?"

"Just run!"

Carl ran.

Two minutes. There was a second, smaller closet to his right—overflow supplies for administration, Carl had once told him. Mostly empty. Kevin leapt for the closet and pulled the door open.

How much explosive did it take to blow a building this size? Kevin was staring at the answer. Black wires protruded from five shoeboxes and met in a contraption that looked like the inside of a transistor radio. Slater's bomb.

"Jennifer!" he yelled. He twisted for the door and yelled again, at the top of his lungs. "Jennifer!"

His voice echoed back. The building was empty. Kevin ran his hands through his hair. Could he carry this thing outside? It'll blow there. That's where the people are. You have to stop it! But how? He reached for the wires, paused, and pulled back.

Pulling the wires would probably set it off, wouldn't it?

You're going to die, Kevin. Any split second it could go. He could set it off early.

"Kevin!" Jennifer's scream carried down the stairs. "Kevin, for God's sake, answer me! Get out!"

He fled the supply room in a full sprint. He'd seen the movies a hundred times—the explosion behind, the billows of fire, the diving hero rolling to freedom just out of the blast's reach.

But this wasn't a movie. This was real and this was now and this was him.

"Kevin—"

"Get out!" he yelled. "The bomb's in here!" He cleared the first four steps, and his momentum carried him to the top in two more bounds.

Jennifer was at the door, holding it open, face white. "What are you thinking?" she snapped at him. "It could go early. You'll get us both killed!"

He ran out and tore for the parking lot. Jennifer kept pace.

A huge arc of onlookers stood a hundred yards off, watching them run. "Get back!" she yelled, sprinting for them. "Farther back! Get—"

A deep, dull *whomp* cut her off. Then a louder, sharp blast and the crash of shattering glass. The ground shook.

Jennifer grabbed Kevin by the waist and pulled him down. They landed together and rolled. She threw her arms over his head. "Stay down!"

He lay smothered by her for a few long seconds. Screams rolled across the lawn. Jennifer pushed herself halfway up and looked back.

Her leg was over the backs of his legs and her hand pressed into his back for support. Kevin twisted and followed her gaze.

Half of the Divinity School of the Pacific's crown jewel lay in a heap of smoking rubble. The other half jutted to the sky, stripped of glass, naked.

"My God, my God, help us all," Jennifer said. "He blew it early, didn't he? I could kill Milton."

Still breathing hard from the run, Kevin dropped back down and buried his face in the grass.

19

THE LIBRARY EXPLOSION on the heels of the bus bomb put Long Beach at the world's center stage. All the networks played and replayed live footage of the library being blown to smithereens, courtesy of an alert student. Helicopters circled the hole that had been a building and relayed stunning images to millions of glued viewers. The world had seen this before and everyone had the same question on their minds: Terrorism?

But the explosion was the work of a madman known only as the Riddle Killer, the networks all said. Miraculously, no one had been hurt in the blast; in fact, no life had been taken by any of the three incidents. Nevertheless, they all knew it was only a matter of time. He'd killed in Sacramento; he would kill in Long Beach. Unless the authorities stopped him first. Unless his intended victim, Kevin Parson, confessed what the killer demanded he confess. Where was Kevin Parson? He'd last been seen running from the building with a woman, an FBI agent by some accounts. They had them on the student's video. Stunning footage.

The ATF had entered the fray after the first bomb; now they came in force. The state police, local police, sheriff, a half-dozen other task forces all poured over the library.

Jennifer did her best to keep Kevin beyond the reach of the media's long tentacles while making sense of the scene. She avoided Milton, for the simple reason that she didn't trust herself in his presence. He'd come within a few seconds of killing Kevin and countless others by talking to the press. If she'd been frustrated with him before, the sight of him running to and fro made her seethe now.

Still, he was an integral part of the investigation, and she couldn't avoid him once he finished his rounds with the press.

"You knew this was coming?" he demanded.

"Not now, Milton."

He took her arm and steered her away from the onlookers, squeezing with enough force to hurt her. "You were here. That means you knew. How long did you know?"

"Let go," she snapped.

He released her arm and glanced over her shoulder, smiling. "The word *negligence* mean anything to you, Agent Peters?"

"The word *carnage* mean anything to you, Detective Milton? I knew because he wanted me to know. You didn't know about the library because he said that if you were told, he'd blow the building early. In fact, he did blow it early, because you had to announce to the world that we'd found Kevin. You, sir, are lucky we got out when we did or you'd have *at least* two dead bodies on your hands. Don't ever touch me again."

"We could have put a bomb squad in there."

"Is there something with the air down here that messes with your hearing? What part of 'he told us he'd blow the building early' didn't penetrate that thick skull of yours? You almost killed us!"

"You're posing a danger to my city, and if you think I'm just going to stand by and let you, you're naive."

"And you're posing a danger to Kevin. Take it up with the bureau chief."

His eyes narrowed for a brief second, then he smiled again. "We're not through with this."

"Sure we are." She walked away. If not for the fact that half the world was watching, she might have taken the man's tie and shoved it down his throat. It took her thirty seconds to put the man out of her mind. She had more important things to dwell on than an overzealous fool. So she told herself, but in reality Milton sat in her gut like a sour pill.

Two questions soon reoccupied her mind. First, had anybody seen a stranger enter the library in the past twenty-four hours? And second, had anybody seen *Kevin* enter the library in the last twenty-four hours? Samantha had raised the question of Kevin's involvement, and although Jennifer knew the idea was ridiculous, the question raised others. Samantha's theory that someone on the inside might be somehow tied to Slater bothered her.

The Riddle Killer was remarkably elusive. The last three days were no exception. Sam was in Texas, flushing out something that had her hopes high. No doubt she'd come waltzing in tomorrow with a new theory that would set them back to square one. Actually, the CBI agent was beginning to grow on her, but jurisdiction had a way of straining the best relationships.

As it turned out, no one had seen a stranger around the library. And no one had seen Kevin. The front desk receptionist would have remembered Kevin—he was an avid reader. Short of bypassing the security system, of which there was no evidence, the likelihood of anyone entering the library unseen was small. Carl had been in the closet yesterday morning and there'd been no bomb, which meant Slater had found a way in since then, either at night or under their noses, unrecognized. How?

An hour after the explosion, Jennifer sat across from Kevin in a small Chinese restaurant and tried to distract him with small talk while they ate. But neither of them was good at small talk.

They went back to the warehouse at nine, this time armed with high-powered halogens that lit up the interior like a football field. Kevin walked through the scene with her. But now it was nearing midnight, and he was half-asleep on his feet. Unlike the library, the warehouse was still silent. No police, no ATF, only FBI.

She hadn't bothered to tell Milton about the incident at the warehouse. She would as soon as she was done with it. She'd explained the situation to Frank, and he'd finally agreed to her reasoning, but he wasn't happy with it. He was getting an earful from a dozen different sources. The governor wanted this tied up now. Washington was starting to apply pressure too. They were running out of time. If another bomb went off, they might take the case from her.

Jennifer glanced at Kevin, who leaned his head back against the wall in the reception area, eyes closed. She entered a ten-by-ten office storage room where they were compiling evidence for delivery to the lab. Under other circumstances, she would probably be doing this back at her desk, but Milton would be breathing down her neck. Besides, proximity favored the storage room, so Galager had transferred what he needed from the van and set up temporary shop here.

"Any conclusions, Bill?"

Galager leaned over a drawing of the warehouse floor plan, on which he'd painstakingly redrawn the footprints as they appeared.

"Best as I can tell, Slater entered and left through the fire escape. We have a single set of footprints coming and going, which correlates with the testimony. He walks up and down the hall a half-dozen times, waiting for Kevin to show, descends the stairs at least twice, springs his trap, and ends up in this room here." He tapped the room next to Kevin's hiding place.

"How did he lock the door? He shut it with the string, but Sam told me it was open when they first arrived."

"We can only assume that he had the lock rigged somehow. It's feasible that with a hard knock the lock could engage."

"Seems thin," Jennifer said. "So we have him entering and leaving through the fire escape. Kevin enters and leaves through the front door. What about the footprints themselves?"

"When all is said and done, there are only four clear prints, all of which we've casted and photographed. Problem is, they're all from the hallway and the stairs where both Kevin and Slater walked. Same size. Same basic shape. Both hard-soled and similar to what Kevin is wearing—impossible to visually determine which is which. The lab will break it down."

Jennifer considered his report. Sam hadn't entered the building, which was good thinking. But she hadn't seen Slater come or go either.

"What about the recording?" Galager had already transferred the data to a tape, which he had in a small recorder on the table.

"Again, the lab will have to tell us what they can come up with, but it sounds clean to me. This is the first recording from the hotel room." He punched the play button. Two voices filled the speaker. Slater and Samantha.

"There, that's better, don't you think? The game won't last forever; we might as well make this more interesting."

Low and gravelly. Breathy. Slater.

"What good is a game that you can't lose? It proves nothing."

She recognized Sam's voice. The tape played to the end of the conversation and clicked off.

"Here's the second recording, made while we were here earlier this evening." Galager punched it up. This time it was Kevin and Slater.

Kevin: *"H . . . hello?"*

Slater: *"H . . . hello? You sound like an imbecile, Kevin. I thought I said no cops."*

The recordings were clear and clean. Jennifer nodded. "Get them to the lab with the footprints immediately. Any word yet on the dagger tattoo or the blood work from the warehouse?"

"Blood's too old for anything but type. They're having trouble even with that, though. Twenty years is a long time."

"So it is twenty years old?"

"Best estimate, seventeen to twenty. Follows his confession."

"And the type?"

"They're having a hard time typing it. On the other hand, we do have something with the tattoo. A parlor in Houston says they have a large man with blond hair who comes in on occasion. Same tattoo as the one Kevin drew us. Says he's never seen a tattoo like it except on this man." Galager grinned deliberately. "The report came in about an hour ago. No current address, but the parlor says the man was in last Tuesday around ten o'clock."

"In Houston?" That's where Sam had gone. "Slater was in Houston last week? Doesn't sound right."

"Houston?" Kevin asked behind her. They turned to see him standing in the door. He walked in. "You have a lead in Houston?"

"The tattoo—"

"Yeah, I heard. But . . . how could Slater be in Houston?"

"Three-hour flight or a very long day's drive," Galager said. "Possible he's going back and forth."

Kevin's brow furrowed. "He has a dagger tattoo? What if this guy turns out to be the boy, but not Slater or the Riddle Killer? You pick him up and now he knows about me, where I live. All I need is another wacko after me."

"Unless this guy lives in a cave," Galager said, "he's heard the confession and seen your face on television. There's a chance he *is* Slater. And there's an even better chance that Slater is the boy. We have a man threatening you who all but admits that he's the boy; a boy who has reason to threaten you, identified with a very unique tattoo. And now we have a man with the same tattoo. Circumstantial, I realize, but it sounds pretty plausible to me. We make busts on less."

"But can you put someone behind bars with that?"

"Not a chance. That's where the physical and forensic evidence comes in. As soon as we have a suspect in custody, we measure him up against the evidence we've gathered, which is substantial. We have Slater's voice on tape. We have his shoe print. We have several bombs, all of which were made somewhere. We have six bugs—all this in three days. A virtual windfall in cases like this. I'd say Slater's getting sloppy."

And more so today than yesterday. "He's at least pushing the pace," Jennifer said. "Getting caught doesn't seem to concern him. Which isn't good."

"Why?" Kevin asked.

She looked at his haggard face. A blade of grass from the library lawn was still stuck in his shaggy hair. His blue eyes looked more desperate than enchanting now. He didn't tap his foot or rake his hair as frequently. The man needed rest. "Based on his profile, my guess is that he's closing in on his objective."

"Which is what?"

Jennifer glanced at Galager. "Good work, Bill. Why don't you wrap it up and call the locals?" She took Kevin's arm and led him out. "Let's take a walk."

Two of the streetlights nearest the warehouse were either shut down on energy conservation timers or burned out. A cool ocean breeze drifted over Long Beach. She'd shed her jacket and wore a sleeveless gold blouse with a black skirt—it was actually a bit chilly at this hour.

She crossed her arms. "You okay?"

"Tired."

"Nothing like fresh air to clear the mind. This way." She led him toward the fire escape in the back.

"So, what is Slater's objective?" Kevin asked again, shoving his hands in his jeans pockets.

"Well, that's a problem. I've been giving it a lot of thought. On the surface it seems simple enough: He wants to terrorize you. Men like Slater do what they do for a variety of reasons, usually to gratify some twisted need they've grown into over many years, but almost without exception they prey on the weak. Their focus is on their own need, not on the victim."

"Makes sense. And Slater's different?"

"I think so. His objective doesn't seem to be himself as much as you. I mean you specifically."

"I'm not sure I understand."

"Take your typical serial offender. Say a pyromaniac bent on burning down houses. He doesn't care whose house it is as long as it fits his needs. He needs to see the flame engulfing this structure—it excites him and gives him a feeling of power beyond his reach in any other way. The house is important—it has to be a certain size, maybe a certain build, maybe a symbol of wealth. In the same way a sex offender might prey on women he considers appealing. But his focus is on himself, not the victim. The victim is almost incidental."

"And you're saying that Slater hasn't chosen me for what I can do for him, but for what he can do to me. Like he did with your brother."

"Maybe. But this is playing out differently than Roy's murder. The Riddle Killer filled his thirst for bloodshed by killing Roy and killing him quickly. Slater is playing with you, over three days now. I'm beginning to question our initial assumption that Slater and the Riddle Killer are the same person." The Riddle Killer didn't seem to know his victims, other than Roy, whom he'd selected for her benefit. She rubbed her arms against the cold.

"Unless all that was just a cover-up for what he's doing now. Unless extracting revenge for what I did to him was the game all along."

"That's the obvious assumption. I'm not sure anymore. Revenge would be a simple matter. Assuming Slater is the boy you locked up, he could have found a hundred opportunities over the years to extract his revenge. His most obvious course would have been to hurt or kill you. I don't think Slater's interested in killing you. Not anytime soon, anyway. I think he wants to change you. He wants to force your hand somehow. I don't think the game's the device; I think the game's the objective."

"But that's crazy!" Kevin stopped and put both hands into his hair. "What is there about me? Who? Who would want to . . . to force my hand?"

"I know it doesn't all fit yet, but the sooner we narrow down Slater's true motivation, the higher our chances of getting you out of this mess."

They were at the back, by the fire escape. A ladder reached up to the second floor and curved into a window. Jennifer sighed and leaned against the tin siding.

"Bottom line is that if I'm right, then the only way to understand Slater's true motivation is to understand you, Kevin. I've got to know more about you." He was pacing, staring at the concrete, hands still in his hair.

"I want to know about the house," she said.

"There's nothing to know about the house," he said.

"Why don't you let me judge that?"

"I can't talk about the house!"

"I know you don't think you can, but it may provide our best clues now. I know it's hard—"

"I don't think you have a clue about how hard it is! You didn't grow up there!" He paced and smoothed his hair frantically, and then flung his arms wide. "You think any of this means anything? You think this is reality? A bunch of ants running around the globe, hiding their secrets in their deep dark tunnels? We *all* have our secrets. Who's to say that mine have anything to do with anything? Why don't the rest of the ants have to crawl out of their tunnels and broadcast their sins to the world?"

Kevin was baring himself, and Jennifer needed him to do just that. Not because she would ever exploit him, but because she needed to understand his secrets if she hoped to help him.

And she did hope to help him. More now than a day ago, even if Slater wasn't her brother's killer after all.

"You're right," she said. "We're all fallen, as my priest used to say. I'm not interested in your sin. I wasn't even in favor of the initial confession, remember? I'm interested in you, Kevin."

"And who am I?" He was desperate. "Huh? Answer me that. Who am I? Who are you? Who is anybody? We are what we do! We are our secrets. I *am* my sin! You want to know me, then you have to know my sin. Is that what you want? Every little dirty secret out on the table so that you can dissect it all and know Kevin, the poor tormented soul?"

"That's not what I said."

"You might as well have, because it's true! Why is it fair that I should spill my guts when the pastor next-door has as many nasty secrets as I do? Huh? If we want to know him, we have to know his secrets, is that it?"

"Stop it!" Her anger surprised her. "You're *not* your sin! Who ever told you that lie? Aunt Balinda? I've seen you, Kevin. You asked me what my profile for you was. Well, let me be more specific. You are one of the kindest, gentlest, most interesting, appealing men I know. That's who you are. And don't insult my intelligence or my feminine discernment by dismissing my opinion." She took a breath and a guess. "I don't know what Slater's up to, or why, but I guarantee you're doing exactly what he wants you to do when you start to believe that you're trapped. You've come out of that. Don't go back."

She knew by his blink that she was right. Slater was trying to pull him back to the past, and the thought so terrified him that he was breaking down. Which was exactly how Slater would accomplish his objective. He would trap Kevin in his past.

Kevin stared at her, stunned. It occurred to her then, looking back into his wide eyes, that she didn't merely like Kevin, she cared for him deeply. She had no business caring for him; she didn't even *want* to care for him, not in that way. Her empathy had risen to the surface, unbidden. She'd always been a sucker for the downtrodden. She had always had a soft spot for men who were hurting in some way. Now her soft spot had found Kevin.

But this didn't feel like a soft spot. She actually found him appealing, with his ragged hair and his charming smile. And those eyes. That wasn't empathy, was it?

She closed her eyes and swallowed. *God forbid, Jennifer. And when was the last time you dated a man, anyway? Two years ago? That hillbilly from Arkansas who came from good stock, so says Mom?* She'd never known the full meaning of boring until then. She would prefer a man with a goatee who rode a Harley and winked frequently.

Jennifer opened her eyes. Kevin was seated on the concrete, cross-legged, head in his hands. The man never ceased to surprise her.

"I'm sorry, I'm not sure where all that came from," she said.

He lifted his head, closed his eyes, and took a deep breath. "Please, don't be sorry. That was the nicest thing I've heard in a long time." His eyes fluttered open, as if he'd just heard himself. "Maybe *nicest* is the wrong word choice. It was . . . I think you're right. He's trying to pull me back, isn't he? That's his objective. So who is he? Balinda?"

Jennifer sat down beside him and folded her legs to the side. Her skirt wasn't exactly dress of choice for concrete sitting, but she didn't care.

"I need to tell you something, Kevin. But I don't want it to upset you."

He stared ahead and then turned to her. "You went to the house, didn't you?"

"Yes. This morning. It took a few threats to convince Balinda to let me in, but I saw the place and I met Eugene and Bob."

Kevin lowered his head again.

"I know it's hard, but I need to know what happened in that house, Kevin. For all we know, Slater could be someone Balinda hired. That would fit the profile. She wants to change you. But without knowing the whole story, I'm floundering here."

"You're asking me to tell you something no one knows. Not because it's so horrible—I know I'm not the only one who's had a few challenges along the way. But it's dead and buried. You want me to bring it back to life? Isn't that what Slater's trying to do?"

"I'm not Slater. And frankly, it doesn't sound dead and buried to me."

"And you really think this whole game has to do with my past?"

She nodded. "I'm assuming that Slater has an objective that is tied to your past, yes."

Kevin remained quiet. The silence stretched, and Jennifer sat beside him feeling his tension, hearing his breathing. She wondered if it would be appropriate to put a hand on his arm but immediately decided it wouldn't.

He suddenly groaned and rocked. "I don't think I can do this."

"You can't slay the dragon without luring it out of its hole. I want to help you, Kevin. I need to know."

For a long time he just sat there rocking. Then he stilled and his breathing slowed. Maybe it was too much too fast. He'd faced more than most could stomach these last three days and she was pushing him even further. He needed sleep. But she was running out of time. Slater was escalating.

She was about to suggest that they get some rest and consider it in the morning when he turned his face to the night sky.

"I don't think Balinda's intentions were necessarily evil." He spoke in a soft monotone. "She wanted a good playmate for Bob. He was eight when they adopted me; I was one. But Bob was retarded. I wasn't, and Balinda couldn't accept that reality."

He paused and took several deep breaths. Jennifer shifted and leaned on her arm so that she could watch his face. His eyes were closed.

"Tell me about Balinda."

"I don't know her story, but Balinda creates her own reality. We all do, but Balinda only knows absolutes. She decides what part of the world is real and what part isn't. If something isn't real, she makes it go away. She manipulates everything around her to create an acceptable reality."

He stopped. Jennifer waited a full thirty seconds before prodding him. "Tell me what it was like to be her son."

"I don't know it yet, because I'm too young, but my mom doesn't want me to be smarter than my brother. So she decides to make me retarded too because she's already tried to make Bob smarter but she can't."

Another stall. He was switching tenses, dipping into the past. Jennifer felt her stomach turn.

"How does she do that? Does she hurt you?"

"No. Hurting is evil in Balinda's world. She won't let me out of the house because the world outside isn't real. The only real world is the one she makes inside the house. She is the princess. She needs me to read so that she can shape my mind with what she makes me read, but she cuts up stories and makes me read only things she decides are real. I'm nine years old before I know there are animals called cats because Princess thinks cats are evil. I don't even know there is evil until I'm eleven. There's only real and unreal. Everything real is good and everything good comes from Princess. I don't do anything bad; I only do things that aren't real. She makes the things that aren't real go away by starving me of them. She never punishes me; she only helps me."

"When you do something that's not real, how does she punish you?"

He hesitated. "She locks me in my room to learn about the real world or makes me sleep so I'll forget the unreal world. She takes away food and water. That's how animals learn, she says, and we are the best animals. I can remember the first time because it made me confused. I was four. My brother and I are playing servant, folding dishtowels for Princess. We have to fold them over and over until they're perfect. Sometimes it takes all day. We don't have toys because toys aren't real. Bob asks me what one plus one is because he wants to give me two towels, but he doesn't know what to call it. I tell him that I think one plus one is two and Princess overhears me. She locks me in my room for two days. Two towels, two days. If Bob doesn't know how to add, then I can't either, because it isn't real. She wants me to be dumb like Bob."

An image of Balinda seated under a stack of clipped newspapers filled Jennifer's mind and she shivered.

Kevin sighed and changed tenses again. "She never held me. She hardly even touched me unless it was by mistake. Sometimes I went without food for days. Once a whole week. Sometimes we couldn't wear clothes if we did unreal things. She deprived us both of anything she thought might feed our minds. Mostly me, because Bob was retarded and he didn't do as many things that weren't real. No school. No games. Sometimes no talking for days. Sometimes she made me stay in bed all day. Other times she made me sit in the bathtub in cold water so I couldn't sleep all night. I could never ask her why, because that wasn't real. Princess was real, and if she decided to do something, anything else was unreal and couldn't be talked about. So we couldn't ask questions. Even questions about real things, because that would question their reality, which was unreal."

Jennifer filled in the blanks. The abuse wasn't primarily physical, not necessarily even emotional, although there was some of both of those. It was primarily psychological. She watched Kevin's chest rise and fall. She desperately wanted to reach out to him. She could see the boy, sitting alone in a bathtub of cold water, shivering in the dark, wondering how to make sense of his horrible world that he'd been brainwashed to think was good.

She fought back tears. *Kevin, dear Kevin, I'm so sorry!* She reached out her hand and put it on his arm. Who could do such terrible things to a little boy? There was more, details, stories that could undoubtedly fill a book to be studied by universities across the country. But she didn't want to hear more. If she could only make it all go away. She might be able to stop Slater, but Kevin would live with this past until the day he died.

A brief absurd image of her lying down beside him and holding him gently in her arms ran through her mind.

Kevin suddenly groaned and then chuckled. "She's a twisted, demented lunatic."

Jennifer cleared her throat. "Agreed."

"But you know what?"

"What?"

"Telling you about it makes me feel . . . good. I've never told any-one."

"Not even Samantha?"

"No."

"Sometimes talking about abuse helps us deal with it. Our tendency is to hide it, and that's understandable. I'm glad you're telling me. None of it was your fault, Kevin. It's not your sin."

He pushed himself up. His eyes were clearer. "You're right. That old goat did everything in her power to hold me back."

"When did you first realize that Balinda's world wasn't the only one?"

"When I met Samantha. She came to my window one night and helped me sneak out. But I was trapped, you know. I mean mentally. For a long time I couldn't accept that Balinda was anything but a loving princess. When Samantha left to study law, she begged me to go with her. Or at least somewhere away from Balinda, but I couldn't leave. I was twenty-three before I finally worked up the courage to leave. Balinda went ballistic."

"And you've done all this in five years?"

He nodded and grinned softly. "Turns out that I was fairly intelligent. It only took me a year to get my general education papers, and four years to graduate from college."

It occurred to Jennifer that she was treating him like a patient with these short, probing questions, but he seemed to want it now.

"Which is when you decided to become a minister," she said.

"That's a long story. I suppose because of my strange rearing the subject of good and evil held unusual fascination for me. Naturally I gravitated toward the church. Morality became somewhat of an obsession, I guess. I figured the least I could do was spend my life showing some small corner of the real world the way to true goodness."

"As opposed to what?"

"As opposed to the false reality we all create for ourselves. Mine was extreme, but it didn't take me long to see that most people live in their own worlds of delusion. Not so different from Balinda's, really."

"Observant." She smiled. "Sometimes I wonder what my delusions are. Is your faith personal?"

He shrugged. "I'm not sure. The church is a system, a vehicle for me. I wouldn't say that I know God personally, no. But my faith in a God is real enough. Without an absolute, moral God, there can be no true morality. It's the most obvious argument for the existence of God."

"I grew up Catholic," she said. "Went through all the forms, never did quite understand it all."

"Well, don't tell Father Bill Strong, but I can't say I do either."

Sitting next to him now, just a few minutes since his confession, Jennifer had difficulty placing Kevin in the context of his youth. He seemed so normal.

He shook his head. "This is incredible. I still can't believe I just told you all that."

"You just needed the right person," she said.

The sound of feet running on the pavement sounded behind them. Jennifer twisted around. It was Galager.

"Jennifer!"

She stood and brushed her skirt.

"We have another riddle!" Galager said. He held a sheet of notebook paper in his hand. "Mickales just found this on the windshield of Kevin's car. It's Slater."

"My car?" Kevin jumped to his feet.

Jennifer took the note. Yellow pad. The scrawling was black, familiar. The milk jug from Kevin's refrigerator. She read the note quickly.

$3+3 = 6$.

    Four down, two to go. You know how I like threes, Kevin. Time's running out. Shame, shame, shame. A simple confession would do, but you force my hand.

    Who escapes their prison but is captive still?

    I'll give you a hint: It isn't you.

    6 A.M.

Kevin gripped his hair and turned away.

"Okay," Jennifer said, turning for the street. "Let's get moving."

20

SAMANTHA WAS TIRED. The Pakistani had insisted they meet at a Mexican restaurant five miles out of town. The light was too low, the music was too loud, and the place smelled of stale cigarettes. She stared the witness directly in the eye. Chris had sworn that Salman would cooperate and he had. But what he had to say wasn't exactly what Sam wanted to hear.

"How do you know it was a dagger if you never saw it?"

"He told me it was. I have the tattoo on my back, and he said he had one like it on his forehead."

"Did you see any scarring or discoloration that might indicate he had the tattoo removed?"

"Perhaps. He wore his hair over his forehead. Didn't matter—he said he had it removed and I believed him."

They'd been over all of this at least once; he'd already described the tattooed man with remarkable detail. Salman was a tailor. Tailors notice these things, he said.

"And this was while you were in New York, four months ago. And you saw him five or six times at a bar named Cougars over the course of about a month?"

"That is what I have said. Yes. You may check with the bar owner; he may remember the man as well."

"So according to you, this man who had a dagger tattoo and who called himself Slater was in New York while the Riddle Killer was killing victims in Sacramento."

"Yes, definitely. I remember watching the news while I was in New York the very night after I had talked to Slater."

Salman had spilled enough details in the previous hour to make his testimony credible. Sam had been in New York four months ago. She knew the pub Salman referred to, a low-class joint frequented by your typical mix of unsavory characters. A CIA task force had set up a sting at the joint to flush out an Iranian whom they suspected had ties to a bombing in Egypt. The man had exonerated himself.

"Okay." She turned to Steve Jules, the agent who'd accompanied her from the Houston office. "I'm done. Thank you for your time, Mr. Salman. It was invaluable."

"Perhaps I could make you a suit," he said with a grin. "I have a new shop here. There aren't so many tailors in Houston as in New York."

She smiled. "Maybe next time I'm in Houston to escape the heat."

They left the bar in Steve's car. This wasn't what she'd wanted to hear. In fact, it was downright dreadful. What if she was right about the rest of it? *Dear God, dear God.*

She wanted only one thing now: to be with Kevin. Kevin needed her more now than ever. The despondent look on his face as she sped off to the airport haunted her.

Her childhood friend had grown into quite an incredible man, hadn't he? Tormented by his past, perhaps, but he'd escaped that hellhole he called a home and flourished. Part of her wanted nothing more than to run back to him and throw herself in his arms and beg him to marry her. Sure he had his demons; everyone did. Yes, he had a long struggle ahead of him; didn't they all? But he was the most genuine man she'd ever known. His eyes shone with the excitement and wonder of a child, and his mind had absorbed the world with stunning capacity. His progress was nearly superhuman.

On the other hand, she could never marry Kevin. Their relationship was too valuable to compromise with romance. He saw that too, otherwise he never would have allowed room for any attraction to Jennifer. Their occasional romantic innuendo was simply teasing. They both knew that.

She sighed.

"Tough interview," Steve said beside her.

She picked up her cell phone and punched in her boss's number. It would be late, but she had to get this to him. "I thought it went pretty smoothly," she said.

Roland picked up the phone on the fourth ring. "It's midnight."

"He was two hours late," Sam said.

"And?"

"And he knew Slater."

"Our guy?"

"Very possible. Tattoo like that is extremely unusual. But he claims to have known Slater in New York."

"So."

"So it was four months ago. Over a period of about a month. The Riddle Killer was in Sacramento then, killing Roy Peters."

"So Slater's not the Riddle Killer."

"That's right."

"Copy cat?"

"Could be."

"And if Slater is the boy, he's no longer walking around with a dagger tattoo on his forehead because he had it removed."

"So it seems."

Roland covered the phone and spoke to someone—probably his wife unless he was in a late meeting, which was entirely possible.

"I want you back in Sacramento tomorrow," he said. "If Slater isn't the Riddle Killer, he's not your concern."

"I know, sir. I have three days left on my leave, remember?"

"We called you back in, remember?"

"Because we believed that Slater was the Riddle Killer. If he's not, the trail's cold."

Roland considered her argument. He wasn't the most reasonable man when it came to time off. He put in eighty hours a week and expected his subordinates to do the same.

"Please, sir, I go way back with Kevin. He's practically family to me. I swear, three more days and I'll be back in the office. You have to let me do this. And there's still the chance that I'm wrong about Salman's testimony."

"Yes, there is."

"It's still possible that Slater knows the Riddle Killer."

"Possible."

"Then give me more time."

"You heard about the library?"

"The whole world heard about the library."

He sighed. "Three days. I expect to see you at your desk Thursday morning. And please, tread lightly down there. This is unofficial. From what I've heard the whole scene is one big snake pit. Every agency in the country has a stake in this."

"Thank you, sir."

Roland hung up.

Sam considered calling Jennifer but decided it could wait until morning. She could tell her only that Slater wasn't the Riddle Killer. She needed to satisfy herself as to the rest before she said anything that might do Kevin more harm than good.

She'd already checked on flights back. No red eyes, one at 6 A.M. and one at 9 A.M. She needed sleep. The nine o'clock United flight would have to do. It would take her through the Denver hub and put her in Long Beach at noon.

|||

"Okay . . ." Kevin watched Jennifer pace the warehouse floor. They'd delayed plans to share details of the warehouse with the police and instead decided to use the place as a staging area. It was the only way to keep Milton off her back, Jennifer said.

"Let's review what we *do* know."

Agents Bill Galager and Brett Mickales straddled chairs by the table, chins in their hands, focused on Jennifer. Kevin leaned against the wall, arms crossed. It was hopeless. They were beat; they were clueless; they were dead. They'd rehashed a hundred ideas in the two hours since Slater's note had been discovered.

"We know that he's escalating. Car, bus, building. We know that all of his other threats made reference to damage of some kind. This one did not. We know that we have until 6 A.M. to solve or . . . or what we don't know. And we know the riddle. *Who escapes their prison but is captive still?*"

Jennifer spread her hands.

"You're forgetting the most crucial bit of knowledge," Kevin said.

"Which is?"

"The fact that we're toast."

They stared at him as if he'd just walked in and flashed his pecs. A wry grin crossed Jennifer's face. "Humor's good."

"People," Mickales said. "He's gonna do people this time."

"There were people every time."

"But he went after a car, a bus, and a building. This time he goes straight after people."

"Kidnapping," Kevin said.

"We've suggested that. It's a possibility."

"If you ask me, it's the best one," Mickales said. He stood up. "It fits."

Jennifer crossed to the table, eyes suddenly wide. "Okay, unless anybody has a better idea, we'll chase that."

"Why would Slater kidnap anyone?" Kevin asked.

"For the same reason he threatened to blow up a bus," Mickales said. "To force a confession."

Kevin stared at the man, suddenly overwhelmed. They'd been at it ad nauseam and they kept coming up with the same thing, which was essentially nothing. In the end it always came back to his confession.

"Look." He could feel the heat rising up his spine. He shouldn't be doing this—he was beyond himself. "If I had the slightest clue as to what this wacko wanted me to confess, you think I would hold out?"

"Easy, man. Nobody's suggesting—"

"I don't have the foggiest notion what his crazy confession is! He's nuts!" Kevin stepped toward them, aware that he'd crossed a line already. "They're out there screaming bloody murder for Kevin's confession. Well, I gave them one, didn't I? I told them I killed someone as a kid. But they want more. They want real blood. They want me to bleed all over their gossip columns! Kevin, the kid killer who brought down Long Beach!"

His fingers were trembling. They looked at him in silence.

He ran his fingers through his hair. "Man . . ."

"Nobody's screaming bloody murder out there," Jennifer said.

"I'm sorry. I'm just . . . I don't know what to do. This isn't all my fault."

"You need rest, Kevin," Jennifer said. "But if Slater's planning to kidnap someone, you may be a target. I know he said it wasn't you, but I'm not sure what that means." She turned to Galager. "Keep the watch on the house, but I want a transponder on him. Kevin, we're going to give you a small transmitting device. I want you to tape it where it won't be found. We'll leave it inactive—this guy's into electronics; he may scan for signals. Anything happens, you turn it on. The range is roughly fifty miles. Fair enough?"

He nodded.

She walked toward him. "Let's get you home."

Galager headed for the van, which was still parked on the street. Kevin walked outside with Jennifer. The weight of two days without sleep descended on him. He could hardly walk straight, much less think straight.

"I'm sorry. I didn't mean to blow up."

"No apology needed. Just get some sleep."

"What are you going to do?"

She looked off to the east. The helicopters were down for the night. "He said no cops. We could put a guard on likely targets, but for all we know, he's planning on kidnapping the mayor. Or it could be another bomb." She shook her head. "You're right, we're pretty much toast."

They stopped at the car. "It meant a lot," he said. "Talking to you tonight. Thank you."

She smiled, but her eyes were tired. How much sleep had she gotten in the last three days? He suddenly felt terrible for her. Flushing out Slater was more than a job for her.

"Go home and get some sleep," she said, squeezing his arm. "Galager will follow you home. We have someone outside. If Slater makes contact—if *anything* happens—call me."

Kevin looked up to see Galager pull up in the black car. "Somehow I doubt it'll be me. That's not what he wants. I'll be fine. The question is, who won't be?"

What if it was Jennifer? Sam was in Houston.

"What about you?" he asked.

"Why would he want to kidnap me?"

Kevin shrugged. "It's not like I have a lot of friends."

"I guess that makes me a friend. Don't worry, I can handle myself."

By the time Kevin finished with Galager's little lecture on the operational procedures for the transmitter and climbed into bed, the three o'clock hour had come and gone. His head was numb before it hit the pillow. He fell into an exhausted sleep within the minute, lost to the horrors of his new life.

For an hour or three.

III

Slater stands by the fence, stock-still in the darkness. He's given them until six, but this time he will be done before six, before the first light grays the sky. He said six because he likes threes, and six is three plus three, but he can't risk doing this in the light.

No one has stirred in the house since his arrival thirty minutes ago. When he first conceived the plan, he considered just blowing up the house with all its occupants trapped inside. But after thinking very carefully about his ultimate objective, because that's what Slater does the best, he settled on this plan. Putting this woman in a cage will send the city through the roof. It's one thing to wonder which unnamed citizens might be the next to discover a bomb under their bed; it's far more disturbing to know that Mrs. Sally Jane who lives on Stars and Stripes Street and buys her groceries at Albertsons is locked up in a cage, waiting desperately for Kevin Parson to fess up.

Besides, Slater's never kidnapped anyone before. The thought brings a chill to his spine. The sensation of pleasure so intense that it runs up and down the spine is interesting. It is not boring like teenagers poking holes in their noses.

Slater looks at his watch. 4:46. Is 4:46 divisible by three? No, but 4:47 is. And that's one minute away. Perfect. Perfect, perfect, perfect. The pleasure of his brilliance is so intense that Slater now begins to shiver a little. He stands by the fence with perfect discipline, resisting a desperate urge to run for the house and drag her out of bed. He is perfectly disciplined and he is shivering. Interesting.

He's waited so long. Eighteen years. Six times three. Three plus three times three.

The two minutes crawl by very slowly, but Slater doesn't mind. He is born for this. He glances at his watch. 4:47. He can't stand it any longer. It's one minute early. Three is divisible by one. Close enough.

Slater walks up to the sliding glass door, pulls out the pick with a gloved hand, and disengages the lock in less than ten seconds. His breathing comes thick, and he pauses to still it. If the others wake, he will have to kill them, and he doesn't want to mess with that. He wants the woman.

He eases into the kitchen and leaves the door open. They have no dogs or cats. One child. The husband is Slater's only concern. He stands on the tile floor for a full minute, adjusting his eyes to the deeper darkness, breathing in the home's smells. The senses are the key to living life to its fullest. Tastes, sights, smells, feelings, sounds. Eat what you like, watch what you can, touch who you want. That's what he wants Kevin to do. To taste and touch and smell his true self. It will destroy him. The plan is perfect. Perfect, perfect, perfect.

Slater takes one deep breath, but very slowly.

He walks through the living room and puts his hand on the door-knob to the master bedroom. It opens without a sound. Perfect. The room is dark. Pitch-black. Perfect.

He walks slowly to the bed and stands over the woman. Her breathing is quicker than the man's. She faces him, mouth slightly parted, hair tangled on the pillow. He reaches out a hand and touches the sheet. Soft and smooth. Two hundred thread count at least. He could stand here over them for an hour and breathe in their smells without being seen. But the light is coming. He doesn't like the light.

Slater reaches into his shirt pocket and withdraws a note, which he sets on the dresser. For Kevin. He slips his hand into his coat and takes out a roll of gauze and a bottle of chloroform. He unscrews the bottle and dips the roll into the liquid. The smell fills his nostrils and he holds his breath. It has to be strong enough to put her under without a struggle.

He replaces the lid on the bottle, drops it into his pocket, and eases the roll of soaked gauze in front of the woman's nose, careful not to touch it. For a moment she doesn't stir, then she whimpers in her dreams. But she doesn't move. He waits twenty seconds, until her breathing slows enough to persuade him that she's unconscious. He shoves the roll into his jacket.

Slater settles to his knees, as if bowing before his victim. A sacrifice for the gods. He lifts the sheet and slips his hands under the body until his elbows are directly under her. She lies limp, like a noodle. He gently pulls her toward his chest. She slides off the bed and sags in his arms. The husband rolls half a turn and then settles. Perfect.

Slater stands and carries her out of the house without bothering to shut the doors. The clock in his car reads 4:57 when he settles behind the wheel with the woman breathing slowly in the backseat.

Slater starts the car and drives away. He could have carried her to the hiding on foot and returned later for the car, but he doesn't want to leave the vehicle in front of the house any longer than absolutely necessary. He's too smart for that. It occurs to him that this will be the first time he's ever brought a guest to the hiding. When she awakes, her eyes will be the first besides his own to see his world. The thought brings a moment of panic.

So then, all the more reason not to let her out. It's what will happen anyway, isn't it? Even if Kevin confesses, Slater has always known that she will have to die. His exposure to another human being will be temporary. He can live with that. Still, why hasn't this detail

occurred to him earlier? It isn't a mistake, just an oversight. But oversight can lead to mistakes. He chides himself and turns down the dark
street.

Slater doesn't bother with stealth now. The woman is stirring, so
he gives her another healthy dose of chloroform, yanks the body out
of the rear seat, and heaves it over his shoulder. He hurries for the
door, opens it with a key, and enters the small room. Close door, feel
for chain, pull on overhead light.

A dim light exposes the space. Down a flight of steps. Another
chain, another light. Through the tunnel. Open the second door with
a second key. The hiding. Home, sweet home.

The thought of sharing his home with another person for a little
while suddenly doesn't seem so bad. In fact, it holds its own excitement. Everything he needs is here. Food, water, a bathroom, a bed,
clothing, the electronics—of course, she won't be sharing any of those
amenities.

The woman is stirring again.

He crosses to the room he's prepared. The walk-in closet once
stored materials he's used in his games, but he's cleared it for her. Can't
take the chance that she knows how to set off dynamite now, can he?
The room is seven by seven and solid concrete all around except the
ceiling, which is heavily insulated wood. The door is steel.

He places her onto the cement floor and steps back. She groans
and rolls to one side. Good enough.

He closes the door, locks it with a deadbolt, and stuffs a rolled-up
rug into the crack at the bottom. Lights out.

21

KEVIN HEARD THE RINGING long before he awoke. It sounded like a high-pitched laugh. Or an intermittent scream. Then there was the pounding, a thumping that could be his heart. But it sounded more like banging on the door.

"Sir?" Someone was yelling, calling him sir.

Kevin's eyes somehow managed to open. Light shone through the window. Where was he? Home. His mind started to drift. He would have to get up eventually and go to class, but at the moment he felt as though he'd met the wrong end of a rhino charge. He closed his eyes.

The muffled voice came again. "Kevin? The phone . . ."

His eyes snapped open. Slater. His life had been turned upside down by a man called Slater who called on the phone. The phone was ringing.

He spilled out of bed. The clock said 7:13. Slater had given them until 6 A.M. He ran to the bedroom door, twisted the lock, and yanked it open. One of the agents watching his house stood there, the cordless phone from the kitchen in hand.

"I'm sorry to wake you, but your phone's been ringing on and off for fifteen minutes. It's a pay phone. Jennifer told us to wake you."

Kevin stood in his pinstriped boxer shorts. "Has . . . has anything happened?"

"Not that I've heard."

Kevin took the phone absently. "Okay. I'll answer it this time."

The agent hesitated, expressionless, and then walked down the stairs for the door. Kevin didn't even know his name. He wore a dark navy jacket and tan slacks; black hair. Walked stiffly, like maybe his underwear were too tight. But the man had a name and maybe a wife and some kids. A life. What if Slater had gone after this man instead of Kevin? Or gone after someone in China, unknown to the West? For that matter, how many men or women were facing their own Slaters throughout the world? It was an awkward thought, standing there at the top of his stairs, watching the agent leave through the front door.

Kevin walked back into his bedroom. He had to call Jennifer. Six o'clock had come and gone—something had to have happened.

The phone suddenly rang. He picked up the receiver.

"Hello?"

"Kevin?" It was Eugene. Kevin felt himself shutting down immediately. The sound of that voice. They didn't have a phone in the house. He was calling from a pay phone.

"Yes."

"Thank God! Thank God, boy. I don't know what to do! I just don't know what I should do . . ."

You could start by drowning yourself. "What's wrong?"

"I'm not sure. It's just that Princess isn't home. I woke up and she was gone. She never leaves without telling me. I thought maybe she went down for some dog food because we threw it away, you know, but then I remembered that we burned the dog and—"

"Shut up, Eugene. Please, just shut up and try to make some sense for once. Her name is Balinda. So Balinda left without telling you. I'm sure she'll be back. You can live without her for a few hours, can't you?"

"This isn't like her. I have a very bad feeling, Kevin! And now I've gotten Bob worried. He keeps looking in all the rooms, calling for Princess. You have to come—"

"Forget it. Call the police, if you're so worried."

"Princess won't allow that! You know . . ."

He talked on but suddenly Kevin wasn't hearing. His mind had turned over a stone. What if Slater had kidnapped Balinda? What if the old hag was really gone?

But why would Slater take Balinda?

Because whether you like it or not, she is your mother, Kevin. You need her. You want her to be your mother.

A cold sweat broke out on his temples and he wasn't sure why. He had to call Jennifer! Where was Samantha? Maybe Jennifer had heard from her.

He interrupted Eugene's rambling. "I'll call you back."

"You can't call me! I have to go home!"

"Then go home."

Kevin hung up. Where was Jennifer's number? He ran downstairs, still in his boxers, snatched her card from the counter with a trembling hand, and dialed the number.

"Good morning, Kevin. I'm surprised you're not still sleeping."

"How did you know it was me?"

"Caller ID. You're on your home phone."

"Have you heard anything?"

"Not yet. I just got off the phone with Samantha. It seems we were wrong about Slater being the Riddle Killer."

"We may have a problem, Jennifer. I just got a call from Eugene. He says that Balinda's missing."

Jennifer didn't respond.

"I was just thinking, do you think Slater could have—"

"Balinda! That's it. It makes perfect sense!"

"It does?"

"Stay put. I'll swing by in ten minutes."

"What? Where are we going?"

She hesitated. "Baker Street."

"No, I can't! Really, Jennifer, I don't think I can go in there like this."

"Don't you see? This could be the break we need! If he took her, then Slater's tied to Balinda and Balinda is tied to the house. I know this may be hard, but I need you."

"You don't know that."

"We can't risk me being wrong."

"Why can't you just go?"

"Because you're the only one who knows how to beat him. If Slater did take Balinda, then we know that this whole thing goes back to the house. To the past. There has to be a key to it all, and I doubt that I'm the one who's going to find it."

He knew what she was saying, and it sounded more like psycho-babble than truth. But she could be right.

"Kevin? I'll be there with you. It's paper and boards; that's all it is. I was there yesterday, remember? And Balinda's gone. Ten minutes?"

Balinda was gone. Bob wasn't the problem—he was a victim in this mess. Eugene was just an old fool without Balinda. The witch was gone.

"Okay."

|||

The white house stood as ominously as always. He stared at it through the windshield, feeling silly next to Jennifer. She was looking at him, knowing him. He felt naked.

Balinda wasn't in the house. Unless she'd come back. If so, he wouldn't go in. Jennifer might want him to. She seemed pretty convinced that there was more to this than he'd told her, but in all honesty, he couldn't think of anything. Slater was the boy and the boy had nothing to do with the house.

"When is Sam coming?" he asked, stalling.

"She said noonish, but she has a few errands to run."

"I wonder why she didn't call me?"

"I told her you were sleeping. She said she'll call you as soon as she can." Jennifer looked at the house. "You didn't tell Sam about locking the boy in the cellar—how much does Sam really know about your childhood, Kevin? You two have known each other for years."

"I don't like to talk about it. Why?"

"Something's bothering her. She wouldn't tell me, but she wants to meet later this afternoon. She's convinced that Slater isn't the Riddle Killer. I can buy that, but there's more. She knows something else." Jennifer hit the steering wheel. "Why do I always feel like I'm the last to know what's going on here?"

Kevin stared at the house. She sighed. "I had to tell Milton about this. He wants to talk to you this morning."

"What did you say?"

"I said he would have to take it up with the bureau chief. We still have official jurisdiction. The rest are still running their investigations, but on the ground everything goes through us. The thought of Milton interviewing you gives me the creeps."

"Okay, let's go," Kevin said, distracted. They might as well get this over with. She would never know how much better he felt with her here. On the other hand, she was a psychologist—she probably *would* understand. He opened his door.

Jennifer put her hand on his arm. "Kevin, I need you to know something. If we discover that Slater did take Balinda, there's no way we can keep it from the media. They'll want to know more. They can be nosy."

"So then my whole life gets dissected by the press."

"Pretty much. I've done my best this far—"

"That's what Slater wants. That's why he took her. It's his way of exposing me." He dropped his head and ruffled his hair.

"I'm sorry."

Kevin stood from the car and slammed the door. "Let's get this over with."

Walking across the street and up the steps to the front door, Kevin made a firm decision. Under no circumstances would he blubber or show any more emotion in front of Jennifer. He was leaning on her too much already. The last thing she needed was a basket case. He would walk in, give Bob a hug, slug Eugene, do his I'm-looking-for-the-key-to-Slater routine, and leave without so much as batting an eye.

His foot crossed the threshold for the first time in five years. The tremble started in his fingers. It spread to his knees before the door closed behind him.

Eugene let them in. "I don't know. I just don't know where she could have gone. She should have been back by now!"

Bobby stood at the end of the hall, grinning wide, beaming. He started to clap and hop in place without leaving the ground. A lump the size of a boulder filled Kevin's throat. What had he done to Bob? He'd abandoned him to Princess. He'd been punished his whole life in part because of Bob, but that didn't make Bob guilty.

"Kevin, Kevin, Kevin! You came to see me?"

Kevin quickly walked to his brother and hugged the man tight. "Yes. I'm sorry, Bob. I'm so sorry." The tears were leaking already. "Are you okay?"

Eugene watched dumbly; Jennifer wrinkled her brow.

"Yes, Kevin. I'm very good."

He didn't seem so concerned about the old bat's disappearance.

"Princess has gone away," he said, smile suddenly gone.

"Why don't you show me your bedroom," Jennifer said to Eugene.

"My, my, my, my. I don't know what I'll do without Princess," Eugene said, heading off to the left.

Kevin let them go. "Bob, could you show me your room?"

Bob lit up and skipped through the narrow passage between the stacks of newspapers. "You want to see my room?"

Kevin walked down the hall on numb legs. It was surreal, this world he'd escaped. An issue of *Time* poked out of the stack to his right. The face on the cover had been replaced by a smiling image of Muhammad Ali. Only God, the devil, and Balinda knew why.

Bob hurried into his room. He snatched something off the floor. It was an old beat-up Game Boy, a monochrome version. Bob had himself a toy. Balinda had softened in her old age. Or was it because Kevin had left?

"It's a computer!" Bob said.

"Nice. I like it." Kevin peeked into the room. "Do you still read stories that Bal—Princess gives you to read?"

"Yes. And I like them a lot."

"That's good, Bob. Does she . . . make you sleep during the day?"

"Not for a long time. But sometimes she won't let me eat. She says I'm getting too fat."

Bobby's room looked just as it had five years earlier. Kevin turned back into the hall and pushed open the door to his old room.

Unchanged. Surreal. He set his jaw. The flood of emotions he'd expected didn't come. The window was still screwed down and the bookcases were still full of bogus books. The bed he'd spent half his childhood in was still covered by the same blanket. It was as if Balinda was waiting for him to return. Or maybe his leaving didn't fit into her reality, so she refused to accept it. With her mind there was no telling.

No keys to Slater here.

A wail—Eugene—carried through the house. Bob turned and ran for the sound. So it was true.

Kevin walked back out to the living room, ignoring the sounds of lament issuing from the back bedroom. He should take a torch to this place. Burn out the rat's nest. Add a few more ashes to the backyard. The stairwell to the basement was still choked off with a mountain of books and magazines, stacks that hadn't been touched for years.

Jennifer stepped out of the master bedroom. "He took her."

"So I gathered."

"He left a note." She handed him a blue slip of paper. Three words were scrawled in the familiar handwriting.

Fess up, Puke.

"Or what," he said. "You'll dump her in the lagoon?"

Kevin stared at the words, numb from four days of horror. Part of him didn't care, part of him felt sorry for the old hag. Either way, all of his deepest secrets would soon be on the table for the world to pick through. That was the point. Kevin wasn't sure how much he cared anymore.

"Can we go now?"

"Are you finished?"

"Yes."

She looked around. "The health department is going to have a field day once this gets out."

"They should burn it."

"That's what I was thinking," she said. Her eyes settled on his. "Are you okay?"

"I feel . . . confused."

"As far as the rest of the world is concerned, she's your mother. They may wonder why you don't seem to care. She may be a witch, but she's still human. Only God knows what he'll do to her."

The emotions came from his gut, unexpectedly and in a rush. He suddenly felt suffocated in the small, dark space. She was his mother, wasn't she? And he was horrified by the fact that he even *thought* of her as a mother, because in reality he hated her more than he hated Slater. Unless they were one and the same and she had kidnapped herself.

A confusing mixture of revulsion and sorrow overcame Kevin. He was falling apart. His eyes swam with tears and his face wrinkled.

Kevin turned for the door. He could feel their stares on his back. *Mommy.* Fire burned through his throat; a tear spilled from his left eye.

At least they couldn't see. He would never allow anyone to see this. He hated Balinda and he was crying for her and he hated that he was crying for her.

It was too much. He hurried for the door, crashed through with far more noise than he wanted, and let out a soft sob. He hoped Jennifer couldn't hear; he didn't want her to hear him acting this way. He was just a lost boy and he was crying like a lost boy and he really just wanted to be held by Mommy. By the one person who had never held him.

"Kevin?" Jennifer was running after him.

He only wanted to be held by Princess.

22

Monday
Afternoon

THE QUESTIONS HAD NAGGED at Samantha through the night. The scenario fit some unseen hand like a glove; the question was, which hand? Who was Slater?

She'd talked to Jennifer upon waking and heard about the note on Kevin's windshield. She should have taken an earlier flight! Jennifer suspected kidnapping, but as of seven this morning there had been no evidence of foul play.

Sam told Jennifer about Salman. If the Pakistani Salman had indeed met with Slater in New York, then whoever the FBI had located with a tattoo could not be Slater, because Slater's had been removed. Furthermore, Slater couldn't be the Riddle Killer—he'd been in New York at the time of Roy's murder. Jennifer hadn't been ready to accept her conclusion out of hand, but the two cases did have a few significant disparities that were obviously weighing on her mind. She talked about objectives. She was beginning to suspect that the Riddle Killer and Slater weren't similarly motivated.

As for the tattoo, they would know within a few hours.

Sam's plane landed at LAX at 12:35. She rented a car and headed south for Long Beach. Traffic on 405 was as bad as it got for a weekday. She called Jennifer. The agent answered on the first ring.

"Hi, Jennifer, it's Sam. Anything?"

"As a matter of fact, yes. The tattoo is a bust. Our man works on an oil rig six months a year. He's been out on one for the last three weeks."

"Makes sense. Any word on a kidnapping?"

Jennifer hesitated and Sam sat up. "Balinda was taken from her home last night," Jennifer said.

"Balinda Parson?" Sam's pulse spiked.

"One and the same. No contact, no leads, nothing but a note left in Slater's writing: 'Fess up, Puke.' Kevin took it pretty hard."

Sam's mind was already whirling. Of course! Taking Balinda would force media attention on Kevin's family. His past. "Does the media know?"

"Yes. But we're keeping them away from Baker Street under the claim that it could trigger Slater. There's wall-to-wall coverage on this thing. I've spent the last hour handling interagency concerns. The bureaucracy's enough to drive me nuts. Milton's ticked off, the ATF wants the evidence from Quantico—it's a mess. Meanwhile we're dead in the water."

Jennifer sounded tired. Sam braked and came to a stop behind a pickup truck billowing black smoke. "How is he?"

"Kevin? He's dead to the world. I left him at his house about two hours ago, sleeping. God knows we could all get some rest."

Sam pulled around the truck. "I have some ideas, Jennifer. Is there a chance we could meet sooner?"

"What is it?"

"I . . . I can't explain right now."

"Come by the station. Unless something breaks, I'll be here."

"Okay. But I have to chase something down first."

"If you have information that's pertinent to the investigation, I expect to be told. Please, Sam, I can use all the help I can get here."

"I promise you I'll call the second I know anything."

"Sam. Please, what's on your mind?"

"I'll call you," Sam said and hung up.

Without evidence her fears would have to remain the paranoia of a close friend, desperate for answers. And if she was right? God help them. God help Kevin.

She drove south, ticking off the facts. Slater had been in New York at the same time she'd been there. Slater knew her, a small detail she'd withheld from the CBI. Knowing Roland, he'd yank her from the case.

Slater was obsessed with Kevin's past; Slater was the boy; Sam had never seen the boy; all of the riddles had to do with opposites; all demanded a confession. Slater was trying to force Kevin back into his past. Who was Slater?

A chill snaked down her arms.

Samantha approached Kevin's house from the west, parked two blocks down, and took to foot, careful to keep yard fences between herself and the black car parked up the street. She had to do this without causing a fuss, and the last thing she wanted to do was wake Kevin if he was asleep.

Dread swelled in her chest as she neared. The notion that Kevin might indeed be Slater refused to budge from her tired mind.

She had to wait for the agent up the street to turn his head before crossing from the neighbor's fence into Kevin's backyard. She hurried up to the sliding glass door and knelt so that Kevin's picket fence blocked her head from the car's line of sight. Working quickly above her head, she inserted a thin pick into the lock and worked it with as much precision as she could from the awkward angle. The pin fell and she pried up the latch. She wiped a bead of sweat from her cheek, glanced back at the black car, slid the glass door open a foot, and slipped past the pulled blinds. She reached back through and closed the door.

If they'd seen her, they would be moving already. They hadn't.

Sam looked around the house. A two-by-four-foot travel poster of a bikini-clad native walking down a white beach said that New Zealand promised paradise. *Dear Kevin, you want so much. I should have known how badly you were hurting, even when we were children. Why did you hide it from me? Why didn't you tell me?*

The house's silence engulfed her. So peaceful, so quiet, asleep while the world crumbled. She crossed to the stairs and took them on her tiptoes. Kevin's bedroom was to the left. She eased the door open, saw him on the bed, and walked quietly up to him.

He lay sprawled on his belly, arms above his head, as if surrendering to some unknown enemy beyond the mattress. His head rested on its side, facing her, lower cheek bunched, mouth closed. His face didn't speak of surrender, only sleep. Deep, deep, sweet sleep.

He was dressed in street clothes; his tan Reeboks sat on the floor, nudging the bed skirt.

Sam briefly wondered if Jennifer had stayed with him until he fell asleep. Had she seen him like this? This sweet boy of hers? This stunning man who bore the weight of a hundred worlds on his shoulders? Her champion who'd slain the wicked boy on Baker Street?

What did Jennifer see when she looked at him? *She sees the same as you do, Sam. She sees Kevin and she can't help but to love him as you love him.*

Sam reached out, tempted to brush his cheek. *No, not as I love him. No one can love him as I love him. I would give my life for this man.* She withdrew her hand. A tear broke down her right cheek. *Oh, how I love you, dear Kevin. Seeing you these last three days has reminded me how desperately I love you. Please, please tell me that you will slay this dragon. We will, Kevin. Together we will slay this beast, my knight.*

The childhood role-playing reference flooded her with warmth. She turned away and walked into his closet. She wasn't sure what she was looking for. Something that Slater had left. Something that the

FBI missed because they wouldn't have guessed that it belonged to Slater.

Kevin had ordered his clothes neatly. Slacks and shirts hung in a row, jeans and cargo pants folded and stacked, shoes on a rack. Seminary dress to the right, casual dress to the left. She smiled and ran her fingers through the slacks. She smelled the shirts. His scent lingered. Amazing how she recognized it after so many years. He was still a boy. *A man, Sam. A man.*

She searched the closet and then slowly worked her way through the rest of his room, walking around him, careful not to make any sound. Other than the rise and fall of his back, Kevin did not move. Sam found nothing.

The bathroom proved no better, and her spirit lightened. She didn't want to find anything.

His study. Sam shut the door and sat at his desk. She ran a finger over his books: *Introduction to Philosophy. Sociology of Religion. Hermeneutics Revealed.* Two dozen others. He was in his first semester at the divinity school but he'd bought enough texts for two years, easily.

On the floor beside the desk she saw a small pile of paper, which she picked up. A paper he'd titled "The True Natures of Man." He was a true man.

Please, Sam, let's cut the romantic drivel and do what you came to do.

She was less concerned about noise; there were two doors between her and Kevin. She searched the drawers and removed the books one by one. This is where Slater would leave a clue. This was the room of the mind. He was obsessed with numbers and mind games. The mind. Somewhere, somewhere.

A small stack of business cards, topped by a slip of paper bearing her own number, sat by a calculator that looked fresh out of the box, perhaps never used. The first card belonged to John Francis, Ph.D.,

Academic Dean, Divinity School of the Pacific, South. Kevin had spoken at length about the man. Surely Jennifer had already interviewed him.

And what if she hadn't? The last four days rushed by without time for standard procedure or a thorough investigation. She picked up the phone and called the number on the card. A receptionist with a nasal voice asked her if she wanted to leave a message. No, thank you. She hung up, turned over the card, and saw that Kevin had scribbled another number with the same prefix. She dialed it.

"Hello, this is John."

"Hello, Dr. John Francis?"

"Yes, this is he."

"This is Samantha Sheer with the California Bureau of Investigation. I'm working with an agent Jennifer Peters on the Kevin Parson case. Are you familiar with it?"

"Of course. Agent Peters was here yesterday morning."

"Kevin speaks highly of you," Sam said. "You have a doctorate in psychology, isn't that right?"

"Correct."

"What is your assessment of Kevin?"

"That's a bit like asking which animals live in the sea. Kevin's a wonderful man. I can't say there's anyone else I'd rather tangle my wits with. Extraordinary . . . genuine."

"Genuine. Yes, he is genuine. Nearly transparent. Which is why it's strange he can't remember this sin Slater demands he confess, don't you think? I'm wondering, is there anything that's occupied him in these last few weeks? Any reoccurring themes, projects, papers?"

"As a matter of fact, yes. He was quite interested in the natures of man. You might say consumed with the subject."

Sam picked up the rough draft of the paper. "The true natures of man," Sam said. "And what are the natures of man? Or what would Kevin say are the natures of man?"

"Yes, well, that's the mystery, isn't it? I'm not sure I can tell you what Kevin would say. He told me he had a new model, but he wanted to present them cohesively in his paper."

"Hmm. And when is this paper due?"

"He was scheduled to turn it in this Wednesday."

"For what class?"

"Introduction to Ethics."

"One more question, Doctor, and I'll let you go. You're a religious man with an education in psychology; would you say that the natures of man are primarily spiritual, or psychological?"

"I know that Freud would turn in his grave, but in my mind there's no doubt. Man is primarily a spiritual being."

"And Kevin would agree to that?"

"Yes, I'm sure he would."

"Thank you for your time, Doctor. You sound like a reasonable man."

He chuckled. "They pay me to be; I do try. Anything else, don't hesitate to call."

She set the phone down. Ethics. She scanned the paper and saw that it was hardly more than the recitation of several theories on man's natures. It ended with a new heading: "The True Natures." She set the pages down. Where would Kevin keep his notes on the natures of man?

She stepped over to the bookcase and reached for a large gray book titled *Morality Redefined.* The book was used, frayed around the edges, pages yellowing. She lifted the cover, saw that it was a library book. Copyright 1953.

Sam flipped through the pages, but there were no notes. She was about to replace the book when the back cover fell open. Several loose sheets of white paper dropped to the floor. On the top of one in Kevin's handwriting: *The True Natures of Man, an Essay.*

Samantha withdrew the pages and sat down at the desk. They were only notes. Three pages of notes. She scanned them, a simple outline with headings that fit the subject. Summaries.

We learn as we live, and we live what we learn, but not so well.

How can a nature be dead and yet live? He is dead in the light, but thrives in the dark.

If Good and Evil could talk to each other, what would they say?

They are all pretenders, who live in the light but hide in the dark.

Insightful. But there was nothing here that Slater would have . . .

Sam froze. There at the bottom of page four, three small words.

I AM I.

Sam recognized the handwriting immediately. Slater! "I am I."

"Dear God!"

Sam set the pages on Kevin's desk with a trembling hand. She began to panic.

No. Stop. *What does "I am I" even mean, Sam? It means Slater is Slater. Slater snuck in here and wrote this. That proves nothing except that he has his nose in every part of Kevin's life.*

If Good and Evil could talk to each other, what would they say?

Then how had Kevin and Slater talked to each other? The FBI had a recording. How, how? Unless . . .

A second cell. He's using another cell phone!

Sam ran for Kevin's room. *Dear God, let me be wrong!* He hadn't moved. She crept up to him. Where would he keep the phones? The one Slater had left him was always in his right pocket.

There was only one way to do this. Quickly, before she awakened him. Sam slipped her hand into his right pocket. He wore cargo pants, loose, but his weight pressed her hand into the mattress. She touched the phone, felt the recording device on the back. Slater's.

She rounded the bed, crawled up for better access, and slid her hand into his left pocket. Kevin grunted and rolled to his side, facing her. She stayed still until his breathing returned to a deep slow rhythm and then tried again, this time with his left pocket exposed.

Her fingers felt plastic. Sam knew then that she was right, but she pulled it out anyway. A cell phone, identical to the one Slater had left for Kevin, except black instead of silver. She flipped it open and scrolled through the call history. The calls were to the other cell phone. One to the hotel room phone. Two to Kevin's home phone.

This was the cell phone Slater had used. To talk, to detonate the bombs. Sam's mind throbbed. There could be no doubt about it.

They would crucify him.

23

SAM ROLLED OFF THE BED, closed Kevin's door, and flew downstairs. She gripped the phone Slater had used to make his calls in her right hand—for now Slater wouldn't be making those calls, at least not on this phone. She didn't bother being discreet on her exit but walked right out the back, turned up the street, and ran for her car.

I, Slater, am I, Kevin. And that had been Samantha's greatest fear. That her childhood friend had a multiple personality disorder as she'd suggested to Jennifer a day earlier, and then immediately rejected because Kevin was in the room when Slater called. But it struck her as she lay trying to sleep last night that Slater had not *talked* to her while Kevin was in the room. The phone had only rung while he was in the room. Kevin was in the hall before she picked up and heard Slater. Kevin could have simply pushed the send button in his pocket and then talked to Sam once in the hall. Could multiple personalities work that way?

She'd been with Kevin in the car when Slater called, just before the bus blew. But she had no proof that Slater was actually on the line then. They had no recording of that call.

It was absurd. It was impossible! But try as she might in sleepless fits, Sam couldn't account for a single definitive situation that necessarily proved they couldn't be the same man. Not one.

Mere conjecture! It had to be coincidence!

Now this.

If Good and Evil could talk to each other, what would they say?

Sam reached her car, stomach in knots. This might not be enough. She'd been irresponsible to suggest the possibility to Jennifer in the first place. The man you think you might be falling in love with is insane. And she'd said it so calmly for the simple reason that she didn't believe it herself. She was only doing what she was trained to do. But this . . . this was an entirely different matter.

And Kevin *wasn't* insane! He was merely role-playing, as he had learned to do with Balinda for so many years. He had split into a divergent personality when he first began to comprehend true evil. The boy. He had been the boy! Only he didn't know that he was the boy. To Kevin at age eleven, the boy was an evil person who needed to be killed. So he killed him. But the boy had never died. Slater had simply remained dormant until now, when somehow this paper on the natures of man had allowed him to resurface.

She could still be wrong. In true cases of multiple personality disorders, the subjects were rarely conscious of their alternate personalities. Slater wouldn't know that he was Kevin; Kevin would not know that he was Slater. Actually they *weren't* each other. Physically, yes, but in no other way. Slater could be living right now as Kevin slept, plotting to kill Balinda, and Kevin wouldn't have a clue. Some things Slater did would be merely imagined; others, like the bombs and the kidnapping, would be acted out.

She tossed Kevin's phone on the seat and punched Jennifer's number into her own.

"Jenn—"

"I need to meet you! Now. Where are you?"

"Sam? I'm down at the PD. What's wrong?"

"Have you gotten the lab reports on the shoe prints and the recordings yet?"

"No. Why? Where are you?"

"I was just in Kevin's house and I'm headed your way." She pulled onto Willow.

"How's Kevin?"

Sam took a deep breath and let it out slowly. "He's asleep. I found a second phone on him, Jennifer. It was the phone used to call the cell with the recording device. I don't know how else to say this. I think Kevin is Slater."

"That's . . . I thought we'd already been over this. He was in the room when Slater—"

"Listen, Jennifer, I've come at this from a hundred different angles in the last twelve hours. I'm not saying that I can prove it; God knows I don't want it to be true, but if it is, he needs help! He needs you. And he's the only one who can take us to Balinda. Kevin won't know, but Slater will."

"Please, Sam, this is crazy. How could he have pulled this off? We've had people on the house. We've been listening to him in there! How did he get out to kidnap Balinda?"

"It's his house; he knows how to get out without your boys catching on. Where was he between 3 A.M. and 5 A.M. last night?"

"Sleeping . . ."

"Kevin may have thought he was, but was he? I don't think he's had six hours' sleep in the last four days. Trace it back. He hasn't gotten any phone calls while you were listening, at least not in the house. I hope I'm wrong, I really do, but I don't think you'll find a discrepancy. He's too intelligent. But he wants the truth out. Subconsciously, consciously, I don't know, but he's getting sloppy. He wants the world to know. That's the answer to the riddle."

"*What falls but never breaks? What breaks but never falls?* Night and day," Jennifer said. "Opposites. Kevin."

"Kevin. *Kevin* was the boy; that's why I never saw the boy when we were kids. He was in that warehouse cellar, but only him, no second boy. He hit himself. Check the blood type. The confession Slater wants isn't that Kevin tried to kill the boy, but that he *was* the boy. That Kevin is Slater."

"I am my sin," Jennifer said absently. There was a tremor in her voice.

"What?"

"Something he said last night."

"I'll be there in ten minutes," Sam said. "Don't let Kevin leave the house."

"But only Slater knows where he has Balinda? Kevin truly doesn't know?"

"That's my guess."

"Then we need Slater to find Balinda. But if we send the wrong signal, Slater may go into remission. If he does and Kevin doesn't know where Balinda is, we may have our first actual victim in this case. Even if we hold Kevin in a cell, she could starve to death." Jennifer was suddenly sounding frantic. "He's not the Riddle Killer; he hasn't killed anyone yet. We can't let that happen."

"So we let him walk out?"

"No. No, I don't know, but we have to handle this with kid gloves."

"I'll be right there," Sam said. "Just make sure Kevin doesn't leave that house."

|||

The sound of his bedroom door closing pulled Kevin from sleep. It was 3:00. He'd slept over four hours. Jennifer had insisted that he not be bothered unless absolutely necessary. So why were they in his house?

Unless *they* weren't in his house. Unless it was someone else. Someone like Slater!

He slid out of bed, tiptoed to the door, eased it open. Someone was opening the sliding glass door to the back lawn! *Just ask who it is, Kevin. It's the FBI, that's all.*

But what if it wasn't?

"Hello?"

Nothing.

"Is anyone here?" he called, louder this time.

Silence.

Kevin descended the stairs and stepped cautiously into the living room. He ran over to the window and peered out. The familiar Lincoln was parked half a block down the street.

Something was wrong. Something had happened. He walked to his kitchen phone and instinctively felt for the cell phone in his right pocket. Still there. But something wasn't right. What?

The cell phone suddenly vibrated against his leg and he jumped. He shoved his hand back into the pocket and pulled out the silver phone. The other phone, the larger VTech, was in his left hand. For a moment he stared at them, confused. *Did I pick that up? So many phones,* his mind was playing tricks on him.

The cell vibrated madly. *Answer it!*

"Hello?"

Slater's voice ground in his ear. "Who thinks he's a butterfly but is really a worm?"

Kevin's breathing smothered the phone.

"You're pathetic, Kevin. Do you have knowledge of this obvious fact yet, or am I going to have to beat it out of you?" Slater breathed heavily. "I have someone here who wants to hold you and for the life of me I can't understand why."

Blood flushed Kevin's face. His throat felt as though it was locked in a vise. He couldn't speak.

"How long do you expect me to play tiddlywinks, Kevin? You're obviously too dense for the riddles, so I've decided to up the ante. I know how conflicted you are about Mommy, but by now I have it under reliable advisement that you aren't so conflicted about me. In fact, you hate me, don't you, Kevin? You should—I've destroyed your life."

"Stop it!" Kevin screamed.

"Stop it? Stop it? That's all you can manage? You're the only one with the power to stop anything. But I don't think you have the guts. You're as yellow as the rest of them; you've made that abundantly clear. So here's the new deal, Kevin. *You* come and stop me. Face to face, man to man. This is your big chance to blow away Slater with that peashooter you obtained illegally. Find me."

"Face me, you coward! Come out and face me!" Kevin shouted.

"Coward? I'm petrified. I can hardly move, much less face you." Pause. "Do I have to chisel it on your forehead? You find *me!* Find me, find me! The game ends in six hours, Kevin. Then I kill her. You fess up or I slit her throat. Are we properly motivated now?"

The detail about the six hours hardly registered. Slater wanted to meet him. Kevin shifted on his feet. He actually wanted to meet him. But where?

"How?"

"You know how. It's dark down here. Alone, Kevin. All alone, the way it was meant to be."

Click.

For an endless moment Kevin stood glued to the linoleum. Blood throbbed through his temples. The black VTech phone trembled in his left hand. He roared and slammed it on the counter with all of his strength. Black plastic splintered and scattered.

Kevin shoved the cell phone in his pocket, whirled around, and flew up the stairs. He'd hidden the gun under his mattress. Three bullets left. Two days earlier the thought of going after Slater would have terrified him; now he was consumed with the idea.

It's dark down here.

He shoved his hand under the mattress, pulled out the gun, and crammed it behind his belt. Dark. Down. *I've got a few ideas about dark and down, don't I? Where the worms hide their nasty little secrets. He knew, he knew!* Why hadn't he thought of this earlier? He had to get out unseen and he had to go alone. This was now between him and Slater. One on one, man on man.

The FBI car was still somewhere down the street. Kevin ran out the back and sprinted east, the opposite way. One block and then he cut south. They would know that he'd left. In fact, they would have recorded Slater's last call to him through the home surveillance. What if they came after him? He had to tell Jennifer to stay away. He could use the cell phone, but the call would have to be short, or they would triangulate his position.

If *dark* and *down* was where he thought it might be . . . Kevin ground his teeth and grunted. The man was a pervert. And he would kill Balinda—empty threats weren't part of his character.

What if the FBI sent out helicopters? He turned west and hugged a line of trees by the sidewalk. The gun jutted into his back.

He started to jog.

|||

"Now! I need some facts now, not in ten minutes," Jennifer snapped.

Reports normally came in from Quantico at intervals established by the agents in charge. The next report window was in ten minutes, Galager had explained.

"I'll call, but they've only had the evidence for a few hours. This stuff can take up to a week."

"We don't have a week! Do they know what's happening down here? Tell them to turn on the television, for heaven's sake!"

Galager dipped his head and left.

Her world had collapsed with the call from Sam two minutes ago. She still didn't want to accept the possibility that Kevin could have blown up the bus or the library.

From her corner station Jennifer could see the exit across a sea of desks. Milton barged out of his office, grabbed his coat, and headed for the door. Where was he going? He paused, glancing back, and Jennifer instinctively turned her head to avoid eye contact. When she glanced back, he was gone. An inexplicable rage flashed through her mind. But really none of this was Milton's fault. He was simply doing his job. Sure he liked the cameras, but he arguably had a responsibility to the public. She was directing her frustration and anger at him without appropriate cause—she knew this but it didn't seem to calm her.

It wasn't Kevin, she reminded herself. Even if Kevin was Slater, which hasn't been established, the Kevin she knew wouldn't blow anything up. A jury would take one look at his past and agree. If Slater was Kevin, then he was part of a fractured personality, not Kevin himself.

A thought smacked her and she stopped. Could Slater be framing Kevin? What better way to drag the man down than to frame him as the lunatic who tried to blow up Long Beach? She sat behind the desk, grabbed a legal pad, and penciled it out.

Slater is the boy; he wants revenge. He terrorizes Kevin and then convinces the world that he is Kevin, terrorizing himself because he is Slater. Kevin is ruined and Slater escapes. It would raise the bar for perfect crimes.

But how could Slater pull that off? Sam had found *two* phones. Why would Kevin be carrying around two phones without knowing it? And how could the numbers that Slater called be on that second phone? An electronic relay that duplicated the numbers to make it look like the phone had been used. Possible. And how could Slater have placed the phone in Kevin's pocket without Kevin's knowledge?

It would have had to be while Kevin slept, this morning. Who had access to Kevin . . .

Her phone rang and she snatched it up without thinking.

"Jennifer."

"It's Claude, surveillance. We have a situation at the house. Someone just called Kevin."

"Who?" Jennifer stood, knocking her chair back.

Static. "Slater. We're pretty sure. But that's not all."

"Hold on. You have the recording from Kevin's cell phone?"

"No, we have a recording from inside the house. Someone who sounded like Slater called Kevin from *inside* Kevin's house. I . . . uh, I know it sounds strange, but we have both voices inside the house. I'm sending the recording down now. He threatened to kill the woman in six hours and suggested that Kevin meet him."

"Did he say where?"

"No. He said Kevin would know where. He said it was dark down here, that's it."

"Have you talked to Kevin?"

"We made the decision to enter premises." He paused. "Kevin was gone."

Jennifer collapsed in her chair. "You let him *walk?*"

Claude sounded flustered. "His car's still in the garage."

She closed her eyes and took a calming breath. What now? "I want that tape here now. Set up a search in concentric circles. He's on foot."

She dropped her phone on the table and closed her fingers to still a bad tremble. Her nerves were shot. Four days and how much sleep? Twelve, fourteen hours? The case had just gone from terrible to hopeless. He was going to kill Balinda. Inevitable. *Who* was going to kill Balinda? Slater? Kevin?

"Ma'am?"

She looked up to see one of Milton's detectives in the door. "I have a call for you. He says he tried your personal line but couldn't get through. Wouldn't give his name."

She nodded at the desk phone. "Put it through."

The call transferred and she picked up. "Peters."

"Jennifer?"

It was Kevin. Jennifer was too stunned to respond.

"Hello?"

"Where are you?"

"I'm sorry, Jennifer. I'm going after him. But I have to do this alone. If you come after me, he'll kill her. You're recording the house, right? Listen to the tape. I can't talk now, because they'll find me, but I wanted you to know." He sounded desperate.

"Kevin, you don't have to do this. Tell me where you are."

"I *do* have to do this. Listen to the tape. It's not what you think. Slater's doing this to me. Don't bother calling me; I'm throwing this phone away." He abruptly clicked off.

"Kevin?"

Jennifer slammed the phone in its cradle. She ran her hands through her hair and picked up the phone again. She dialed Samantha's number.

"Hello?"

"Kevin's gone, Sam," Jennifer said. "He just received a call from Slater threatening to kill Balinda in six hours. He baited Kevin to meet him, said he would know where and that it was dark. As far as I know, that's it. The tape's on the way down."

"He's on foot? How could they let him walk out?"

"I don't know. The point is, we're now on a very tight time line and we've lost contact."

"Slater's cell—"

"He said he was getting rid of it."

"I'll go back," Sam said. "He can't get far."

"Assuming you're right about Kevin, Slater's drawing him to a place they must both know from their childhood. Any ideas?"

Sam hesitated. "The warehouse?"

"We'll check it out, but it's too obvious."

"Let me think about it. If we're lucky, we pick him up. Concentrate the search to the west—closer to Baker Street."

"There's another possibility, Sam. I know it may sound like a stretch, but what if Slater's framing Kevin?"

The phone was quiet.

"Forensics will give us a better picture, but the cell could have been planted and the call log duplicated by relay. The objective fits: Kevin is branded a psychopath who terrorized himself, he's ruined, and Slater skips free. Childhood grudge revenged."

"What a tangled web we weave," Sam said quietly. "Get the data on the recordings; hopefully it'll tell us more."

"I'm working on it." Galager walked in and sat down, file in hand. Jennifer stood. "Call me if you think of anything."

"One last thing," Sam said. "I talked to Dr. John Francis and he mentioned that you'd spoken to him already, but you might want to consider breaking this down with him. He knows Kevin well and he's in your field. Just a thought."

"Thank you, I will."

She set the phone down. Galager was back. "Well?"

"Like I said, not done. But I do have something. Ever hear of a seismic tuner?"

"A what?"

"Seismic tuner. A device that alters voice patterns."

"Okay."

"Well, I could record my voice and program this thing to match it to yours."

"So? The sample we sent them of Kevin's voice sounds nothing like Slater's—what's your point?"

"I talked to Carl Riggs at the lab. He says that even if they do determine that both Slater's voice and Kevin's voice have the same vocal patterns, someone who knew what they were doing could manufacture the effect with a seismic tuner."

"I'm not following. Bottom line, Galager." Her frustration was overflowing now.

"Bottom line is that Slater could have altered his voice to make it sound like a derivative of Kevin's voice. He could have obtained a sample of Kevin's voice, broken it down electronically, and then reproduced its vocal patterns at a different range and with different inflections. In other words, he could be speaking through a box that makes it sound like he's Kevin, trying not to be Kevin. Follow?"

"Knowing that we would analyze the recording and conclude that both voices were Kevin's." She blinked.

"Correct. Even though they aren't."

"As in, if he wanted to frame Kevin."

"A possibility. Riggs said there's an open case in Florida where a guy's wife was kidnapped for a ransom of a million dollars. The community came together in a fund drive and raised the money. But it turns out the kidnapper's voice was a recording of the husband's, manipulated by a seismic tuner. He evidently kidnapped his own wife. It's going to trial next month."

"I didn't know there was such a thing as a seismic tuner."

"There wasn't until about a year ago." Galager stood. "Either way, even if both voiceprints match Kevin's, we won't know if both really are his until we rule out the use of a seismic tuner. Riggs won't have the voice report until tomorrow. They're on it, but it takes time."

"And the shoe prints?"

"Should have that this evening, but he doesn't think it'll help us either. Not distinctive enough."

"So what you're telling me is that none of this matters?"

"I'm telling you none of this may matter. In the end."

He left and Jennifer sagged into her chair. Milton. She would have to depend on him now. She needed every available patrol car in the city to join the search for Kevin, and she needed the search conducted without risking a leak to the media.

Jennifer closed her eyes. Actually, none of that mattered. What mattered was the fact that Kevin was lost. The boy was lost.

She suddenly wanted to cry.

24

KEVIN KEPT TO THE SIDE STREETS, jogging as naturally as he could despite the pounding in his head.

When cars or pedestrians approached, he either changed directions or crossed the street. At the least lowered his head. If he had the luxury of a direct route, the crosstown jog would be half what it was with all of his side jaunts.

But Slater had said alone, which meant avoiding the authorities at all costs. Jennifer would have the cops out in force this time. She would be desperate to find him before he found Slater because she knew that Kevin didn't stand a chance against Slater.

Kevin knew it too.

He ran with the dread knowledge that there was no way he could face Slater and survive. Balinda would die; he would die. But he had no choice. Although he thought he'd freed himself, he'd really been slumping around in that dungeon of the past for twenty years. No longer. He would face Slater head-on and live, or die in this last-ditch effort to reach freedom.

What about Jennifer? And Sam? He would lose them, wouldn't he? The best things in his life—the only things that mattered now— would be ripped away by Slater. And if he found a way to escape Slater this time, the man would be back to hunt him down again. No, he had to end this once and for all. He had to kill or be killed.

Kevin swallowed hard and ran on through unsuspecting residential neighborhoods. Helicopters chopped through the sky. He couldn't quickly differentiate the police from others, so he hid from them all, which slowed his progress even more. Eleven police cars crossed his path, each time forcing him to alter direction. He ran for one hour and still was only halfway there. He grunted and pushed on. The hour stretched into two. With every step, his determination increased until he could almost taste his bitterness toward Slater, the coppery taste of blood on his dry tongue.

The warehouse district dawned on him without warning. Kevin slowed to a walk. His wet shirt clung to his torso. He was close. His heart began to pound, as much from his nerves as from exertion now.

Five P.M. Slater had given them six hours. Three plus three. The ultimate in this sick little game of threes. By now the whole city would be on a desperate manhunt to find Balinda before the nine o'clock deadline. The FBI would have listened to the surveillance from the house and, with Sam, they would be pounding their collective skulls against the wall trying to decode Slater's cryptic message. *You'll know, Kevin. It's dark down here.*

Would Sam figure it out? He'd never told her about the place.

Kevin crossed railroad tracks and slipped into a patch of trees sequestered away here on the outskirts of the city. Close. So close.

You're going to die, Kevin. His skin felt like a pincushion. He stopped and looked around. The city noise sounded distant. Birds chirped. A lizard scurried over dead leaves to his right, stopped, craned a bulging eye for a view of him, and then darted for the rocks.

Kevin walked forward. What if he was wrong? It could have been the warehouse where he'd trapped the boy, of course—that was dark down here. But Slater would never be so obvious. Cops would be crawling all over the place, anyway. No, this had to be it.

He caught sight of the old toolshed through the trees and stopped.

What little paint remained flaked gray with age. Suddenly Kevin wasn't sure he could go through with it. Slater was probably hidden behind one of the trees at this very moment, watching. What if he did run, and Slater stepped out from his hiding place and shot him? He couldn't call for help—he'd dumped the cell phone in an alley behind a 7-Eleven five miles east.

Didn't matter. He had to do this. The gun dug into his belly where he'd moved it when it rubbed him raw at his back. He touched it through his shirt. Should he pull it out now?

He eased the gun from his belt and walked forward. The shack sat undisturbed, hardly more than an outhouse. Breathing deliberately through his nose, Kevin approached the rear door, eyes glued to the boards, the cracks between them, searching for a sign of movement. Anything.

You're going to die in there, Kevin.

He crept up to the door. For a moment he stood there, shaking badly. To his right, deep tire marks ran through the soft earth. A rusted Master Lock padlock hung from the latch, gaping. Open. It was never open.

He eased the lock out of the latch and set it on the ground. Put his hand on the handle and pulled gently. The door creaked. He stopped. A small gap showed pitch-blackness inside.

Dear God, what am I doing? Give me strength. Did the light even work anymore?

Kevin pulled the door open. The shack was empty. *Thank God.*

You came to find him, and now you're thanking God that he isn't here?

But if he's here, he's under that trapdoor, down the stairs, through the tunnel. That's where "dark down here" is, isn't it?

He stepped in and pulled a chain that hung from a single light bulb. The bulb glowed weakly, like a dim lounge lamp. Kevin closed the door. It took him a full five minutes, trembling in the dim yellow light, to work up enough courage to pull the trapdoor open.

Wood steps descended into black. There were footprints on the steps.

Kevin swallowed.

|||

A mood of pending doom had settled over the conference room and two adjacent offices in the Long Beach police headquarters where Jennifer and the other FBI agents had worked feverishly over the past four days.

Two hours of methodical searching, both on the ground and from the air, had turned up nothing. If Slater's *dark down here* place was the warehouse cellar, he would walk in to find two uniformed policemen with weapons drawn. Sam had called in twice, the last time after giving up her ground search. She wanted to check into something that she didn't elaborate on. Said she would call back. That was an hour ago.

The forensic report on the shoe prints had come in—inconclusive. Jennifer had retraced every detail of the past four days, scrutinizing them for clues to which of the two new theories held more water. Either Kevin was Slater, or Slater was framing Kevin by seeding evidence to make it appear that he was Slater.

If Kevin really was Slater, then at least they had their man. No more games for Slater. No more victims. Unless Slater killed Kevin, which would be tantamount to suicide. Or unless Slater killed Balinda. Then they'd have two dead bodies lying in a place that's dark down here. Even if Slater didn't kill Balinda, Kevin would have to live with what he did as Slater for the rest of his life. The thought brought a lump to Jennifer's throat.

If Slater were someone else, Kevin would merely be the poor victim of a horrible plot. Unless he was killed by Slater, in which case he'd be the dead victim of a horrible plot.

The clock ticked on. 5:30. Jennifer picked up the cell phone and called Sam.

"Sam, we're dead down here. We don't have a thing. The shoe prints came back inconclusive. Please tell me you have something."

"I was just going to call. Have you talked to John Francis yet?"

"No. Why?"

"I've been at Kevin's house digging through his writings, papers, books, anything where he might have made reference to his past, a clue to a place that's dark. I knew Kevin was intelligent, but I never expected quite this—mind blowing. No obvious references at all to Slater or anything that even hints at multiple personalities."

"Which could support our theory that he was framed," Jennifer said.

"Maybe. But I did find this in a periodic journal he keeps on his computer. Listen. Written two weeks ago.

"'The problem with most of the best thinkers is that they dissociate their reasoning from spirituality, as if the two exist in separate realities. Not so. It's a false dichotomy. No one understands this more than Dr. John Francis. I feel like I can trust him. He alone truly understands me. I told him about the secret today. I miss Samantha. She called . . .'"

"It continues about me," Sam said. "The point is, I think Dr. John Francis may know more than he may realize."

"The *secret,*" Jennifer said. "Could be a reference to something he never told you. A place he knew as a child."

"I want to talk to him, Jennifer."

It was the only glimmer of light Jennifer had seen in two hours. "You have his address?"

"Yes."

Jennifer grabbed her coat. "I'll meet you there in twenty minutes."

|||

The descent into the bomb shelter and through the tunnel had wrung a gallon of sweat from Kevin's glands. The door at the bottom of the stairwell into the basement stood wide open. Kevin leaned forward and peered into the room for the first time in twenty years, numb on his feet.

A shiny black floor with patches of concrete showing through. A chest freezer to the right, next to a white stove and a sink. A metal desk to the left, piled with electronics. Boxes of dynamite, a file cabinet, a mirror. Two doors that led . . . somewhere.

Kevin held the gun out with both hands, breathless. Sweat stung his eyes. This was it! Had to be. But the room was empty! Where was Slater?

Something bumped against the door to his right and Kevin jerked the gun toward it. Gray carpet had been rolled and stuffed into the crack at its base.

Thump, thump, thump. A muffled cry.

Kevin's body went rigid.

"Is someone there?" He could barely make out the words. "Pleeeease!"

Balinda. The room started to move. He shoved a foot forward and steadied himself. Frantic, he searched the room again. Where was Slater?

"Pleeeease, please." She sounded like a mouse. Kevin took another step. Then another, gun wavering before him.

"I don't want to die," the voice wept. "Please, please, I'll do anything."

"Balinda?" Kevin's voice cracked. The sounds stopped. A thick silence settled.

Kevin struggled to breathe. Slater had left Balinda here for him to find. He wanted Kevin to save his mommy, because that's what little boys do for their mommies. He had deserted her, and now he would rescue her to make up for the horrible sin. Kevin's world started to spin.

"Kevin?" The voice whimpered. "Kevin?"

"Mommy?"

Something scraped the concrete behind him. He whirled, gun extended.

A man stepped out of the dark shadows, sneering. Blond hair. *No shirt.* Beige slacks. White tennis shoes. *No shirt.* A tattoo of a heart over his left breast with the word *Mom* stenciled in black. He held a large silver gun at his side. *No shirt.* His naked torso struck Kevin as obscene. Slater, in the flesh.

"Hello, Kevin," Slater said. "I'm so glad you found us." He edged to his right.

Kevin followed him with the gun, finger tightening. *Do it! Shoot. Pull the trigger.*

"I wouldn't shoot just yet, Kevin. Not until I tell you how you can save Mommy. Because I swear if you kill me now, she's dead meat. Do you want Mommy to be dead meat?" Slater grinned and moved around slowly, gun still at his side. "Well, yes, I suppose you might want Mommy to be dead meat. That would be understandable."

A fist thumped into the door. "Kevin! Help me!" Balinda's muffled voice cried.

"Shut up, witch!" Slater yelled, face flushed red. He caught himself and smiled. "Tell her it isn't real, Kevin. That the darkness isn't really dark. Tell her that if she's a good girl, you'll let her out. Isn't that what she told you?"

"How do you know me?" Kevin asked, voice cracking.

"You don't recognize me?" Slater exposed his forehead with his left hand. "I had the tattoo removed."

He was the boy, but Kevin already knew that. "But . . . how do you know about Balinda? What are you doing?"

"You still don't get it, do you?" Slater edged closer to the door Balinda was thumping on. "Four days of crystal-clear clues and you still are as stupid as you look. Do you know how long I've waited for this? Hmm? Planned for this. It's brilliant. Even if you think you know, you don't. Nobody will know. Ever. That's the beauty of it."

Slater giggled. His face twitched.

"Drop the gun," Kevin said. He had to know what Slater meant. He wanted to shoot the man. He wanted to send a piece of lead through his forehead, but he wanted to know what Slater was saying.

"Drop the gun."

Slater reached for the doorknob, twisted it, pushed the door open. Balinda sat on the floor, hands bound behind her back, foot against the door. Slater calmly pointed his pistol at her white, stricken face.

"Sorry, Kevin," Slater said. "Toss me the peashooter, or I shoot Mommy."

What? Kevin felt his face flush with heat. He could still shoot and Slater would be dead before he could kill Balinda.

"Drop it!" Slater said. "I've got this trigger milled down to a hair. You shoot me and my finger twitches and she's dead."

Balinda started to cry. "Kevin . . . honey . . ."

"Now! Now, now, now!"

Kevin lowered the gun slowly.

"I know how fond you are of it, but when I say drop, I really do mean drop. Now!"

Kevin dropped the gun and stepped back, panicked.

Slater slammed the door shut on Balinda, stepped forward, and scooped up the gun. "Good boy. Mommy will be proud of you." He shoved Kevin's gun into his own belt, walked toward the door to the stairwell, and shut it.

"There."

Balinda's feet thumped the door again. "Kevin? Pleeeease . . ."

"Ahhhhh!" Slater screamed and ran at the door. He kicked it hard enough to put a dent in the steel. "Shut up! One more peep and I'll staple your mouth shut!"

Slater stood back, panting. Balinda quieted.

"Don't you hate these women who don't know how to keep their yappers shut?" Slater turned around. "Now, where were we?"

A strange resolve settled over Kevin. He was going to die down here after all. He really had nothing to lose. The twisted boy had grown up into a pathetic monster. Slater would kill both him and Balinda without a fleeting thought of remorse.

"You're sick," Kevin said.

"Now there's a novel thought. Actually, you're the sick one. That's what they suspect now and, believe me, by the time I'm done here, they won't have any reason to think differently."

"You're wrong. You've already proved your insanity. You've torn this city to shreds and now you've kidnapped an innocent—"

"Innocent? Hardly, but that's not the point. The point is, *you* kidnapped her." Slater grinned wide.

"You're not making sense."

"Of course not. I'm not making any sense to you because you're not thinking. You and I both know that I did all those nasty things. That Slater called Kevin, and Slater blew up the bus, and Slater is holding the old witch in a cement box. Problem is, they think that Kevin is Slater. And if they don't yet, they will soon enough. Kevin is Slater because Kevin is crazy." Grin. "That's the plan, puke."

Kevin stared, mind numb. "That's . . . that's not possible."

"Actually, it is. Which is why it'll work. You don't think I'd go for something implausible, do you?"

"How could I be you?"

"Multiple Personality Disorder. MPD. You're me without even knowing that you are me."

Kevin shook his head. "You're actually stupid enough to think that Jennifer—"

"Sam believes it." Slater walked over to the desk and touched a black box that looked like an answering machine. He'd lowered the pistol to his side, and Kevin wondered if he could rush him before he had a chance to lift it and shoot.

"She found the cell phone I used in your pocket—that alone's enough for most juries. But they'll find more. The recordings, for instance. They'll show that my voice is really your voice, manipulated to sound like a terrible killer named Slater." Slater feigned horror and shivered. "Oooo . . . chilling, don't you think?"

"There are a thousand holes! You'll never get away with it."

"There are no holes!" Slater snapped. Then he grinned again. "And I already *am* getting away with it."

He picked up a picture. It was a photograph of Sam, taken at a distance with a telephoto lens. "She's really quite beautiful," he said, lost in the image for a moment. He reached up and ripped down a large black sheet that hung on the wall. Behind it, fifty or sixty pictures had been affixed to the concrete.

They were all of Samantha.

Kevin blinked and took a step forward. Slater's gun came up. "Stay back."

Pictures of Sam on the street, New York, Sacramento, through a window, in her bedroom . . . Heat spread down Kevin's neck.

"What are you doing?"

"I wanted to kill her once." Slater slowly faced Kevin, eyes sagging. "But you know that. You wanted her, so you tried to kill me instead."

Slater's lips began to quiver and his breathing came in short quick drags. "Well, now I *am* going to kill her. And I'm going to show the world who you really are, because you're no better than I am. You're the pretty boy down the street she loves to play with. But does that make you better? No!" He screamed the last word and Kevin jumped.

"Hang out with me for a while and we'll see how sweet you are." He leaned forward and tapped Kevin's chest with the gun barrel.

"Deep down inside you're no different than I am. If you'd met me before you met Samantha, we'd both have been at her window, licking the glass. I know that, because I was just like you once."

"That's what this is about?" Kevin demanded. "A jealous schoolboy come back to butcher the boy across the street? You're pathetic!"

"And so are you! You're sick like the rest of them." Slater spat a thimbleful of saliva at the cement. It landed with a smack. "Sick!" He took two steps forward and shoved the gun into Kevin's cheek. Pain flashed up his jaw. "I should just end this now. You and all the freaks who pretend to be so sweet on Sundays! You may not be me but really you are me, you slug."

Slater's body shook against Kevin's.

Kevin's mind began to shut down. *You're going to die, Kevin.*

|||

Slater fights a desperate urge to pull the trigger. He knows that he can't do it. This isn't the plan. Not this way. Not yet.

He stares at Kevin's round eyes. The smell of fear and sweat wafts through his nostrils. Impulsively he sticks out his tongue and presses it firmly against Kevin's jaw. He draws it all the way up his cheek to his temple, as if he's licking an ice-cream cone. Salty. Bitter. Sick, sick, sick.

Slater shoves Kevin and steps back. "Know what I taste? I taste Slater. I'm going to kill her, Kevin. I'm going to kill both of them. But that's not what the world will think. They're going to think that you did it."

Kevin straightens and glares at him. The man has more spunk than Slater estimated. Enough to come here, he'd guessed as much. But he can't forget that this man also locked him in that cellar once, when he was still a boy. They might be more alike than even Slater realizes.

He takes a deep breath. "Now, let's calm down, shall we? I have a new game I would like to play."

"I'm not going to play any more games," Kevin says.

"Yes, you are. You'll play more games or I'll cut up Mommy, one finger at a time."

Kevin glances at the door that holds the old woman.

"And if we still aren't properly motivated, I'll start on *your* fingers. Are we still all stuffed and cocky?"

Kevin just stares at him. At least he isn't whimpering and crying like the old hag.

"Let's face it, Kevin. You came here with one thing on your mind. You wanted to kill. Kill, kill, kill. That's another way you and I are alike." Slater shrugs. "True, the object of your blood lust is me, but when you cut away all the face-saving, it's the same instinct. Most humans are truly murderers, but I didn't bring you here to lecture. I brought you here to kill. I'm going to give you your wish. You came to kill me, but that doesn't suite my tastes, so I've chosen to flip things a bit."

Kevin doesn't flinch.

"We already have one, but we need the other." Slater looks at the wall, the collage of pictures. It's in part her beauty that he hates so much. It's why he keeps the photographs covered. By nine o'clock she will be dead.

"Kill me," Kevin says. "I hate you." He speaks the last words with such contempt that Slater feels a sliver of shock.

But Slater doesn't show shock. He shows anger and hatred, but not shock, because shock is weakness.

"So courageous. So noble. How can I refuse such a sincere request? Consider yourself dead already. We all die; yours will be a living death until you finally do kick the bucket. In the meantime, we must lure in our second victim. She will fly to your rescue. Her knight is in peril."

"I despise you."

"You will help me or Mommy will begin to scream!" Slater says.

Kevin glares at him and then closes his eyes slowly.

"Just a simple call, Kevin. I would do it, but I really need her to hear your voice."

Kevin shakes his head and is about to speak, but Slater doesn't want to hear it. He steps forward and slams the gun against the side of Kevin's head.

"I'll kill her, you perverted little brat!"

Blood oozes down Kevin's face. This excites Slater.

Kevin's face wrinkles and he begins to cry. Better, much better. He sinks slowly to his knees and for the first time since his nemesis entered the room, Slater knows he will win.

|||

Samantha raced through Long Beach. Secret. What secret? Kevin had hidden his dealing with Slater as a boy and he'd remained quiet about his home life, but the journal entry had to be something else. Something the professor knew.

She was a block away when her cell phone rang. She couldn't imagine how investigators had managed before the advent of cellular technology. On the other hand, criminals took advantage as well. Slater certainly had.

"Sam."

"This is Kevin."

"Kevin!"

" . . . no one else. Do you understand?" His voice sounded flat—horrible. He was reading, being forced. Sam veered for the curb, ignoring a honk behind.

"Kevin, if you're with Slater keep talking and don't cough. If you're not, cough. Yes, I do understand." Actually, she'd missed what she was supposed to understand. And she quickly considered asking him to repeat it, but that might endanger him.

Kevin didn't cough.

"We're playing a new game," he said. "This game's for you, Sam. If you can find us before nine, he'll set me and Mommy free." His voice wavered. She heard a muffled voice in the background. Slater.

"I will give you the first clue. If you find it, there will be another one. No authorities can be involved, including that wench, Jennifer." Slater chuckled in the background. His voice suddenly filled the phone, loud and eager.

"First clue: *Who loves what he sees, but hates what he loves?* You might find a clue in his house; you might not. Hurry to the rescue, Princess." The phone went dead.

"Slater? Kevin!" Sam threw the phone against the windshield. "Aaaahh!"

Who loves what he sees, but hates what he loves? Her mind was blank. 6:27. Less than three hours. She had to get back to Kevin's house. The answers had to be in his papers. His journal. Somewhere!

She roared through a U-turn and headed back north. What was the chance that Slater had found a way to monitor her phone calls? If he knew electronics well enough to pull off a frame on Kevin, he knew more than she. No authorities involved, he'd said.

Sam bent for her cell on the floor and swerved badly enough to force a second attempt. She caught the phone, fumbled with the battery, which had jarred loose. Power on. Redial.

|||

"Thank you again for your time, Dr. Francis. As I explained on the phone—"

"Yes, yes, of course." The professor waved her in. "Please come in, dear. Believe me, I will do whatever I can for that boy."

Jennifer paused. "You understand why I'm here? It seems that you know more about Kevin than you first suggested. At least Kevin believes you do."

"I know him better than most, yes. But nothing that I haven't told you."

"That's what we're going to find out. With your help." She stepped into the house. "We're running out of time, Professor. If you can't help us, I'm afraid no one will be able to. You talked to Samantha Sheer from CBI earlier today; she'll be here shortly." Her cell went off and she pulled it from her waist. "Excuse me."

It was Sam. She'd heard from Kevin. Jennifer instinctively turned back toward the door and listened while Sam ran through the details.

"So you're headed *back* to the house?"

"Yes. Review the clue with Dr. Francis. *Who loves what he sees, but hates what he loves?* You got it? Review *everything* with him. He has to know something."

"I have to report this."

"Slater said no cops, and he mentioned you by name. You won't be out of the loop. Just stay where you are. Don't brief Milton. Let me work alone; that's all I ask. If you think of anything, call me. But this is between us now. Kevin, Slater, and me. Please, Jennifer."

Jennifer hesitated. "Okay. I'll give you an hour. Then I call this in, understood? I'm over my head here."

"I'll call you."

"One hour." She closed the cell.

"Anything wrong?" Dr. Francis asked.

"Everything's wrong, Doctor."

25

"WHO LOVES WHAT HE SEES, but hates what he loves?" Dr. Francis said. "Every man, every woman, every child beyond the age of accountability."

"He loves the ice cream, but hates the fat it puts on his waist," Jennifer said.

"Yes. She loves the wrong man, but hates what he does to her life. The dilemma goes back to Eve and the apple in the garden. Sin."

"I don't see how that helps us," Jennifer said. "The reference has to be personal, something that only Sam or Kevin might know. Something the three of them knew when they were children."

"Three children? Or two? Sam and Kevin, who had his alter ego—the boy?" Dr. Francis sat in a large leather recliner and leaned forward. "Tell me everything. From the beginning. Time is slipping."

He listened, eyes sparkling, with only the occasional frown to betray his anxiety over Kevin's predicament. In many ways he reminded Jennifer of Kevin, genuine to the bone and thoroughly intelligent. It was the first time she'd run through the last four days aloud and with such comprehensive minutiae with anyone except Galager. The first call, the car bomb, the second call regarding the doghouse. Then the bus, Kevin's flight with Sam to Palos Verdes, the warehouse, the library, the kidnapping, and now this death threat.

She told it all in one long run-on, interrupted only by his prodding for further detail. He was a thinker, among the best, and he seemed to like playing detective. So did most people. His questions were insightful. How do you know that Kevin was inside his house when the second phone call was made? Is there a way to intercept a laser signal? All the questions lent themselves to whether Kevin could logically be Slater.

Twenty minutes and Sam still hadn't called. Jennifer stood and paced, hand on chin. "I can't believe it's coming down to this. Kevin's out there somewhere in the dark with a madman and we're . . ." She ran her hands through her hair. "It's been like that since I got down here. Slater's always one step ahead, and we're running around like a bunch of toy monkeys."

"You remind me of Kevin when you do that."

He was looking at her hands, still in her hair. She sat down on the couch and sighed. "So now I'm Kevin as well."

He chuckled. "Hardly. But I do agree that the primary question is who, not what. Who is Kevin? Really."

"And?"

He leaned back and crossed his legs. "Multiple Personality Disorder. It's referred to as Dissociative Identity Disorder these days, isn't it? Where two or more personalities inhabit a single body. As you know, not everyone acknowledges such an animal. Some spiritualize the phenomenon—demon possession. Others discount it outright or think of it as commonplace, a gift even."

"And you?"

"While I do believe in spiritual forces and even demon possession, I can assure you that Kevin is not possessed. I've spent many hours with the boy, and my own spirit isn't so callous. The fact of the matter is, all of us experience some level of dissociation, more so with age. We suddenly forget why we walked into the bathroom. Or we have strange déjà vu. Daydreaming, highway hypnosis, even losing yourself in a book or movie. All forms of dissociation that are thoroughly natural."

"A far cry from the kind of dissociation that would be required for Kevin to be Slater," Jennifer said. "As you said, you've spent time with him, so have I. Kevin doesn't have a trace of Slater in him. If both personalities share the same body, they are completely unaware of each other."

"*If.* That is the operative word here. If Kevin is also Slater. Frankly, your theory that Slater may be framing Kevin makes as much sense. But . . ." Dr. Francis stood and paced to the fireplace and back. "But let's assume Kevin is Slater for the moment. What if there was a child, a boy, who from a very young age was isolated from the real world."

"Kevin."

"Yes. What would that child learn?"

"He would learn whatever he was taught from his surroundings: the environment he could touch, taste, hear, smell, see. If he were alone on an island, he would think the world was a small piece of dirt floating on the water, and he would wonder why he didn't have fur like the rest of his playmates. Like Tarzan."

"Yes, but our child does not grow up on an island. He grows up in a world of shifting realities. A world where realities are merely slips of paper cut up into truth. There are no absolutes. There is no evil and, by extension, there is no good. Everything is pretend, and only that which you decide to be real is actually real. Life is merely a string of role-playing adventures."

Dr. Frances lifted his hand to his beard and pulled lightly at the gray strands. "But there *is* an absolute, you see. There is good and there is evil. The boy feels a void in his soul. He longs for an understanding of those absolutes, good and evil. He is abused in the most mentally strenuous ways, causing his mind to separate into dissociative realities. He becomes a master role-player, and finally, when he is old enough to understand evil, he subconsciously creates a personality to play the part. Because that's what he's learned to do."

"The boy. Slater."

"A walking, living personification of man's dual nature. The natures of man could be playing themselves out through personalities he's created. It does follow, doesn't it?"

"Assuming man has more than one nature. It could also be a simple fracture—common dissociation."

"Man does have more than one nature," the professor said. "The 'old man,' which is our flesh, and the fingerprint of God, the good."

"And for those of us who don't necessarily believe in the spirit of God? Who aren't religious?"

"A person's inner natures have nothing to do with religion. They are spiritual, not religious. Two natures battling. Good and evil. They are the good that we would do but do not do, and they are that which we would not do, but still do. The apostle Paul. Romans chapter seven. The capacity for good and evil is within every person from birth, I think. The spirit of God can regenerate man, but it is the human spirit I'm talking about here. Not a separate nature, although I would say that the struggle between good and evil is hopeless without divine intervention. Perhaps that's what you think of when you say 'religious,' although really religion has little to do with divine intervention either."

He offered a quick smile. For the second time in as many days he was tempting her to discover his faith. Right now, however, she didn't have the time.

"So you're thinking Kevin, as a young boy, simply struggled to make sense of the conflict within him, between basic good and evil. He dealt with it the way he learned to deal with all reality. He creates roles for each persona and plays them out without knowing that he's doing it."

"Yes, that's exactly what I'm thinking," the professor said, standing and pacing to his right. "It's possible. Entirely possible. It may not even be classical Dissociative Identity Disorder. Could be Post-traumatic Stress Disorder, which is even more likely for this kind of unconscious role-playing."

"Assuming Kevin is Slater."

"Yes, assuming Kevin is Slater."

| | |

Sam poured through Kevin's journal, searching desperately for a key to the riddle. *Who loves what he sees, but hates what he loves?* When that yielded no answer, she paged through his class notebooks.

The most obvious answer was mankind, of course. Mankind looks and sees and loves and then hates. The story of humanity in one sentence. Not quite up there with Descartes's "I think therefore I am," but obvious enough.

Who loves what he sees, but hates what he loves? Who, who? Slater. Slater was who. Despite Jennifer's theory, Kevin had to be Slater. If so, Slater was the hater of the two.

She sighed. Something common to all three of them triggered this riddle. But what? She had only two hours to win this mad game. And even if she did find them, Slater surely wouldn't let them all go. Someone would die in the next two hours. Kevin had saved her from the killer once; he'd risked his life. Now it was her turn.

6:59. And this riddle was only the first clue.

She mumbled through gritted teeth. "Come on, Kevin! Tell me something."

| | |

"Then Slater's the boy, stalking Sam, but he's really Kevin's evil alter ego," Jennifer said.

"And Kevin doesn't like the evil boy, so he kills him," the professor said.

"But isn't that evil? To kill?"

"God killed a few men in their time. Read the Old Testament. Kevin tries to kill the boy because the boy threatens to kill his childhood friend."

"But the boy is really Kevin. So Kevin would have killed Samantha if he hadn't dealt with the boy?"

"Think of it—a personality that embodies only evil would be quite a little monster. Slater, the evil in Kevin, sees that Samantha favored Kevin over him. Slater decides he must kill Sam."

"And now that monster has come back to life and is stalking Kevin," Jennifer said. "In this scenario of yours."

"That monster never died. That would require more than Kevin was capable of on his own. Death to the old self." Dr. Francis paused and then continued. "As Kevin matured, he recognized Balinda's folly, but he didn't recognize his dual nature. He did, however, successfully climb out of his past, leave the house, and embrace the real world."

"Until three months of seminary and discussions of his one obsession, the natures of man, finally brings Slater back to the surface," Jennifer finished.

The professor lifted an eyebrow. "It's possible."

As a clinical theory the possibilities were interesting, but Jennifer was having difficulty accepting it as reality. Theories abounded in the study of the mind, a new one every month, it seemed. This was a theory. And time was still ticking away, while the real Kevin possibly sat at the real Slater's gunpoint, praying desperately for someone to burst through the doors and save him.

"But why the game? Why the riddles?"

"I don't know." His eyes glimmered mischievously. "Perhaps the whole thing was really Kevin's idea."

"I don't follow."

"Evil only survives in the dark. This isn't religious either, by the way. The simplest way to deal with evil is to force it into the light of truth. Expose its secret. Sun on the vampire. Sin thrives in the dungeon, but slap it on the table for all to see, and it withers rather quickly. It was one of Kevin's greatest complaints about the church, actually. That everyone hides their evil. Their sin. Pastors, deacons, bishops—they perpetuate the very nature they are in business to destroy by covering it up. No confession allowed except in secret."

"Now you sound like a skeptic."

"I'm a skeptic of religious systems, not of the faith. Someday I will be happy to discuss the difference with you."

"How does this make the riddles Kevin's idea?"

"Perhaps subconsciously Kevin knows that Slater still lurks. What better way to destroy him than to expose him? Kevin could be forcing Slater's hand, forcing him to reveal himself. Ha! I'm telling you, Kevin is genuine enough to conceive of just such a plan! Slater thinks he has Kevin where he wants him by forcing a confession, when it's the very confession that will destroy Slater, not Kevin! It's like the cross all over again."

Jennifer rubbed her temples. "I can just hear the court case now. This all assumes Slater isn't framing Kevin."

"Yes. But either way, we've pieced together his framework. At least the logic of it." Dr. Francis sat and faced her with his fingers touching each other in a tepee. "My goodness. You came here to find out who Kevin really is. I think I've just stumbled on it, my dear."

"Tell me, who is Kevin?"

"Kevin is every man. And woman. He is you; he is me; he is the woman who wears a yellow hat and sits on the third pew every Sunday. Kevin is the natures of humanity personified."

"Please, you can't mean that everyone's a Slater."

"No, only those who do as Slater does. Only those who hate. Do you hate, Jennifer? Do you gossip?"

|||

Who loves what he sees, but hates what he loves? The simplicity of it hit Sam midstride, as she paced Kevin's living room, staring at the travel posters. The windows to the world. It wasn't *who;* it was the *seeing!* Who had *seen?* Slater had seen her and wanted her. But where had he seen her?

The window. Her window! The boy Slater had watched her from the window and seen what he desperately wanted but could not have. And he hated her.

The answer to the riddle was her window!

Sam stood still, stunned, then ran for her car. She fired the engine and roared down the street. 7:23.

Sam punched in Jennifer's cell number.

"This is—"

"I think I have it! I'm on my way now."

"What is it?" Jennifer demanded.

Sam hesitated. "This is for me—"

"Just tell me where, for heaven's sake! I know it's for you, but time's running out here!"

"The window."

"Kevin's window?"

"My window. That's where Slater saw me. That's where he hated me." She glanced in her rearview mirror. Clear. "I need more time, Jennifer. If Slater even gets a whiff of anyone else snooping around this, he may pull the trigger. You know that."

No response.

"Please, Jennifer, there's no other way."

"We could have a dozen of the best minds on this."

"Then get them on it. But no one from the investigation and, without question, no locals. We can't risk a leak. Besides, no one's going to know these riddles like I do. This is about me now."

Silence.

"Jennifer—"

"Just hurry, Samantha."

"I'm doing sixty in a thirty-five as it is." She hung up.

Hold on, Kevin. Please don't do anything stupid. Wait for me. I'm coming. I swear I'm coming.

26

WHETHER THE BOY WAS IMAGINARY OR REAL, he knew Sam and he wants her to come," Dr. Francis said as Jennifer closed her phone. "He's luring her in. You see that, don't you? The riddles are only to continue the game."

Jennifer sighed. "And if Sam finds them? He'll kill them all and I'll have done nothing."

"What can you do?"

"Something. Anything! If I can't save him, then I should report this."

"Then report it. But what can any of your colleagues do?"

He was right, of course, but the idea of sitting here in his living room discussing the natures of man was . . . impossible! Roy had been killed in similar circumstances by the Riddle Killer. True, Slater probably wasn't the same man who'd killed Roy, but he represented the same kind of man. Unless Kevin was Slater.

Did Slater live in her? Do you hate, Jennifer? Milton?

"Perhaps the most you can do is try to understand, so that if an opportunity does come, you're better equipped," the professor said. "I know how frustrating it must be, but now it's up to Sam. She sounds like someone who can handle herself. If I'm right, Kevin will need her."

"How so?"

"If Kevin is Slater, he'll be powerless to overcome Slater on his own."

Jennifer looked at him and wondered what movies he watched.

"Okay, Professor. We still don't know if Kevin is Slater or not. Theories are fine, but let's try the logistics on for size." She pulled out her notebook and crossed her legs. "Question: From a purely logistical and evidentiary perspective, could one person have done what we know to have happened?"

She opened the book to the list she'd made two hours earlier, after Sam's call suggesting for the second time that Kevin was Slater. She ticked the first item with her pencil. "Kevin gets a call in his car."

"Although you said there's no evidence of that first call, correct? The cell phone was burned. The entire call could have been in Kevin's mind, two voices talking. Same with any unrecorded conversation he had with Slater."

She nodded. "Number two. The car blows up three minutes after the call, after Kevin has escaped."

"The personality that is Slater carries a sophisticated cell phone in his pocket—Kevin's pocket. This device is a secure telephone and a transmitting device. After the imaginary conversation giving him three minutes, the Slater personality triggers a bomb he's planted in the trunk. It explodes, as planned. He detonates all of the bombs in similar fashion."

"The second phone Sam found."

"Follows," Dr. Francis said.

"Where does the Slater personality make all these explosives? We found nothing." Jennifer had her own thoughts but she wanted to hear the professor.

He smiled. "Maybe when I'm done playing scholar, I'll apply for a job with the FBI."

"I'm sure we would welcome you. Understanding of religion is a hot recruitment criterion these days."

"Slater obviously has his hiding place. Likely the place he's hidden Balinda. Kevin takes frequent trips to this location as Slater, totally unaware. The middle of the night, on the way home from class. He remembers nothing of them because it is the Slater personality, not Kevin, who is actually going."

"And his knowledge of electronics. Slater learns, but not Kevin."

"So it would seem."

She looked at her list. "But the warehouse is different because he calls the room phone and talks to Samantha. It's the first time we have him on tape."

"You said the phone rang while he was in the room, but Slater didn't speak until Kevin was out. He reaches into his pocket and presses send on a number he's already entered. As soon as he's in the hall, he begins to speak."

"Sounds far-fetched, don't you think? Somehow I don't see Slater as a James Bond."

"No, he's probably made his mistakes. You just haven't had the time to find them. For all you know, the recording will bear that out. We're just reconstructing a possible scenario based on what we do know."

"Then we can assume he planted the bomb in the library the night before last somehow, while he was supposedly in Palos Verdes with Samantha. Maybe he slipped out at night or something. The library's not exactly a high-security facility. He, meaning Slater, did everything either while our eyes were off him or remotely using the cell phone."

"If Kevin is Slater," the professor said.

She frowned. The scenario was plausible. Too plausible for her own comfort. If it bore out, the scientific journals would be writing about Kevin for years.

"And the Riddle Killer?" she asked.

"As you said earlier. Someone Slater imitated to throw the authorities off. What do you call it—copy cat? It's only been four days. Even the wheels of the FBI can turn only so fast. Perpetuating the double life beyond a week might be impossible. Four days is all he evidently needed."

Jennifer closed the notebook. There were a dozen more, but she saw with a glance that they weren't so unique. What they really needed was the analysis of the two recordings from Kevin's cell phone. It was the second call that interested her. If this theory held water, the same person had made and received the call that had sent them running for the library. It couldn't have been imagined by Kevin because it was recorded.

She sighed. "This is way too complicated. There's something missing here that would make all of this much clearer."

The professor ran his fingers over his bearded chin. "Maybe so. Do you rely on your intuition very often, Jennifer?"

"All day. Intuition leads to evidence, which leads to answers. It's what makes us ask the right questions."

"Hmm. And what does your intuition tell you about Kevin?"

She thought about it for a moment. "That he's innocent, either way. That he's an exceptional man. That he's nothing like Slater."

His right eyebrow went up. "This after four days? It took me a month to conclude the same."

"Four days of hell will tell you a lot about a man, Professor."

"'Yea, though I walk through the valley of the shadow of death, I will fear no evil.'"

"If he is Slater, do you think Kevin's afraid?" she asked.

"I think he is petrified."

|||

Baker Street was black and still, shrouded in the long line of elms standing like sentinels. The drive had sliced twenty-one minutes off the clock, thanks to an accident on Willow. 7:46. She passed Kevin's old house—light glowed behind the drapes where Eugene and Bob might very well still be crying. Jennifer had kept the media at bay for the day, but it wouldn't last. By tomorrow there would probably be at least a couple vans parked out front, waiting for a snapshot of the crazies inside.

What loves what it sees? She slowed the car to a crawl and approached her old house. A porch light glared angrily. The hedges were ragged, not trimmed like her father had kept them years earlier. She'd already decided that she wouldn't bother the residents for the simple reason that she couldn't think of a decent explanation for why she would want to snoop around the bedroom window without causing alarm. She hoped they didn't have a dog.

Sam parked the car across the street and walked past the house, then cut into the neighbor's yard. She rounded the house and headed for the same old fence she and Kevin had wriggled through on a hundred occasions. Unlikely the boards were still loose.

She crouched by the fence and ran along it toward the east side of the yard, where her old bedroom faced. A dog barked several houses down. *Settle down, Spot, I'm just going to take a peek.* Just like Slater used to take peeps. Life had come full circle.

She poked her head over the fence. The window was opaque, slightly obscured by the same bushes she'd crawled over as a child. Vacant? No dog that she could see. The boards she'd once been able to slip through wouldn't budge. Up and over—the only way.

Sam grabbed the fence with both hands and vaulted it easily. She had a body built for gymnastics, a coach had told her in law school. But you don't start taking gymnastics at age twenty and expect to make the Olympics. She had opted for dance classes.

The lawn was wet from a recent watering. She ran for the window and knelt by the hedge. What was she looking for? Another clue. A riddle maybe, scratched in the ground. A note taped to the brick.

She slid in behind the bushes and felt the wall. The musty smell of dirt filled her nose. How long had it been since anyone had climbed through this window? She eased her head up and saw that the window not only was dark, but had been painted black on the inside.

Her pulse spiked. Did Slater live here? Had he taken residence in her old house? *I can't have you, so I'll take your house.* For a moment she just stared at the window, caught off guard. Someone laughed inside. A man. Then a woman, laughing.

No, they'd probably just turned the room into a darkroom or something. Photography buffs. She exhaled and resumed her search. Time was ticking.

She felt along the ledge, but there was nothing she could feel or see. The ground was dark at her feet, so she knelt and groped around in the dirt. Her fingers ran over a few rocks—he could have written a message on a rock. She held them up to what little light reached her from the warehouses across the street. Nothing. She dropped the rocks and stood again.

Had she been wrong about the window? There was a message here; there had to be! The dial on her watch glowed green, 7:58. She felt the first tendrils of panic tickle her spine. If she was wrong about the window, she'd have to start over—the game would be lost.

Maybe she shouldn't be looking for a written message.

She groaned and stepped back into the lawn. The panic was growing. *Take a breath, Sam. You're smarter than he is. You have to be. For Kevin's sake. Play his game; beat him at his own game.*

She paced the lawn, uncaring of her exposure now. She wore black slacks and a red blouse, dark colors that wouldn't easily be seen from the street. Time was running out.

Sam walked to the fence and faced the window. Okay, is there something in the bushes? An arrow? That was stupid movie stuff. She followed the roofline. Did it point anywhere? There were two second-story windows above the one down here, forming a triangle of sorts. An arrow.

Enough with the arrows, Sam! This is something that you couldn't mistake. Not something cute out of a Nancy Drew mystery. What's changed here? What is altered to make a statement? What's altered that could make a statement?

The window. The window is painted black, because it's now a darkroom or something. So really it's not a window any longer. It's a dark sheet of glass. No light.

It's dark down here, Kevin.

Sam let out a small cry and immediately swallowed it. That was it! *No* window. What used to have light but does no more? What has no window?

Sam ran for the fence and slung herself over it, spilling to the ground on her landing. Was it possible? How could Slater have pulled it off?

She felt for her gun. *Okay, think. One hour.* If she was right, she didn't need five minutes, much less sixty, to find Kevin.

| | |

"And how is a man or a woman set free from this hideous nature?" Jennifer asked.

"You kill it. But to kill it you must see it. Thus the light."

"So just like"—Jennifer snapped her fingers—"that, huh?"

"As it turns out, no. It needs a daily dose of death. Really, the single greatest ally of evil is darkness. That is my point. I don't care what faith you have or what you say you believe, whether you go to church every Sunday or pray to God five times a day. If you keep the evil nature hidden, like most do, it thrives."

"And Kevin?"

"Kevin? I don't know about Kevin. If he is Slater, I suppose you would need to kill Slater the way you kill the old self. But he can't do it alone. He wouldn't even know to kill him. Man cannot deal with evil alone."

III

Kevin had never shown her the inside of the old shed because he said it was dark inside. Only he hadn't just said inside, he said *down* there. She remembered that now. Nobody used the useless old shack in the corner of the lawn. The old bomb shelter turned toolshed on the edge of the ash heap.

The window that wasn't really a window had to be Kevin's window. In Slater's mind he might have used another riddle: *What thinks it's a window but really isn't?* Opposites. As a boy, Kevin thought he'd escaped his tortuous world through his window, but he hadn't.

The old toolshed in the corner of Kevin's lawn was the only place Sam knew of that had a basement of sorts. It was dark down there and it had no windows, and she knew that she knew that she knew that Slater was down in that bomb shelter with Balinda.

Sam held the nine millimeter at her side and ran for the shack, bent over, eyes fixed on its wood siding. The door had always been latched and locked with a big rusted padlock. What if it still was?

She should call Jennifer, but therein lay a dilemma. What could Jennifer do? Swoop in and surround the house? Slater would do the worst. On the other hand, what could *Sam* do? Waltz in and confiscate all illegally obtained firearms, slap on the handcuffs, and deliver the nasty man to the county jail?

She had to at least verify.

Sam dropped to her knee by the door, breathing heavily, both hands wrapped around her gun. The lock was disengaged.

Just remember, you were born for this, Sam.

She stuck the barrel of her gun under the door and pulled, using the gun sight as a hook. The door creaked open. A dim bulb glowed inside. She pushed the door all the way open and shoved her weapon in, careful to stay behind the cover of the doorjamb. Slowly, the opening door revealed the shapes of shelves and a wheelbarrow. A square on the floor. The trapdoor.

How deep did the shelter go? There had to be stairs.

She stepped in, one foot and then the second. The trapdoor was open, she could see now. She edged over to the dark hole and peered down. Faint light, very faint, from the right. She pulled back. Maybe calling Jennifer would be the wisest course of action. Just Jennifer.

8:15. They still had forty-five minutes. But what if she waited for Jennifer and this *wasn't* the place? That would leave them with less than half an hour to find Slater. No, she had to verify. Verify, verify.

Come on, Sam, you were born for this.

Sam shoved the gun into her waistband, knelt down, gripped the edge of the opening, and then swung one leg into the shaft. She stretched her foot, found a step. She mounted the stairs and then swung back up. The shoes might make too much noise. She took them off and then settled back on the stairs.

Come on, Sam, you were born for this.

There were nine steps; she counted them. Never knew when she might have to run back up full tilt. Knowing when to duck to avoid a head-on with the ceiling and when to turn right to exit the shack could come in handy. She was telling herself this stuff to calm her nerves, because anything in the dread silence was better than facing the certainty that she was walking to her death.

Light came from a crack below a door at the end of a concrete tunnel. The tunnel led to a basement below Kevin's house! She'd known that some of these old bomb shelters were connected to houses, but she'd never imagined such an elaborate setup beneath Kevin's house. She'd never even known there *was* a basement in his house. Wasn't there a way to the top floor from the basement? Jennifer had been in the house, but she hadn't said anything about a basement.

Sam withdrew her gun and tiptoed down the shaft.

"Shut up." Slater's voice sounded muffled behind the door. Sam stopped. Verified. She could never mistake that voice. Slater was behind that door. And Kevin?

The door was well insulated; they would never hear her. Sam walked to the door, nine millimeter up by her ear. She reached for the doorknob and slowly applied pressure. She didn't plan on bursting in, or entering at all, for that matter, but she needed to know a few things. Whether the door was locked, for starters. The knob refused to turn.

She backed up a foot and considered her options. What did Slater expect her to do, knock? She would if she had to, wouldn't she? There was only one way to save this man, and it was on the other side of that door.

Sam eased down to her belly and pressed her left eye to the crack beneath the door. On the right, white tennis shoes walked slowly toward her. She stilled her breathing.

"Time is most definitely winding down," Slater said. The feet were his, white tennis shoes she didn't recognize. "I don't hear your lover breaking down the door."

"Sam's smarter than you," Kevin said.

The tennis shoes stopped.

Sam jerked her eye to the left, where the voice had come from. She saw his feet, Kevin's shoes, the tan Reeboks she'd seen by his bed a few hours ago. Two voices, two men.

Sam pulled back. Kevin and Slater weren't the same person. She'd been wrong!

Sam flattened herself again and peered, breathing too loudly but not caring now. There they were, two sets of feet. One to her right, white, and one to her left, tan. Kevin tapped one foot nervously. Slater was walking away.

She had to tell Jennifer! In case something happened to her, she had to let Jennifer know who stood behind that door.

Sam slid back and stood. She hurried to the end of the hall. Going up the stairs might be prudent, but at this distance, there was no way Slater could hear. She lifted her phone and hit redial.

"Jennifer?"

"Sam! What's going on?"

"Shh, shh, shh. I can't talk," Sam whispered. "I found them."

A barely audible ring pierced the silence, as if a gunshot had discharged too close to her ear within the last half-hour.

Jennifer seemed incredulous. "You . . . you found Kevin? You actually located them? Where?"

"Listen to me, Jennifer. Kevin's not Slater. Do you hear me? I was wrong. It has to be a frame!"

"Where are you?" Jennifer demanded.

"I'm here, outside."

"You're absolutely positive that Kevin isn't Slater? How—"

"Listen to me!" Sam whispered harshly. She glanced back at the door. "I just saw them both; that's how I know."

"You have to tell me where you are!"

"No. Not yet. I have to think this through. He said no cops. I'll call you." She hung up before she lost her nerve and dropped the phone into her pocket.

Why didn't she just call Jennifer in? What could she possibly do that Jennifer couldn't? Only Slater knew the answer to that. The boy she'd never seen. Until today. *Kevin, dear Kevin, I'm so sorry.*

A shaft of light suddenly cut through the tunnel. She whirled around. The door was open. Slater stood in the doorframe, barechested, grinning, gun in hand.

"Hello, Samantha. I was getting worried. So nice of you to find us."

27

S AM'S FIRST INSTINCT WAS TO RUN. Up the stairs, duck, to the left, into the open. Come back with a flamethrower and burn him out. Her second instinct was to rush him. The rage that flooded her mind seeing him backlit by the light surprised her. She could feel her gun at her waist and she grabbed for it.

"Don't be so predictable, Sam. Kevin thinks you're smarter than me. Did you hear him say that? Prove it, darling." He brought the gun up and aimed it inside to his right. "Come on in here and prove it to me, or I'll cap the kid where he stands."

Sam hesitated. Slater stood with a cocky grin. She walked down the hall. *You were born for this, Sam. You were born for this.*

Slater backed up, keeping his gun aimed to his right. She stepped past the steel door. A single bulb cast dim light over the basement. Shades of black and gray. Stark. Kevin stood in front of a wall of pictures, face ashen. Pictures of her. He took a step toward her.

"Not so fast," Slater snapped. "I know how badly you want to be the hero again, boy, but not this time. Take the gun out slowly, Samantha. Slide it toward me." There wasn't a trace of doubt on Slater's face. He had them precisely where he'd intended.

Sam slid the gun across the concrete, and Slater scooped it up. He walked to the door, closed it, and faced them both. It struck Sam, staring at the man's smirk, that she'd committed a kind of suicide.

She'd stepped into the lair willfully, and she'd just given the dragon her gun.

You were born for this, Sam. Born for what? Born to die.

She turned from him purposefully. *No, I was born for Kevin.* She looked at him, ignoring Slater, who stood behind her now.

"You okay?"

Kevin's eyes darted over her shoulder and then settled on hers. Trails of sweat glistened on his face. The poor man was terrified.

"Not really."

"It's okay, Kevin." She smiled. "I promise you, it'll be okay."

"Actually, it won't be okay, Kevin," Slater said, walking briskly to her right. He wasn't the monster she'd imagined. No horns, no yellow teeth, no scarred face. He looked like a jock with short blond hair, tight tan slacks, a torso cut like a gymnast's. A large, red tattoo of a heart branded over his breast. She could have met this man a dozen times over the years and not taken notice. Only his eyes gave him away. They were far away, light gray eyes, like a wolf's. If Kevin's eyes swallowed her, Slater's were the kind she might bounce off of. He even smiled like a wolf.

"I'm not sure you're aware of what we have here, but the way I see it, you're both in a bit of a pickle," Slater said. "And Kevin is fit to be tied. He's made three phone calls to his FBI girlfriend, and I just sat back and let him do it. Why? Because I know how hopeless his situation is, even if he doesn't. No one can help him. Or you, dear Samantha."

"If you wanted to kill Kevin, you could have done it a dozen times," Sam said. "So what *is* your game? What do you hope to accomplish with all of this nonsense?"

"I could have killed you too, my dear. A hundred times. But this way it's just so much more fun. We're all together like a happy little family. Mommy's in the closet, Kevin's finally come back home, and now his little girlfriend has come to save him from the terrible boy down the street. It's almost like old times. We're even going to let Kevin kill again."

Slater's lips fell flat. "Only this time he's not going after me. This time he's going to put a bullet in your head."

Sam took this in and faced Kevin. He looked so frail in the yellow light. Afraid. Slater was going to force his hand to kill. Her. It all made perfect sense now, although exactly what Slater had in mind, she didn't know.

Surprisingly, Sam felt no fear. In fact, she felt somewhat buoyed, even confident. *Maybe this is how you feel just before you die.*

"So. He's the boy, after all," Sam said to Kevin. Both men were watching her. "How does a big, strong, handsome man like this become so jealous of you, Kevin? Think about it. How could such a powerful, intelligent man be driven to such insane fits over one man? Answer: Because underneath that big, bold, red tattoo and all that bulging muscle, he's only a pathetic little weasel who's never managed to make a friend, much less win a girl."

Slater stared at her. "I'll keep your predicament in mind and forgive the rest of your desperate insults, but I don't think *jealous* is the right word, Samantha. I am not jealous of this piece of meat."

She faced him slowly, wildly bold and unsure why. "Then forgive me for such poor word choice. You're not insanely jealous; you're delighted with the sweet bond of love that Kevin and I have always shared. The fact that I would have shoved a toilet plunger into your face if I'd ever caught you peeping and licking at my window doesn't bother you, does it?"

His mouth was a thin, straight line. He blinked. Again.

"The fact is, *I chose Kevin,*" Sam said. "And Kevin chose me, and neither of us wants anything to do with you. You can't accept that. It drives you crazy. It makes you see red."

Slater's face twisted. "And Kevin doesn't see red?"

Silence settled. Balinda was in the closet. A clock on the wall read 8:35. She should have told Jennifer where they were. Her cell phone was still in her pocket, and she didn't think Slater knew. Could she call Jennifer? If she could slip her hand into her pocket and press the send button twice, it would automatically dial the last number. Jennifer would hear them. A tingle ran through her fingertips.

"You really think Kevin is any different than me?" Slater waved the guns around absently. "You really think this little puke here doesn't want exactly what I want? He'll kill and he'll lie and he'll spend the rest of his life pretending he won't, just like the rest. That's better than me? At least I'm honest about who I am!"

"And who are you, Slater? You're the devil. You're the sickness of this world. You're vile and you're vomit. Go on, tell us. Be honest—"

"Shut up!" Slater screamed. "Shut your disgusting pie hole! This little piece of trash sits in the pew every Sunday, swearing to God that he won't keep doing his secret little sins when he knows as well as I that he will. We know he will because he's made this promise a thousand times and breaks it every time. He's the liar." Spittle flew from his lips. "*That's* the truth!"

"He's nothing like you," Sam said. "See him? He's a terrorized victim whom you've tried desperately to pound to a pulp. See you? You're a revolting monster pounding whoever threatens you into a pulp. See me? I'm neither terrorized nor frightened, because I see you and I see him and I see nothing in common. Please, don't be such a snail."

Slater stared at her, lips parted, stunned. She had pushed him beyond himself with the simple truth, and he was writhing inside already. She shoved her fingers into her pockets and confidently hooked her thumbs.

"Where do they breed your kind, Slater? Is that a mask you're wearing? You look so normal, but I have this unshakable suspicion that if I pulled your ear, the whole mask would come off and—"

Gunfire crashed through the room and Samantha jerked. Slater had fired the gun. A muffled wail cried through the door. Balinda. Sam's pulse quickened. Slater stood without flinching, gun ex-tended to the ground where his bullet had chipped a divot from the concrete. "That hole below your nose is starting to bother me," he said. "Maybe you should think about closing it."

"Or maybe you should consider putting a hole in your head," Sam said.

Slowly a smile formed on his lips. "You have more spunk than I would have guessed. I really should have broken your window that first night."

"You're demented."

"How much I loved to hurt little girls like you."

"You make me very, very sick."

"Take your hands out where I can see them."

He'd noticed. She pulled her hands out of her pockets and re-turned his glare. Neither backed down.

"Enough!" Kevin yelled.

Sam faced him. Kevin scowled at Slater, whose face was red and quivering. "I've always loved her! Why can't you just accept that? Why have you hidden away all these years? Why can't you find some other poor sucker and leave us alone?"

"Because none of them interests me like you do, Kevin. I hate you more than I hate myself, and that, puke face, is quite interesting."

|||

Slater sounds confident, but he's never felt so much unease in all of his life. He has underestimated the strength of the girl. If his plan depends on bending her will, he will have significant challenges ahead. Fortunately, Kevin is more pliable. He'll be the one pulling the trigger.

What is it about her? Her nerve. Her unyielding conviction. Her arrogance! She really does love the fool and she flaunts that love. In fact, she is all about love and Slater hates her for it. He'd seen her smiling, combing her hair, bouncing around her bedroom as a child twenty years ago; he'd seen her run around, locking up criminals in New York, like some kind of superhero on steroids. Happy, happy and snappy. It makes him sick. The look of disdain in her eyes now brings small comfort—it's born out of her love for the worm to his right. So then, all the more reason for Kevin to put a bullet through her pretty white forehead.

He glances at the clock. Nineteen minutes. He should forget the timing and just do it now. A bitter taste pulls at the back of his tongue. The sweet taste of death. He should do it!

But Slater is a patient man, most excellent in all of the disciplines. He will wait, because it is his power to wait.

The game is down to the last test. The last little surprise.

Slater feels a surge of confidence sweep through his bones. He chuckles. But he doesn't feel like chuckling. He feels like shooting his gun again.

Say what you want now, little girl. We'll see who Kevin chooses.

III

Kevin watched Slater, heard him chuckle, knew with awful certainty that things were going to get worse.

He couldn't believe that Sam had actually come in and given up her gun like that. Didn't she know that Slater would kill her? That was his whole point. Slater wanted Sam dead, and he wanted him to kill her. Kevin would refuse, of course, and then Slater would just kill her himself and find a way to frame Kevin. Either way, their lives would never be the same.

He looked at Sam and saw that she was watching him. She winked slowly. "Courage, Kevin. Courage, my knight."

"Shut up!" Slater said. "Nobody talk! My knight? You're trying to make me gag? *My knight?* What rubbish!"

They stared at him. He was losing himself in this game.

"Shall we begin with the festivities?" Slater asked. He shoved Samantha's gun into his waistband, took two long steps to Balinda's door, unlocked it, and threw it open. Balinda sagged against a wall, bound and wide-eyed. Black smudges covered her white lace nightgown. Stripped of makeup, her face looked quite normal for a woman in her fifties. She whimpered and Kevin felt a pang of sorrow knife through his chest.

Slater bent down and hauled her to her feet. Balinda stumbled out of the room, lips quivering, squeaking in terror.

Slater shoved her against the desk. He pointed to the chair. "Sit!"

She collapsed to her seat. Slater waved his gun at Sam. "Hands up where I can see them." She lifted her hands from her waist. Keeping his gun pointed in Sam's general direction, Slater pulled a roll of duct tape from the top drawer, ripped off a six-inch slab with his teeth, and plastered it over Balinda's mouth.

"Keep quiet," he mumbled. She didn't seem to hear. He shoved his face up to her. "Keep quiet!" he yelled. She jumped and he chuckled.

Slater removed the second gun from his pants and faced them. He cocked the guns, raised them to his shoulders. Sweat covered his white chest like oil. He grinned, lowered his arms, and twirled each pistol like a gunslinger.

"I've thought about this moment for so long," Slater said. "The really big moments in life are never as inspiring as you imagine them—I'm sure you've both figured that out by now. What happens in these next few minutes has run so many laps around my mind that I swear there's a groove an inch deep in there. I've taken way too much pleasure from the thoughts already; nothing can possibly compare. That's the downside of dreaming. But it's been worth it. Now I'm going to make it happen, and of course I'll try to spice it up as much as possible to keep things interesting."

He spun each gun again, the left, then the right. "I've practiced, can you tell?"

Kevin looked at Sam, who stood five feet from Slater, staring at the madman with a quiet fury. What was going through her mind? Slater had shifted his focus to her the moment she'd come in. With Kevin, the man showed no fear, but now facing Sam, Slater was trying to hide his fear with this show of his, wasn't he? He was actually afraid. Sam just stared at him, undaunted, hands limp by her hips.

Kevin's heart swelled. She was the true rescuer, always had been. He wasn't the knight; she was. *Dear Sam, I love you so. I've always loved you.*

This was the end; he knew that. They couldn't save each other this time. Had he told her how much he really did love her? Not with romantic love—with something much stronger. A desperate need. The need to survive. The way he loved his own life.

Kevin blinked. He had to tell her how precious she was to him!

"The game is simple," Slater said. "No need confusing the common folk. One out of two people will die"—he glanced at the clock— "seventeen minutes from now. The old woman"—Slater shoved one of the guns to her temple—"who has evidently mistaken life for a Froot Loops commercial. Actually, I like that about her. If you're going to pretend, you might as well do the whole enchilada, right?"

He smiled and slowly aimed the other gun toward Samantha. "Or the bright young maiden." Both arms were fully extended at right angles now, one toward Balinda, the other toward Sam. "Our executioner will be Kevin. I want you to begin thinking about which wench you'll kill, Kevin. Killing neither isn't an option; that would ruin the fun. You must choose one."

"I won't," Kevin said.

Slater tilted the gun and shot him in the foot.

He gasped. Pain throbbed through to his sole and then spiked up his shin; nausea rolled into his gut. The Reebok on his right foot had a red hole in it and was trembling. His horizon tipped.

"You will." Slater blew imaginary smoke from the barrel. "I promise you, Kevin. You most definitely will."

Sam ran for him and caught his sagging body. He let her support him and adjusted his weight to his left foot.

Sam jerked her head toward Slater. "You're sick . . . You didn't need to do that!"

"A hole in the foot, a hole in the head; we'll see who ends up dead."

"I love you, Sam," Kevin said softly, ignoring the pain. "No matter what happens, I want you to know how lost I am without you."

III

Jennifer paced. "I could *strangle* her!"

"Call her," Dr. Francis said.

"And risk exposing her? She could be right outside his door and her cell goes off? Can't do it."

He nodded. "Something doesn't sit right."

She picked up her phone. "I had myself firmly convinced that Kevin was Slater."

"And he isn't."

"Unless—"

Her cell phone chirped. They both looked at it. Jennifer flipped it open.

"Hello?"

"We have the report from Riggs," Galager said. But Jennifer already knew that Slater and Kevin weren't the same person.

"Bit late. We already know. Anything else?"

"No. Just that."

She sighed. "We have a problem, Bill. What's the mood over there?"

"Gloomy. Frantic without direction. The director just called for you. He's getting an earful from the governor. Expect a call any second. They want to know."

"Know what? We don't know where he's stashed Balinda. We're down to a few minutes and we don't have the faintest idea where he's taken her. Tell them that."

Galager didn't respond right away. "If it's any consolation, Jennifer, I think he's innocent. The man I talked to wasn't a killer."

"Of course he isn't a killer," Jennifer snapped. "What do you mean? Of course . . ." She turned to the professor. His eyes were fixed on her. "What did the report say?"

"I thought you said you knew. The voices on the recording are from the same person."

"The seismic tuner—"

"No. The same person. In Riggs's estimation, if the recording is Kevin and Slater, then Kevin is Slater. There's an echo in the background that barely surfaces on the second tape. Both voices are from the same room. Riggs's guess is he's using two cell phones and the recording picks up a faint reproduction of what he's saying on the other phone."

"But . . . that's impossible!"

"I thought it was the prevailing theory . . ."

"But Sam's with them, and she called us. Kevin isn't Slater!"

"And what makes you think you can trust Sam? If she's with them, didn't she tell you where they are? I'd bank on Riggs."

Jennifer stood frozen to the carpet. Was it possible? "I have to go."

"Jennifer, what do I—"

"I'll call you back." She snapped the phone closed and stared at the professor, dumbstruck.

"Unless Sam *didn't* see them both."

"Did you ever meet with Sam?" Dr. Francis asked. "Actually see her with your own eyes?"

Jennifer thought. "No, I didn't. But . . . I talked to her. So many times."

"So did I. But her voice wasn't so high that it sounded necessarily female."

"Could . . . he do that?" Jennifer scrambled for understanding, searched for something, anything Sam had done that might contradict the notion. None came immediately to mind. "Cases of many more than two personalities have been documented."

"What if Slater isn't the only one who's Kevin? What if Samantha is also Kevin?"

"Three! Three personalities in one."

28

SAMANTHA WATCHED THE SECOND HAND tick relentlessly through its slow arc. Kevin sat on the floor, head in hands, distraught. Balinda slumped in her chair five feet to his left, mouth taped gray, eyes flittering over Kevin. If Kevin's aunt could talk now, what would she say? *I'm so sorry, Kevin! I beg your forgiveness! Don't be a coward, Kevin! Get up and kick that man where he'll remember it!*

Balinda never looked at Slater. It was as if he didn't exist. Or she couldn't bear to look at him. For that matter, the woman didn't look at Sam either. Her attention was consumed by Kevin and Kevin alone.

Sam closed her eyes. *Easy, girl. You can do this.*

But in all honesty she was no longer feeling like she could do this or anything. Slater had two guns and a big smile. She had only her cell phone.

"Uh, uh, uh, hands where I can see, darling."

|||

Jennifer ran her hands through her hair. "This is crazy!" Her head hurt and time was running out. *Think!*

"She was always disappearing! She—he could have made it all up. The CBI, the task force, the interview with the Pakistani, all of it! They were all things she could have created in her mind based on information Kevin already knew."

"Or that Kevin simply fabricated," Dr. Francis said. "Kevin concludes that Slater can't be the Riddle Killer because deep in his subconscious he knows that *he* is Slater. Sam, his alter ego, concludes the same. She's working to free Kevin without knowing that she *is* him."

"She kept suggesting that there was someone on the inside! There was—Kevin! He was on the inside. And she was the one who first concluded that Kevin was Slater!"

"And to Kevin, both Slater and Samantha are as real as you and me."

They were running over each other with their words now, connecting dots that formed a perfect picture.

Or did they?

Jennifer shook her head. "But I just talked to Sam and she saw Kevin and Slater while she was *outside* the door. You're saying that I was actually talking to Kevin, and that he was simply imagining himself as Samantha, sneaking up on him and Slater?"

"It's possible," the professor said, excitedly. "You've read the case studies. If Kevin is truly split, Sam would have her own personality. Everything she's done has been done completely in Kevin's mind, but to both of them, it has been completely real."

"So it was Kevin I just talked to."

"No, it was Sam. Sam is distinct from Kevin in his mind."

"But physically, it was Kevin."

"Assuming she is him, yes."

"And why didn't Slater stop him? If Slater was there as well? Kevin picks up the phone and calls me, and in his mind he's really Samantha, outside the door. Makes sense. But Slater's there too. Why doesn't he stop the phone call?"

"I don't know," the professor said, turning with hand on chin. "You'd think he'd stop Kevin. So we could be wrong."

Jennifer massaged her temples. "But if they *are* all Kevin, it would mean he never even had a childhood friend named Samantha. He created her as an escape to fill the void in his life. Then he created Slater, and when he discovered that Slater hated Sam, he tried to kill Slater. Now Slater's come back and so has Sam." She turned. "But her father was a cop! He lived in the house three down from Kevin's."

"Kevin could have known that a cop named Sheer lived in that house and simply built Samantha's reality on that. Do you know whether Officer Sheer even had a daughter named Samantha?"

"Never checked." Jennifer paced, sorting through the tide of thoughts. "It does make sense, doesn't it? Balinda wouldn't let Kevin have a best friend, so he fabricated one. He role-played her."

"This is what Kevin could have meant when he told me he had a new model for the natures of man," Dr. Francis said. "The three natures of man. Good, evil, and the man struggling between! 'The good that I would, that I do not, but that which I would not, that I do.' There are really three natures in there! One, *the good*. Two, *that which I would not*. And, three, *I!*"

"The struggle between good and evil, embodied in a man who is role-playing both good and evil and yet is still himself as well. Kevin Parson."

"The noble child. Every man."

They stared at each other, transfixed by the enormity of it all.

"It's a possibility," the professor said.

"It almost makes perfect sense." Jennifer glanced at her watch. "And we're almost out of time."

"Then we have to tell her," Dr. Francis said, walking for the kitchen. He turned back. "If Sam is Kevin, then she has to be told! *He* has to be told! He can't deal with this on his own. No one can deal with evil on their own!" .

"Call Sam and tell her that she's Kevin?"

"Yes! Sam's the only one who can save him now! But she's power-less without you."

Jennifer took a deep breath. "What if we're wrong? How do I tell her without sounding like an idiot? Excuse me, Sam, but you're not a real person. You're just part of Kevin?"

"Yes. Tell her as if we know it's a fact, and tell her quickly. Slater may try to stop the call. How much time?"

"Ten minutes."

|||

"This is going to be delightful, Samantha," Slater said, clicking the barrels of the two pistols together like drumsticks. He squirmed. "It's starting to give me shivers all over."

The phone was her only hope, but Slater kept insisting that her hands remain where he could see them. If he knew about the phone, he would have insisted she give it up. Either way, it sat like a useless lump in the folds of her slacks. She'd thought through a dozen other possibilities, but none presented themselves as viable. There would be a way—there was always a way for good to triumph over evil. Even if Slater did kill her . . .

A high chirping sound cut through the silence. Her cell!

Slater spun, glaring. She acted quickly, before he could respond. She snatched it from her pocket and flipped it open.

"Hello?"

"Sam, listen to me. I know this may sound impossible to you, but you're one of Kevin's personalities. Both you and Slater, do you hear me? That's why you can see them both. You—we—have to save Kevin. Tell me where you are, please, Sam."

Her mind rocked crazily. What had Jennifer said? She was one of Kevin's . . .

"What . . . what do you think you're doing?" Slater demanded.

"Please, Sam, you have to believe me!"

"You saw me in the car at the bus explosion," Sam said. "You waved."

"The bus? I saw Kevin. I waved to Kevin. You . . . you'd already left for the airport. Listen to me . . ."

Sam didn't hear any more. Slater had recovered from his shock and bounded for her.

"Below the screw," Sam said.

Slater's hand crashed against the side of her head. The cell phone dug into her ear and clattered to the concrete. She instinctively reached for it, but Slater was too quick. He slapped her arm away, scooped up the cell phone, and threw it across the room. It skipped off the floor and shattered against the wall.

He faced her and shoved a pistol under her chin. "Below the screw? What does that mean, you filthy little traitor?"

Sam's mind hurt. *You are one of his personalities,* isn't that what Jennifer had said? *I am one of Kevin's personalities? That's impossible!*

"Tell me!" Slater yelled. "Tell me or I swear I'll put the hole in your head myself."

"And forgo the pleasure of seeing Kevin do it?" Sam asked.

Slater looked at her for a moment, eyes working over her face. He jerked the pistol back and grinned. "You're right. Doesn't matter anyway; they're out of time."

III

"It was her?" Dr. Francis asked.

"Sam. Call was terminated. Sure didn't sound like Kevin to me. She said she saw me at the bus, but I never saw her." Jennifer swallowed. "I hope we didn't just put a bullet in Sam's head."

Dr. Francis sat slowly.

"She told me they were below the screw," Jennifer said.

"The screw?"

Jennifer whirled to him. "The screw that held Kevin's window closed. Below the window, below the house. There's . . ." Could it be so close, right under their noses? "There's a stairwell in the house, clogged with piles of newsprint now, but it leads to a basement."

"Below the house."

"Kevin has Balinda in the basement of their house! There has to be another way in!" Jennifer ran for the door. "Come on!"

"Me?"

"Yes, you! You know him better than anyone else."

He grabbed his coat and ran after her. "Even if we find them, what can we do?"

"I don't know, but I'm done waiting. You said he can't do this without help. God, give us help."

"How much time?"

"Nine minutes."

"My car! I'll drive," the professor said and veered for the Porsche in the driveway.

|||

Samantha had never felt more distracted from the mission at hand than now. What was the mission at hand? Saving Kevin from Slater.

She thought back to her years in college, to her law enforcement training, to New York. It was all fuzzy. Broad sweeps of reality without detail. Not the kind of detail that immediately surfaced when her mind wandered to the past, as a child, sneaking around with Kevin. Not the specifics that flooded her mind when she considered these past four days. Even her investigation of the Riddle Killer now seemed distant, like something she had read, not actually engaged in.

If Jennifer was right, she was really Kevin. But that was impossible because Kevin sat on the floor ten feet away, rocking, deeply withdrawn, holding a red foot, bleeding from his left ear.

Bleeding from his ear. She took a step around for a better view of Kevin's ear. Her cell phone lay in several pieces twenty feet away on the concrete where Slater had hurled it. That was real enough. Was it possible that Kevin had made her up? She looked at her hands—they seemed real, but she also knew how the mind worked. She also knew that Kevin was a prime candidate for multiple personalities. Balinda had taught him how to dissociate from the beginning. If Kevin was Slater, as Jennifer insisted, then why couldn't *she* be as well? And Sam could see Slater because she was there, in Kevin's mind where Slater lived. But Balinda was real . . .

Sam walked up to Balinda. If Jennifer was right, there were only two bodies here—Kevin's and Balinda's. She and Slater were only personalities in Kevin's imagination.

"What's with you?" Slater snapped. "Back off!"

Sam turned to face the man. He had the barrel of his weapon trained on her knee. Did he really have the gun if he was just in her mind? Or was that Kevin, and he only looked like Slater to her?

Slater grinned wickedly. Sweat wet his face. He glanced at the clock behind her. "Four minutes, Samantha. You have four minutes to live. If Kevin chooses to kill his mother instead of you, then I'm going to waste you myself. I just decided that, and it feels pretty good. How does it feel for you?"

"Why is Kevin bleeding from the ear, Slater? You hit me in the ear, but did you hit him in his ear?"

Slater's eyes shifted to Kevin and then back. "I love it. This is the part where the clever agent begins to play mind tricks in a last-ditch effort to confuse the nasty assailant. I really do love it. Back away from the bait, precious."

Sam ignored him. Instead she reached out and pinched Balinda on the cheek. The woman clenched her eyes and made a squeak. Thunder crashed through the chamber; white-hot pain seared through Sam's thigh. Slater had shot her.

Sam gasped and grabbed her thigh. Blood spread through her black capris. Her head swam. The pain was real enough. If she and Slater weren't real, then who was shooting whom?

Kevin jumped to his feet. "Sam!"

"Stay!" Slater said.

Sam's mind climbed from the pain. Kevin was shooting himself? Any normal person viewing this would see that he'd just shot himself in the thigh.

The details began to fall into order, like dominoes slowly toppling in a long line. So then if Kevin shot Sam in the head, he'd really kill whom? Himself? He was going to kill either Balinda or himself! And even if Slater killed Sam, he would really be pulling the trigger on Kevin, because all three of them occupied the same body. No matter who shot whom, Kevin's body would receive the bullet!

Sam felt a swarm of panic. *Tell Kevin,* Jennifer had said.

"When I say back off, I mean back off—not pinch her, not lick her, not spit on her," Slater said. "Back off really does mean back off. So . . . *back off!*"

Sam took a side step away from Balinda. *Hurry, Jennifer, please hurry! Beneath the screw. That means the basement; you know about the basement, don't you? Dear God, help them.*

"Hurts, doesn't it?" Slater's eyes danced around. "Don't worry, a bullet to the head does wonders for the odd surface wound. *Pow!* Works every time."

"He's bleeding in the ear because you hit *me* in the ear," Sam said. "He's bleeding in the leg too, isn't he?" She followed Slater's glance. Kevin stood, weaving on his feet, stricken with empathy. Blood soaked both his shoe and his right pant leg. He didn't feel the pain because in his mind it hadn't happened to him. Their personalities were completely fragmented. And what about Slater? She dropped her eyes to his thigh—a red spot was spreading on his tan slacks. Slater had shot Sam, but the wound appeared on both Kevin and Slater. She looked at Slater's ear. Then at his shoe. Blood there too.

"I'm so sorry, Sam," Kevin said. "This isn't your fault. I'm sorry I got you into this. I . . . I shouldn't have called you."

"You called her because I told you to call her, you idiot!" Slater said. "And now you're going to kill her because I'm telling you to kill her. Don't slip into Mommy's land of Froot Loops on me, Kevin. I swear I'll kill every one of you if you don't play nicely."

The truth of the matter struck Sam as she watched the deepening lines of sorrow in Kevin's face. This was the confession that Kevin had to make. The whole game was really *Kevin's*, a desperate attempt to flush his evil nature out of its hiding place. He was trying to expose the Slater in him. He'd reached out to her, the Samantha in him, the good in him. He was exposing the good and the bad in him to the world, in a desperate attempt to be rid of Slater. Slater thought he was winning, but in the end Kevin would be the victor.

If he survived. He'd already shot himself twice, once in the foot and once in the thigh.

"I have a theory," Samantha said, voice unsteady.

"The old Colombo trick," Slater said. "Let's stall the nasty man with the I've-got-a-theory routine. Can it! Time's ticking."

Sam cleared her throat and pressed on. "My theory is that I'm not really real."

Slater stared at her.

"I'm a childhood friend Kevin created because that's what he learned to do when he was a child." She looked into his eyes. "You made things up, Kevin. Only I'm not really made up—I'm part of you. I'm the good part of you."

"Can it!" Slater said.

"Slater isn't real either. He's another personality, and he's trying to trick you into killing either me or your mother. If you choose me, you'll be killing the good in you, maybe even yourself. But if you choose Balinda, you'll be murdering another living person. Your mother, for all practical purposes."

"That's a lie, you foul-mouthed, sick . . ." Slater's tirade sputtered short. His eyes bulged from a red face. "That's the stupidest thing I've ever heard!"

"That's not possible," Kevin said, face round in confusion. "That can't be, Sam! Of course you're real! You're the most real thing I've ever known."

"I *am* real, Kevin. I'm real and I love you desperately! But I'm part of you." Hearing herself say it, she sounded foolish. How could she possibly not be real? She felt and looked and even smelled real! But it did make sense on some unspeakable level.

"Look at your leg. You're bleeding because I was shot," she said. "I'm you. And so is Slater. You have to believe me. You've taken the good and the evil in you and turned them into imaginary people. Personalities. It's not really that strange, Kevin. You're acting out the struggle between good and evil every human being engages in. Slater and I are only the players in your own mind. But neither of us can do anything unless you give us the power to do it. He can't pull that trigger unless you do. Do you—"

"Shut up! Shut up, you lying piece of trash!" Slater jumped across the room and shoved a gun into Kevin's hand. He lifted the hand and pointed it toward Samantha.

"You have fifty seconds, Kevin. Fifty, tick, tick, tick." He lifted his own pistol and pressed the barrel against Balinda's temple. "Either you shoot Sam or I shoot Froot Loops."

"I can't shoot her!" Kevin cried.

"Then Mommy dies. Of course you can! You pull that trigger, or I swear I'm going to take care of Mommy and then finish you off for being a bad sport, you hear me? Forty seconds, Kevin. Forty, tick, tick, tick."

Slater's face glistened in the dim light. Kevin held the gun by his side. His face wrinkled; tears hung in his eyes.

"Point the gun at Samantha, you idiot! Lift it up. Now!"

Kevin lifted it slowly. "Sam? I can't let him kill Balinda, right?"

"Please don't get all sentimental on us," Slater said. "It's good for the mood, I realize, but it makes my stomach turn. Just put a bullet through her forehead. You heard her, she's not real. She's a figment of our imaginations. Of course, so am I; that's why you have two bullet holes in your leg." He chuckled.

Sam's mind hurt. What was really happening? What if she was wrong? Never before had she held a notion to be so utterly impossible and so utterly true at once. And she was now telling Kevin to gamble his very life on that notion. *Dear God, give me strength.*

"Look at your leg, Kevin," Sam said. "You shot yourself. Please, I'm begging you. Don't let Slater kill her. He can't shoot unless you give him the power. He's you."

29

THE DOOR at the end of the tunnel was unlocked. Jennifer could hear Sam's voice begging inside. She wasn't sure what she would find when she crashed in, but time was gone. Dr. John Francis breathed raggedly behind her.

They'd come to the house, barged past Eugene to find the stairwell still blocked with books. After frantically searching the perimeter, they found the stairs in the old bomb shelter. No telling how often or how long Kevin had been here over the years thinking he was Slater.

"Here we go."

She twisted the knob, took a deep breath, and threw her weight forward, gun extended.

The first thing she saw was Balinda, seated in a wooden chair, bound and gagged with gray duct tape. The second was the man standing over her. Kevin.

Kevin had a gun in each hand, one outstretched and pressed into Balinda's temple, and the other crammed against his own head like a man about to commit suicide. No Samantha, no Slater. Just Kevin.

But she knew that Kevin wasn't seeing what she saw. His eyes were clenched tight and he was hyperventilating.

"Kevin?"

He jerked his head toward her, eyes wide.

"It's okay, Kevin," Jennifer said. "I'm here." She held out a hand, urging calm. "Don't do anything. Please, don't pull that trigger."

Sweat covered his upper lip and cheeks. He stood, torn, terrified, furious. Blood leaked from wounds on his right thigh and foot. He'd shot himself! Twice.

"Kevin, where is Samantha?" Jennifer asked.

His eyes jerked to his left.

"Shut up," he snarled. Only it was in Slater's voice, which she now clearly recognized as Kevin's voice, but lower and grating.

"You're not real, Slater," Jennifer said. "You're only a personality Kevin created. You have no power on your own. Sam, do you hear me?"

"I hear you, Jennifer," Sam said—only it wasn't Sam; it was Kevin speaking in a slightly higher voice. Unlike over the phone, Jennifer heard the resemblance now.

"You don't see me, do you?" Sam asked.

"No."

"Listen to her, Kevin," Sam said. "Listen to me. I would die for you, my knight. I would gladly give my life for you, but it's Slater you have to kill, not me. Do you understand? We are you. Only you. And now that you've flushed him out, you have to kill him."

Kevin clenched his eyes and began to shake.

"Shut up!" Slater screamed. "Everyone, shut up! Do it! Do it, Kevin, or I swear I'll put this round in Mommy's forehead! Time's up!"

Jennifer felt frantic. "Kevin—"

"Shoot Slater, Kevin," the professor said, stepping past her. "He can't kill you. Put the weapon on Slater and kill him."

"Won't he shoot himself?" Jennifer demanded.

"You have to separate yourself from Slater, Kevin."

Kevin's eyes fluttered open. He'd recognized the professor's voice. "Dr. Francis?" Kevin's normal voice.

"There are three natures, Kevin. The good, the bad, and the poor soul struggling between them. Remember? You're role-playing those three roles. Listen to me. You have to kill Slater. Take your gun off Sam and point it at Slater. He can't do anything to stop you. Then, when you are sure that you have your gun on Slater, I want you to shoot him. I'll tell you. You have to trust me."

Kevin turned his head, staring to his left and then back to his right. From Kevin's perspective he was looking between Samantha and Slater.

"Don't be a fool!" Slater said. Kevin swung the gun that was on Balinda toward Jennifer. "Drop the gun! Out!" It was Slater and he was frantic.

"Do what the professor says, Kevin," Sam said. "Shoot Slater."

|||

Kevin stared at Slater and wondered why he hadn't fired. The man had swung his gun from Balinda and aimed it at Jennifer, but he wasn't pulling the trigger. The time had come and gone and still Slater hadn't shot.

It occurred to him that he still had the gun in his hand, trained on Sam. He lowered his arm. They wanted him to shoot Slater.

But . . . if Sam and Jennifer were right, that was him over there, threatening Jennifer. And they wanted him to shoot himself? He'd flushed the man out of his hiding and now he was to kill him.

Kevin turned to Sam. She looked so tender, so lovely, eyes drawn with sympathy. *Dear Sam, I love you so.* Her eyes reached into his mind, his heart, melting him with their love.

She took a step toward him. "I should go now, Kevin."

"Go?" The thought frightened him.

"I won't be gone. I'll be with you. I *am* you. Shoot Slater."

"Stop!" Slater screamed. "Stop!" He stepped out and swung his gun on Samantha.

"I love you, Kevin," Samantha said. She stepped up to him, smiled gently, knowingly. "Shoot him. His kind is powerless when you under-stand who holds the true power. I know you're the one who feels pow-erless, and on your own, you are. But if you look to your Maker, you'll find enough power to kill a thousand Slaters, wherever they crop up. He will save you. Listen to Dr. Francis."

She reached out and touched his hand. Her finger went through his skin, into his hand. Kevin watched, mouth gaping. Samantha stepped into him, her knee into his knee, her shoulder into his shoulder. He couldn't feel her. Then she was gone.

Kevin gasped for air. She was him! She'd always been him! The realization fell into his mind like an anvil dropped from heaven. And she was gone, wasn't she? Or maybe closer than ever. A buzz circled his mind.

And if Sam was him, then Slater . . .

Kevin turned to his right. Slater shook from head to foot, gun aimed at Kevin's head now. But that wasn't a real person over there; it was only his evil nature, right?

Kevin looked at Jennifer. Her eyes were begging him. She couldn't stop Slater because she couldn't see him. She only saw him—Kevin.

If he was Slater, then the gun was really in his hand, wasn't it? He could force Slater to lower the gun by lowering it himself, in his mind.

Look to your Maker, Sam had said.

Open my eyes.

Kevin looked at the pathetic man who called himself Slater. He closed his eyes. It occurred to him then that he had two guns in his hands—one at his side and one at his temple. That would be Slater. He lowered the gun; now he had two guns by his side, one in each hand. He opened his eyes.

Slater faced him, gun lowered, face twisted with fury. "You'll never succeed, Kevin. Never! You're just like me, and nothing will ever change that. You hear me? Nothing!"

"Now, Kevin," Dr. Francis said. "Now."

Kevin lifted his right arm, pointed the nine millimeter at Slater's head, and pulled the trigger. The shot echoed loudly. At this range he could hardly miss.

But he did miss. He missed because suddenly there was no target to hit. Slater was gone.

Kevin lowered the gun. The bullet had buried itself in the metal desk behind the spot where Slater had stood, but it hadn't penetrated any flesh and blood. Slater wasn't flesh or blood. He was dead just the same. At least for now.

For a few long seconds the room rang in the aftermath of the detonation. Balinda began to sob. Kevin looked at her and pity, not anger, washed through his mind. She needed help, didn't she? She was a wounded soul, like him. She needed love and understanding. He doubted she would ever be able to return to the false reality she'd created.

"Kevin?"

The world seemed to collapse at the sound of Jennifer's voice. He wasn't certain what had just happened, but if he wasn't mistaken, he'd blown up a bus and a library and kidnapped his aunt. He needed help. Dear God, he needed help!

"Are you all right, Kevin?" Jennifer's voice broke.

He lowered his head and began to cry. He couldn't help it. *Dear God, what have I done?*

An arm settled on his shoulders. He could smell the musty scent of her perfume as she pulled him close.

"It's okay, Kevin. Everything's okay now. I won't let them hurt you, I promise."

He dissolved in sobs at her words. He deserved to be hurt. Or was that Slater's old voice?

Listen to Dr. Francis, Samantha had said. He would. He would listen to Dr. Francis and let Jennifer hold him. It was all he had now. Truth and love.

30

One Week Later

J ENNIFER LOOKED THROUGH the glass door at Kevin, who stood by the flowers in the professor's lawn, touching and smelling the roses as if he'd newly discovered them. Dr. John Francis stood beside her, gazing out. Kevin had spent the last seven days in a prison cell, awaiting an extended bail hearing that had ended three hours earlier. Persuading the judge that Kevin wasn't a flight risk was a simple matter; convincing her that Kevin wasn't a threat to society wasn't. But Chuck Hatters, a good friend to Jennifer and now Kevin's attorney, had managed.

The press had slaughtered Kevin that first day, but as the details of his childhood leaked out over the next week, their tenor had changed—Jennifer had seen to that. She'd held a news conference and revealed his past in all of its horrifying detail. Kevin was simply role-playing as only a child who'd been severely abused and fractured could role-play. If even a single person had been hurt or killed, the public would probably have continued screaming retribution until another earth-shattering event distracted them. But in Kevin's case, pity quickly took precedence over a few destroyed buildings. The Slater personality would never have blown up any bus before it had been evacuated, Jennifer argued. She wasn't sure she believed it, but enough of the public did to swing the tide of outrage. Kevin still had his significant detractors, of course, but they no longer dominated the airwaves.

Was he insane? No, but she couldn't tell them that yet. The courts would put him through the wringer, and legal insanity was his only defense. In many ways, he *had* been legally insane, but he seemed to have emerged from the basement with a full grasp of himself, perhaps for the first time in his life. Patients who suffered from Dissociative Identity Disorder typically required years of therapy to pull themselves free of their alternate personalities.

For that matter, even the diagnosis would take some time. Kevin's admittedly enigmatic behavior didn't fit any classical disorder. Dissociative Identity Disorder, yes, but there were no cases of three personalities carrying on a conversation as she herself had witnessed. Posttraumatic Stress Disorder, perhaps. Or a strange blend of Schizophrenia and DID. The scientific community would undoubtedly argue over this one.

The good news was that Kevin could hardly be better. He would need help, but she'd never seen such a sudden shift.

"I'm curious," Dr. Francis said. "Have you unraveled Samantha's part in all this?"

Samantha? He spoke as if she were still a real person. Jennifer looked at him and caught the smile in his eyes. "I think you mean how Kevin managed to play Samantha without tipping his hand, don't you?"

"Yes. In the public places."

"You were right—another day or two and we'd have caught on. There were only three places where Sam was supposedly exposed to the public. The Howard Johnson hotel, the hotel in Palos Verdes where they spent the night, and when they cleared the bus. I talked to the clerk at the Howard Johnson where Sam stayed. She did remember Sam, if you recall, but the person who she remembers was a man with brown hair and blue eyes. Sam."

"Kevin," the professor said.

"Yes. He actually went over there and checked in as Sam, thinking he really was her. If he'd signed in under Samantha instead of Sam, the clerk would have raised a brow. But to her he was Sam."

"Hmm. And Palos Verdes?"

"The maître d' from the restaurant will be a good witness. Evidently some of the customers complained about the strange behavior of the man seated by the window. Kevin. He was staring directly across the table and speaking to an empty chair in hushed tones. Raised his voice a couple times." Jennifer smiled. "The maître d' approached and asked if everything was okay, and Kevin assured him it was. But that didn't stop him from walking to the dance floor a few minutes later and dancing with an invisible partner before leaving the room."

"Sam."

"Sam. According to Kevin, the only other time they were together in public was when they cleared the bus that blew up. Kevin insisted that Sam was in the car, but none of the passengers remember seeing another person in the car. And when I drove by a few minutes after the explosion, Kevin was alone, although he clearly remembers Sam sitting beside him, talking on her phone to her superiors. The California Bureau of Investigation has no record of her, of course."

"Of course. And I suppose Kevin chose to imitate the Riddle Killer because it offered him a fully fleshed persona."

"Don't you mean *Slater?*"

"Pardon me—Slater." The professor smiled.

"We found a stack of newspaper clippings on the Riddle Killer in Slater's desk. Several were addressed to Kevin's home. He never remembers receiving them. He can't remember how he got into the library undetected or how he planted the bombs in his car or the bus, although the evidence in the basement leaves no doubt that he built all three bombs."

Jennifer shook her head. "Kevin himself, as himself, wasn't aware that he was carrying both Sam's and Slater's cell phones most of the time. You'd think when he wasn't in their personas, he'd be aware of that much, but somehow the alter egos managed to shut off his mind to those realities. Amazing how the mind works. I've never heard of such a clear fragmentation."

"Because the personalities Kevin spun off were so diametrically opposed," Dr. Francis said. "*What falls but never breaks; what breaks but never falls?* Night and day. Black and white. Evil and good. Kevin."

"Night and day. Evil. Some in your camp are calling him possessed, you know?"

"I've heard."

"And you?"

He took a deep breath and let it out slowly. "If they want to attribute his evil nature to a demonic presence or a stronghold, they may do so without argument or endorsement from me. It sounds quite sensational, but it doesn't change the fundamental truth. Evil is evil, whether it takes the form of a devil with horns or a demon from hell or the gossip of a bishop. I believe Kevin was merely playing out the natures that reside in all humans from birth. Like a child might play Dorothy and the Wicked Witch of the West. But Kevin really believed he was both Slater and Samantha, thanks to his own childhood."

The professor crossed his arms and looked back out at Kevin, who was staring at a cloud formation now.

"I do believe that we all have Slater and Samantha living within us as part of our own nature," he said. "You could call me *Slater-John-Samantha.*"

"Hmm. And I suppose that would make me *Slater-Jennifer-Samantha.*"

"Why not? We all struggle between good and evil. Kevin lived that struggle out in dramatic fashion, but we all live the same struggle.

We all struggle with our own Slaters. With gossip and anger and jealousy. Kevin said his term paper was going to be a story—in more ways than one, I think he just lived his paper out."

"Forgive my ignorance, Professor," Jennifer said without looking at him, "but how is it that you, supposedly a 'regenerated' man, devoted servant of God, still struggle with evil?"

"Because I am a creature of free will," Dr. Francis said. "I have the choice at any given moment how I will live. And if I choose to hide my evil in a basement, as Kevin did, it will grow. Those who populate America's churches may not be blowing up buses and kidnapping, to be sure, but most hide their sin just the same. Slater lurks in their dungeons and they refuse to blow the lid off them, so to speak. Kevin, on the other hand, most certainly blew the lid off, no pun intended."

"Unfortunately, he took half the city with him."

"Did you hear what Samantha said in the basement?" the professor asked.

Jennifer had wondered if he would bring up Samantha's words. "'You are powerless on your own. But if you look to your Maker, you'll find enough power to kill a thousand Slaters,'" she said. The words Samantha spoke to Kevin had haunted Jennifer for the last week. How had Kevin known to say that? Was it really as simple as his good nature crying out the truth?

"She was right. We are all powerless to deal with Slater on our own."

He was talking about man's dependence on God to find true freedom. He'd spent long hours with Kevin in his prison cell—Jennifer wondered what had passed between them.

"After seeing what I've seen down here, I'm not going to even try to argue with you, Professor." She nodded at Kevin. "You think he's . . . okay?"

"Okay?" Dr. Francis's right eyebrow went up. He smiled. "I'm sure he'll be delighted to hear the news you have, if that's what you mean."

Jennifer felt exposed. He could see more than she meant for him to see, couldn't he?

"Take your time. I have some calls to make." He walked for his study.

"Professor."

He turned back. "Yes?"

"Thank you. He . . . we . . . *We* owe our lives to you."

"Nonsense, dear. You owe me nothing. You may, however, have a debt to Samantha. And to Samantha's Maker." He grinned deliberately and entered his study.

Jennifer waited until his door closed. She slid the glass door open and stepped onto the patio. "Hello, Kevin."

He turned, eyes bright. "Jennifer! I didn't know you were here."

"I had some time." As much as she tried to ignore the fact, there was a unique bond between them. Whether it was her natural reaction to the sympathy he engendered or her own generous spirit or more, she didn't know. Time would tell. The Riddle Killer was still at large, and yet she somehow felt she'd found herself for the first time since Roy's death.

Kevin glanced back at the roses. His eyes couldn't hold hers unwaveringly as they had before—he'd lost a certain innocence. But she preferred him this way.

"I'm taking a sabbatical," she said.

"From the FBI? You are?"

"I am. I just came from a hearing with Judge Rosewood." Jennifer couldn't contain herself any longer. She smiled wide.

"What?" he asked. Her elation spread to him. "What's so funny?"

"Nothing. She's going to consider my request."

"The judge? What request?"

"You do know that I'm a licensed psychotherapist, don't you?"

"Yes."

"Even if we win your acquittal, which I think we will, the court will insist on therapy. In fact, your treatment will likely begin much sooner. But I don't think we can trust just any psychotherapist to pry around your head."

"Psychobabble," he said. "They . . ." His eyes widened. "You?"

Jennifer laughed. If the judge could see her now, she might reconsider. But she couldn't. In fact, no one could. The professor had retired to his office.

She walked up to him, pulse quickening. "Not your psychotherapist, exactly. But I'll be there, every step of the way, monitoring. I don't intend to let anyone mess with your mind any more than they have to."

He stared into her eyes. "I think I'd let you mess with my mind."

Everything in Jennifer's being wanted to reach out to him then. To touch his cheek and tell him that she cared for him more than anyone she'd cared for in a very long time. But she was an FBI agent, for heaven's sake. The agent in charge of his case! She had to remember that.

"Do I really need a psychotherapist?" he asked.

"You need me." That sounded a bit forward. "I mean you need someone *like* me. There are a lot of issues . . ."

Kevin suddenly leaned forward and kissed her on the cheek. "No, I don't need someone like you," he said. "I need you."

He pulled back, then looked away and blushed.

She couldn't help herself anymore. She stepped forward and kissed him very lightly on his cheek.

"And I need you, Kevin. I need you too."

I do not understand what I do. . . . It is no longer I myself who do it, but it is sin living in me. . . . For what I do is not the good I want to do; no, the evil I do not want to do—this I keep on doing. . . . I find this law at work: When I want to do good, evil is right there with me. . . . I delight in God's law; but I see another law at work in the members of my body, waging war against the law of my mind and making me a prisoner of the law of sin. I myself in my mind am a slave to God's law, but in the sinful nature a slave to the law of sin.

From a letter written by Saint Paul to the church in Rome, A.D. 57.
ROMANS 7:15–25

The Circle

ISBN
1-5955-4021-0

ISBN
1-5955-4034-2

ISBN
1-5955-4035-0

Fleeing assailants through an alleyway in Denver late one night, Thomas Hunter narrowly escapes to the roof of an industrial building. Then a silent bullet from the night clips his head and his world goes black. When he awakes, he finds himself in an entirely different reality—a green forest that seems more real than where he was. Every time he tries to sleep, he wakes up in the other world, and soon he truly no longer knows which reality is real.

Never before has a trilogy of this magnitude—all in hardcover format—been released in an eight-month window of time. On the heels of *The Matrix* and *The Lord of the Rings* comes a new trilogy in which dreams and reality collide. In which the fate of two worlds depends on one man: Thomas Hunter.

Each book in the trilogy is also available in abridged (CD)
and unabridged (CD and cassette) editions.

Discover more at TedDekker.com

Hamburg, Germany
July 17, 1973
Tuesday

ROTH BRAUN slowly twisted the doorknob and gave the door a slight
shove. A familiar medicinal odor stung his nostrils. Outside, the sun warmed
a midsummer day, but here in the dungeon below the house, the old man
lived in perpetual twilight.

Roth imagined a Jew stepping into a delicing shower and let himself
relish the horror he might feel in that moment of realizing that more than
lice were meant to die in this chamber.

Roth was in a very good mood.

The smothering quiet was broken by the sound of the old prune's
tarred, seventy-eight-year-old lungs rasping for relief. Gerhard's wheezing
annoyed Roth, ruining his otherwise perfect mood.

The only living soul he despised more than the Jew who'd stolen his
power was Gerhard, who had allowed the Jew to steal his power.

He glanced at Klaus, the gangly male nurse who had tended his father
for three years. The white-smocked man hovered over Gerhard in the corner
of the room, refusing to meet Roth's eyes. Gerhard Braun sat in a dark-red
leather recliner, gray eyes glaring over the nasal cannula protruding from
each nostril.

"Good morning, Father," Roth said. He closed the door quietly and stepped into the room, pushing aside a curtain of tinkling glass beads that separated it from the entryway. "You wanted to see me?"

His father looked at a servant, who busied himself over the table in the adjacent dining room.

"Leave us."

By the trembling in his voice, either Gerhard really was dying, or something was upsetting him, which invariably sowed its own sort of death. How many men alive today had been responsible for as many deaths as his father? They could be counted on two hands.

Even so, Roth hated him.

The servant dipped his head and exited through a side door. The steel door closed and the nurse flinched. Glass in a cabinet behind the table rattled despite the room's solid-concrete walls. The nineteenth-century Russian crystal—one of dozens of similar collections pilfered during the war—had once belonged to the czar. The Nazis' defeat should have sent Gerhard to the gallows; instead, the war had left his father with obscene wealth. The paintings alone had netted him a significant fortune, and these he owned legally. He'd shipped them to Zurich, where a hotly contested law made them his after remaining unclaimed for five years. Compliments of the Swiss Federation of Art Dealers.

Until the day I suck the energy from your bones, I will love you for showing me the way.

Until the day I suck the energy from your bones, I will despise you for what you did.

Gerhard held up a newspaper. "Have you read this?"

Roth walked across the circular rope rug that covered the black cement slab and stopped five feet from Gerhard. A hawk nose curved over his father's thin, trembling lips. Wispy strands of gray hair backlit by a yellow lamp hovered over his scalp. Skeletal, blue-veined fingers clutched what appeared to be a *Los Angeles Times*. A stack of newspapers—the *New York Times, Chicago Tribune*, London's *Daily Telegraph*, and a dozen others—sat a half-meter thick on the small end table to his left. Gerhard routinely spent six hours each day reading.

Gerhard flung the paper with a flick of his wrist, never removing his eyes from Roth. It landed on the floor with a *smack*.

"Read it."

The male nurse pretended to fiddle with the oxygen tank. Roth stood still. This attitude of Gerhard's was no longer simply ruining his mood, but destroying it altogether.

"I said, 'Read it!'"

Roth calmly bent and picked up the paper. The *Los Angeles Times* was folded around an article in the Life section, "Fortune Goes to Museum." Roth scanned the text. A wealthy woman, a Jew named Rachel Spritzer, sixty-two years of age, had died three days ago in Los Angeles. She'd been survived by no one and had donated her entire estate to the Los Angeles Museum of the Holocaust.

"So another Jew's dead." Roth lowered the paper. "Your legacy lives on."

His father clutched the arms of his chair. "Read the rest." His chest sounded like a whistle.

If Roth wasn't a master of his own impulses, he might have done something stupid, like kill the man. Instead, he set the paper on the windowsill and turned away. "You've read it, Father. Tell me what it says. I have a ten o'clock engagement."

"Cancel it."

Roth walked to the bar. Control. "Just tell me what has you so concerned."

"The Stones of David have me concerned."

Roth blinked. He poured a splash of cognac into a snifter.

"I'm finished chasing your ghosts." He swirled the brandy slowly before sipping it. "If the Stones still exist, we would have found them long ago."

Gerhard managed to stand, trembling from head to foot, red as a rooster around the neck.

"They *have* been found. And you know what that means." He launched into a coughing fit.

Roth's pulse quickened a hair and then eased. If the man wasn't dying, he was losing his mind. Surely the Stones hadn't been found after all this time.

Gerhard staggered three steps to the windowsill, pushing his startled nurse out of the way, and grabbed the newspaper. He leaned on the wall with one hand and held the paper up in the other. He threw the paper toward Roth. It fluttered noisily and landed on the black slab.

"Read it!" Gerhard's eyes drilled him. So then maybe there was something to this.

Roth picked up the paper, found the article, and slowly read down the column. What if Gerhard was right? What if the relics did exist after all? They would be priceless. But the Stones' monetary value didn't interest Gerhard—he already had enough wealth to waste in his final years.

Gerhard's obsession was for the journal that had gone missing with the Stones.

And Roth's obsession was for the power that had gone missing with the Jew who'd taken the journal.

He had spent nearly thirty years tracking down innumerable leads, searching in vain. There was no telling how much wealth had been stripped from the Jews when Hitler had gathered them up and sent them to the camps. Much of the fortune had been confiscated by the Gestapo and recovered after the war, but a number of particularly valuable items—priceless relics that belonged in museums or in vaults—had disappeared. Some of those treasures could be found in this very house. But any well-heeled collector knew that the most valuable collection had vanished for good in 1945.

The Stones of David.

One stunning item in Spritzer's collection is an extremely old golden medallion, better known as one of the five Stones of David. According to legend, the medallions are the actual stones selected by David to kill the giant Goliath. The smooth stones were subsequently gilded and stamped with the Star of David. The collection was last verified in 1307, when they were held by the Knights Templars. The collection was rumored to be held by a wealthy Jewish collector before World War II but went missing before the claim could be verified.

Alone, each medallion may be worth over $10,000,000. But the collection in its entirety is valued at roughly $100,000,000. The relic will be displayed in a museum yet to be disclosed with the following cryptic caption at Rachel Spritzer's request: "The Stones are like the lost orphans. They will eventually find each other."

Sweat cooled Roth's palms. He set the paper on the bar, set an unsteady finger in its margin, and scanned to the end.

—⁓—

Rachel Spritzer lived alone in an apartment complex she owned on La Brea Avenue and died a widow. The complex will be sold by the estate, along with much of Spritzer's noncollectible property.

Rudy and Rachel Spritzer immigrated to the United States sixteen years ago, five years before Rudy was killed in an automobile accident. (See B4.) For a moment Roth's vision clouded. His mouth went dry.

"Now I have your attention?" Gerhard demanded.

Roth read the article again, searching for any phrase that might undermine the possibility that this Jew could be anyone other than whom Gerhard was suggesting.

"She was sixty-two," Gerhard said. "The right age."

Roth's mind flashed back to those war years when he was only ten. Even if the connections were only circumstantial, he could hardly ignore them.

"I *knew* the Jew survived," Gerhard said.

"She donated only one Stone. There were five."

"If one Stone exists, then the journal exists. Someone has that journal!"

"She's dead."

"You will make her speak from the grave." Gerhard swayed on his feet, right fist trembling. His eyes looked black in the basement's shadows. "She knew. She knew about the journal."

"She's dead!" Roth snapped. He took a deep breath, irritated with himself for losing control. The fact was, Gerhard's history with the Stones gave him knowledge that no one else could possibly have.

"You know well enough that the journal implicates the entire line of elders. It lists each of our names and the names of the women we killed. It must be found!"

Mention of the women triggered a coppery taste in the back of Roth's mouth. The last time he'd seen the journal, it contained 243 names. Roth would one day surpass that number, he had vowed it.

But a even a thousand or ten thousand would not compensate for the one that had escaped Gerhard.

"That woman would toy with me even in her death," the old man said. "In her house, in her belongings—somewhere, the old bat left a trail. You will go to Los Angeles." The nurse, Klaus, moved to assist Gerhard back to his seat, but the old man shook him off. Klaus retreated.

—⁓—

Gerhard was right. The Stones could lead to the journal. The journal could lead to the Jew. The Jew would lead to power, a supernatural power that his father had never attained. But Roth would.

The prospect of finding the Jew after so many years felt delightfully obscene.

Roth realized that his fingers were trembling.

"The United States," Roth said absently. "We don't have the same liberties there."

"That's never stopped you before."

The notion swarmed Roth like bees from a disturbed hive. Hope. More than hope—a desperate urgency to possess. Pounding heart, dry mouth. He was no fool. He would neither fight the emotion nor show it. After lingering so long on the edges of his mind, the desire to possess this one lost hope swallowed him. This is what Roth lived for, the purest form of power found in the very emotion that at this very moment raged through his body.

In his mind's eye he was already flying to America. He would have to move quickly, set the trap immediately. There was no telling how long they would keep the old Jew's collectibles in Los Angeles.

Roth stared into his father's blue eyes for a few long seconds, torn between the man's mad obsession with the past and his own with the future. What Roth did for tomorrow, Gerhard did because of yesterday. Who was the better man?

He remembered the first dead Jew he'd seen in the camps twenty-eight years ago. He'd been eating fresh eggs and sausage prepared by one of the Polish servants from the village for breakfast. It was the most delicious breakfast he'd ever tasted. Perhaps leaving his mother in Germany to spend the summer with his father up in Poland would be a good thing after all. He was twelve at the time.

"Papa?"

"What?" his father asked, walking toward the window overlooking the concentration camp.

"Why do Polish eggs taste better than German eggs?"

His father pulled back the curtain, and Roth saw a woman hanging from the main gate. Gerhard answered him, but Roth didn't hear the response. The year was 1942, and hers was the first of many dead bodies Roth would see in Poland. But there was something about the first.

Roth let the memory linger then returned his mind to the Stones. His father's eyes glistened with tears; his face wrinkled.

"The Jew took my soul. *She* took my soul! I beg you, my son." Roth felt a terrible pity for him. A single tear broke free and ran down Gerhard's right cheek.

"If the Jew is alive, she will be drawn by the Stone," Roth said.

"Forget the Jew. I must have the journal. You see that, don't you? More than anything, I must have it." He held out a spindly arm laced with bulging veins. "Swear it to me. Swear you'll bring me what is mine."

Roth looked at the large swastika on the gray wall, sickened by Gerhard's weakness. He would make it right, because the Stones meant far more to him than they could possibly mean to his father.

"Come here," Roth said to the nurse.

Klaus glanced at Gerhard then stepped out from the shadows.

Roth backed up and stepped off the rug. There was the right way and the wrong way to do this, and the purest in mind knew the difference.

"Farther, to the middle of the rug," he said.

Klaus took another step so that he stood near the center of the rug.

"I would like to repay you for your care of my father," Roth said. "Few men could put up with a whining old man the way you do. Is there anything you would like?"

No response. Of course not.

"Anything at all?"

The nurse lowered his head. "No sir."

Roth pulled out his gun and shot Klaus through the top of his head while he was still bent over. The slug likely ended up in his throat.

The man dropped in a pile.

Roth looked at his father. "You should have sent him out."

"You're working against your own kind," Gerhard said. "He was pure."

"Then I did him a favor by sending him to his grave pure."

Also Available from Ted Dekker

BLESSED CHILD
By Ted Dekker and Bill Bright
The young orphan boy was abandoned and raised in an Ethiopian monastery. Now he must flee those walls or die. But the world is hardly ready for a boy like Caleb. When relief expert Jason Marker agrees to take Caleb from the monastery, he opens humanity's doors to an incredible journey filled with intrigue and peril. Together with Leiah, the nurse who escapes to America with them, Jason discovers Caleb's stunning power. But so do the boy's enemies, who will stop at nothing to destroy him. Jason and Leiah fight for the boy's survival while the world erupts into debate over the source of the boy's power. In the end nothing can prepare any of them for what they will find.

A MAN CALLED BLESSED
By Ted Dekker and Bill Bright
In this explosive sequel, Rebecca Soloman leads a team of Israeli commandos deep into the Ethiopian desert to hunt the one man who may know the final resting place of the Ark of the Covenant. But Islamic fundamentalists fear that the Ark's discovery will compel Israel to rebuild Solomon's temple on the very site of their own holy mosque in Jerusalem. They immediately dispatch Ismael, their most accomplished assassin, to pursue the same man. But the man in their sights is no ordinary man. His name is Caleb, and he too is on a quest— to find again the love he once embraced as a child. Tensions sky-rocket as the world awakens to the drama in the desert. The fate of a million souls rests in the hand of these three.

BLINK
By Ted Dekker
Seth Borders isn't your average graduate student. For starters, he has one of the world's highest IQs. Now he's suddenly struck by an incredible power—the ability to see multiple potential futures. Still reeling from this inexplicable gift, Seth stumbles upon a beautiful woman named Miriam, a Saudi Arabian princess who has fled her veiled existence to escape a forced marriage of unimaginable consequences. Cultures collide as they're thrown together and forced to run from an unstoppable force determined to kidnap or kill Miriam.

An intoxicating tale set amid the shifting sands of the Middle East and the back roads of America, *Blink* engages issues as ancient as the earth itself . . . and as current as today's headlines.

Discover more at TedDekker.com

The Martyr's Song Series

HEAVEN'S WAGER

He lost everything he ever wanted—and risked his soul to get what he deserved. Take a glimpse into a world more real and vital than most people ever discover here on earth, the unseen world where the real dramas of the universe—and of our daily lives—continually unfold.

WHEN HEAVEN WEEPS

A cruel game of ultimate stakes at the end of World War II leaves Jan Jovic stunned and perplexed. He's prepared for neither the incredible demonstration of love nor the terrible events that follow. Now, many years later, Jan falls madly in love with the "wrong" woman and learns the true cost of love.

THUNDER OF HEAVEN

When armed forces destroy their idyllic existence within the jungles of the Amazon, Tanya embraces God, while Shannon boldly rejects God, choosing the life of an assassin. Despite their vast differences, they find themselves in the crucible of a hideous plot to strike sheer terror into the heart of America.